Managing change, a quintessentially Chinese idea, is just as applicable to the West as to the East. With its scale, speed and insights from traditional philosophy, China should be the Greatest Show on Earth for anyone interested in world affairs and the future. For someone sitting in Europe, China's Change *tells me lots of things I didn't know. The key thesis, countering all those who argue China will topple over, is a really important one. Through the extraordinary array of people he has known and met over 40 years, Hugh Peyman tells the story of today's China in a way that has never been done before.*

BBC Director-General, Tony Hall.

It is rare for a foreigner to understand China from the ground up. Hugh's advantage is that he got to understand China's diaspora before working in China, going through numbers at the ground level and meeting people engaged in both business and officialdom. This book gives one of the best insights into how China is changing, as she grapples with globalization, one of the truly momentous changes in the 20th and 21st centuries.

China Banking Regulatory Commission former Chief Adviser, head of the Hong Kong Securities and Futures Commission and author of *From Asian to Global Financial Crisis,* Andrew Sheng.

Hugh Peyman knows what he is talking about. Far from seeing China through a Western prism — and consistently getting it wrong — he understands China like few others.

author of *When China Rules the World,* Martin Jacques

A very valuable book. Makes cogent arguments, with a lot of valid, interesting and provocative statements that will help people to think about China.

Pulitzer Prize winner and author of *Wild Grass: Three Stories of Change in Modern China,* Ian Johnson.

China's Change *is essential reading for any serious global investor. China will be the game changer for beta asset diversification and alpha generation. Get insights from the perspective of a researcher who sees things from the top down and bottom up and who has lived in China for 15 years.*

Government Investment Corporation of Singapore former Chief Investment Officer and Adviser to PIMCO, Ng Kok Song.

All travellers to China, whether on business, holiday or study, should take this book. China's Change *has it all on China: history, philosophy, government, politics, business and economics, past, present and future. For Asia and the West this very timely, wide-ranging and original book answers two critical questions. Can China illuminate new paths for us to manage our increasingly disrupted worlds: in our national, work and personal lives? Can China continue to be the main driver of global economic growth?*

Banyan Tree Resorts Founder, Singapore Management University Trustees Chairman and author of *The Ocean in a Drop,* Ho Kwon Ping.

Really like the way you are going for "change". I think you are onto something here and it allows your book to be philosophical economics, which is much more beguiling than straight economics, of course! I too wonder at the capacity of Chinese people to absorb change — this is definitely unusual, I agree.

I was particularly drawn in by the question of "what is China getting right" — there is a clear and valid disconnect that you point out between large parts of the Western narrative and China's result.

Financial Times Emerging Markets Editor
and award-winning author of
China Shakes the World, James Kynge.

Fascinating: you've clearly done a lot of research and have extensive and authoritative experience in Asia. The thing that impressed me the most was how well written it is, you clearly have a flair for making the difficult to grasp and conceptualize into something accessible.

Chatham House Editor, Mike Tsang.

I am impressed with your way of looking at China — putting things against its history, people, religion, philosophy and culture, facing those stereotypes/sensitive topics and addressing them one by one with objective analysis and benchmarking. I am sure it will be much easier for remote China followers to understand China from a unique perspective which is different from the established typical western conventional approach.

You belong to the realistic camp, rather than being simply pessimistic or optimistic. What gives your book more credibility is your 40 years' experience in following and particularly living within China. I am sure this book will prompt people's thinking and will prove in time that you are ahead of the curve, more visionary than most China followers and even lots of Chinese!

Anglo American Group China Chief Representative, William Fu.

Every time the negative alarm sounds about China reach for China's Change*!*

State Street Global Advisors Vice Chairman, Ralph Layman.

China's Change *will be valuable to all investors, because while one-third of global economic growth comes from China — larger than the combined share from the US, Europe and Japan — most of what we read about that country is clouded by misunderstanding and fear.*

Understanding how much China has changed over the past few decades is key to assessing what potential, and problems, lie ahead. China's Change *is a great way to discover how China has evolved from a static, command-economy to one driven by entrepreneurs, and to learn how dramatic income growth has created a thriving middle-class and the world's best consumer story. The book punctures the biggest myths about the Chinese economy, from ghost cities to shadow banks, while maintaining a realistic approach to the risks to future growth. A great read, likely to change many readers' views on China.*

Matthews Asia Investment Strategist,
former US diplomat, Andy Rothman.

Wow! The journalistic skills and realistic perspective (which is long-term) hits this reader squarely on the head with the concise, direct and well written style. Excellent.

South Ocean Management Founder, Brook McConnell.

I found it very good and believe that people outside China could learn a lot from it.

Bing Yuan Founder, Zhou Ping.

China's Change *should be a text book for think tanks and policy units, especially for post-Brexit Britain.*

JP Morgan China Investment Trust Chairman,
William Knight.

Brilliant. It is the book that needs to be written, helping fill the desperate need for all kinds of people to understand China better and understand our future with China better. The content could move people's view of China. It is a monumental book. A great book.

Odin Capital Management Founder, Ulrik Trampe.

China's Change

The Greatest Show on Earth

China's Change

The Greatest Show on Earth

Hugh Peyman

Research-Works, China

NEW JERSEY • LONDON • SINGAPORE • BEIJING • SHANGHAI • HONG KONG • TAIPEI • CHENNAI • TOKYO

Published by

World Scientific Publishing Co. Pte. Ltd.
5 Toh Tuck Link, Singapore 596224
USA office: 27 Warren Street, Suite 401-402, Hackensack, NJ 07601
UK office: 57 Shelton Street, Covent Garden, London WC2H 9HE

Library of Congress Cataloging-in-Publication Data
Names: Peyman, Hugh, author.
Title: China's change : the greatest show on earth / Hugh Peyman (Research-Works, China).
Description: Hackensack, NJ : World Scientific Publishing Co. Pte. Ltd, [2018] |
Includes bibliographical references.
Identifiers: LCCN 2017036862 | ISBN 9789813231429 | ISBN 9789813231993 (pbk)
Subjects: LCSH: China--Economic conditions--2000– | China--Economic policy--2000– |
Social change--China.
Classification: LCC HC427.95 .P49 2018 | DDC 330.951--dc23
LC record available at https://lccn.loc.gov/2017036862

British Library Cataloguing-in-Publication Data
A catalogue record for this book is available from the British Library.

For any available supplementary material, please visit
http://www.worldscientific.com/worldscibooks/10.1142/10748#t=suppl

Desk Editors: Dong Lixi/Judy Yeo

Typeset by Stallion Press
Email: enquiries@stallionpress.com

Printed in Singapore

For Maria Yang Tse Oy

Contents

Preface

Dim, dim, the path in the twilight.

Li Ho (791–817).

If you always do what you always did, you will always get what you always got.

Albert Einstein (1879–1955).

After studying change for five decades, I shall surely be free of serious flaws.

Confucius (551–479 BC), *Analects* 7:17.

Asia and the West face similar challenges. Both need to renew themselves as mounting disruption forges a new era. The question is how: how to change?

"Look to China" is this book's startling answer. After all, Europe, the US and East Asia have copied China before to great effect, so why not now? Managing change is China's X-Factor. The concept of constant renewal, *weixin*, is almost 4,000 years old and the *Book of Change* over 2,000 years old.

Such a provocative idea requires a complete rethink about China, and appreciation that its traditional thought, drawn principally from its turbulent history, provides a roadmap for change. This rethink has to start with the two main narratives of the last quarter of a century about China. Both are now outdated. One is that China is destined to rule the world; the other sees China as seriously, if not fatally, flawed.

Neither China's primacy nor collapse is pre-ordained. Such over-simplistic narratives do not help the growing need to understand

21st-century China, whose rapidly changing reality is driven increasingly by its very demanding consumers, dynamic private companies and new technologies rather than by government or ideology. The state-driven China of recent decades — and still of the popular imagination — is largely passing or passed.

Not before time, much more nuanced narratives are emerging from people everywhere more closely familiar with the new China. As China re-emerges on the world geopolitical scene, Australian China *eminence grise* Stephen FitzGerald gave a lecture, *Managing Ourselves in a Chinese World,* on how to manage relations with China while being true to one's own values. Three McKinsey authors set China in the context of the new global reality in *No Ordinary Disruption,* Edward Tse's *China's Disruptors* captures the entrepreneurial essence of today's China and James Stent's *China's Banking Transformation* describes the reality of one major archetypal state-owned industry.

A large gap in understanding still remains. How has China managed to change so dramatically since 1978? Why has it not gone the way of Japan that also had a very promising three decades? *China's Change* explains that China still has many unused assets to develop but, most of all, China's X-Factor is to manage change by grasping its nature and devising a process to implement it, especially in government, economics and business as well as in life overall. As the *Financial Times* emerging markets editor James Kynge commented when reading an early draft, "I think you are onto something here and it allows your book to be philosophical economics, which is much more beguiling than straight economics, of course! I too wonder at the capacity of Chinese people to absorb change — this is definitely unusual, I agree."

In an increasingly disrupted world, *China's Change* answers two big global questions. How can other countries, firms and individuals find paths out of their dim twilight by adapting Chinese thinking? Can China continue to create one-third of the world's growth, more than the US, EU and Japan combined, to help cure the global economic malaise of the post-2008 stagnation?

Not just in the West: as expectations increasingly are dashed, people everywhere demand new ideas. This includes in the now economically much slower-growing rest of East Asia. As generational change transforms societies and memory of the East Asian Economic Miracle fades, restructuring is needed, even in Southeast Asia's most successful state, Singapore. Hong Kong and Taiwan, once the homes of Asian Tiger economies, Chinese entrepreneurialism and prosperity, have to find new paths before they recede into parochial backwaters.

For a West that has lost its way, a new China narrative and understanding is all the more relevant. Voters say they want change, but the snag is no Western playbook exists to explain how. Instead, only the same old stale thinking, simplistic slogans and recycled policies fill the confused debate about the future, from increasingly inward-looking Asian societies and post-Brexit Europe to culture wars-divided US.

So why not look to the one region in the world that clearly "gets" change, understands its management? Instead of looking inward, look to East Asia's recent past that created the world's greatest economic success of the last half-century, and especially to China, Asia's philosophical home of change, with its unprecedented recent speed and scale of transformation.

While Brexiteers and Trump supporters say they want to take back control but have yet to convince many they know how, China has regained control of its destiny by applying millennia-old Chinese concepts to manage change, with world-altering consequences. Look around: in the last two decades, China has risen from being Asia's pauper to providing the world's most numerous tourists and biggest individual spenders. Even 10% of Antarctica's tourist visitors in 2015–16 came from China, paying up to almost $30,000 each. This is a very different China. Much more important, of course, is that China has lifted 700 million people out of poverty, created a middle class of over 250 million and, as the world's top trader, built the largest foreign exchange reserves.

Only a quarter of a century ago, post-Mao China, already 15 years into reform, was floundering politically and economically. Digging into its traditional philosophy, China used a process that found answers, bit by bit, to its problems. The tools of discovery and implementation, the process, were Chinese, but the means selected were largely Western. Paramount leader Deng Xiaoping's 1992 Southern Tour sparked China's search for the Promethean energy that transformed the West after 1800, establishing its global dominance ever since. Among the means were rules regarding economics and trade, technical requirements like transparency and auditing, and concepts like the rule of law. Very mundane, it is true, but they launched a transformation in ways China did not know.

In what would be an ironic reversal of recent history, why shouldn't others in Asia and the West do what China did in 1992 — look elsewhere for how to conceptualize and implement change? The great strength of traditional Chinese thinking is creating a process to find the means to change: a roadmap. This is not about policy let alone ideology, but about how to handle the future and uncertainty with policies conceived locally. It could be a surprising, dramatic turning of world history's tables.

There is no reason why this cannot happen, once preconceptions are put to one side and misconceptions corrected. *China's Change* tries to provide what Simon Schama did in *Landscape and Memory*:

> a way of looking; of rediscovering what we already have, but which somehow eludes our recognition and our appreciation. Instead of being yet another explanation of what we have lost, it is an explanation of what we may yet find... In offering this alternative way of looking, I am aware that more is at stake than an academic quibble.

I have been lucky enough to have observed, absorbed and analysed Asia's dramatic change over the last 40 years. During this time, an increasingly familiar East Asian movie played out. From a front row seat in Hong Kong, Malaysia, Singapore and, for the last 15 years, China, I have watched as five Confucian-based societies, one after another, became First World economies: Japan, South Korea, Taiwan, Hong Kong and Singapore.

Nothing, though, prepared me for China's Great Change since 1978. China's scale, speed and impact have been literally unprecedented with 1.4 billion people creating the fastest ever prolonged economic spurt. The home of Confucianism is now the Greatest Show on Earth for anyone interested in world affairs, economics, business or their own future. By understanding China's change, anyone can create their own recovery.

Change is China's story. Several times in its long history, China has been in even worse straits than today's West or East Asia, gripped by the same sense of foreboding as poet Li Ho expressed when the great Tang Dynasty began to decline in the 9th century. The path can indeed seem very dim, dim in the twilight.

Gathering gloom and uncertainty has spread through the West in ways not seen since the 1930s. Asia has not been spared. Politics, policy and politicians are at the root of the malaise, stuck in 19th- and 20th-century ideological ruts. Western political and economic thought has all too often become a slave to some long-dead -ism, as economist John Maynard Keynes might have said. Leaders follow George Bush, who proudly proclaimed he did not "do the vision thing". Short-termism has replaced long-term thinking. Priorities are not realistically or clearly defined. Empty, unrealistic slogans dominate policy in the "post-truth" discourse. Philosophy is rarely considered. This was not always so in Asia or the West.

Great scientists like Albert Einstein and Charles Darwin grasped change's critical importance. Statesmen wrought great change through long-term vision, from Abraham Lincoln to Helmut Kohl in the West to Asian leaders from Japan to Singapore, South Korea to Taiwan and Hong Kong. Central to two centuries of Western dominance and the East Asian Miracle was appreciating how change transforms economies and societies, something now largely lost in Western thinking. Scroll back to the early 1860s. Adam Smith's ideas on free trade, after a century of bitter dispute, finally made it into William Gladstone's 1860 budget. Across the Atlantic in 1861, Lincoln reinterpreted the US Declaration of Independence that "all men are created equal", risking civil war to end slavery. On the other side of the world in 1862, explorer McDouall Stuart crossed Australia from south to north, battling interminable, hostile desert. All three showed vision, perseverance, grit and long-term thinking. Nor was this a unique three years; these qualities were not confined to the distant 19th century. William Beveridge's

1942 report led directly to Britain's welfare state and full employment. John Kennedy vowed in 1961 to put a man on the moon that decade, and did. With long-term thinking and a clear set of priorities, Kohl successfully reunited Germany on generous terms in 1990.

Today, such vision and long-term thinking is lacking. Angela Merkel's 2015 call to welcome refugees was firmly rejected by fellow EU governments. Short-term electoral considerations ruled as supposedly core EU humanitarian values of Western liberalism and the Good Samaritan were quickly swept aside. Not even long-term self-interest ruled: no discussion occurred about Europe's demographic problems as its population ages, a real ticking time bomb in full sight.

Everything is about now, the moment and instant solutions, not long-term thinking. The West seems dazed as it struggles to cope with accelerating change, uncertainty and complexity: disruption. The same is starting to happen in parts of Asia. Navigating these clichéd "uncharted waters" requires bold long-term rethinking. To avoid future problems, stagnation and even decline, nations and individuals need to rediscover approaches that made the West so strong for two centuries. These were not all about Empire, glory and Western exceptionalism, let alone divine right.

Managing change has been central to Western and East Asian progress. Heavy long-term investment in technology, science, government and infrastructure laid the economic foundations; steady improvements in housing, sanitation, health and education radically improved living standards; and step-by-step political reform led to votes for all from the UK to Taiwan, US to South Korea. There were struggles, but managing change, overcoming adverse forces, kept things moving. There is no reason this cannot happen again.

I arrived to live in Shanghai from early 2002, shortly after Gordon Chang published *The Coming Collapse of China*. Over 15 years later, China has not collapsed. Instead it has become of ever-growing global importance and endless fascination. Songwriter Graham Earnshaw jokingly captured the essence of 1970s Hong Kong in *Hong Kong Blues,* "I know it is noisy and crowded, dirty and annoying … but it's not boring." China today has the same intense mix of energy, confusion, pace and uncertainty that Hong Kong had in the 1970s, but with so much greater scale and global significance.

Understanding China can be perplexing but also exhilarating. Paradoxes abound. Simultaneously, China can appear to be communist and capitalist, rich and poor, rigidly bureaucratic and manically free-wheeling, traditional and modern, inward-looking and outward-going. Adding further confusion are questions about why China's economy has not collapsed, why it could be the one successful "communist" country. Reconciling all this is a great brain-teaser. Scepticism is rife; myths, misconceptions and complexity obscure the real China. Nonetheless, since my first glimpses in 1977, each decade has seemed to be less — not more — challenging for China. Why? It knows how to manage change, as recent results show.

China's economic re-emergence provides proven, practical and largely universal ideas, not some mysterious, abstract theory from an irrelevant, incompatible country or culture. The concrete fact is that China's real GDP has grown 107% from 2007 to 2016, while the US grew only 12%, UK 9%, EU 5% and Japan 3%: surely a nerve-tingling wake-up call? Solving the China puzzle answers one of today's greatest questions in economics, business and finance, casting light on the world's likely direction and prosperity. That is why, in increasingly disrupted times, fathoming China's change, how it happened and what it might mean, is the Greatest Show on Earth.

Shanghai, December 2017
hughpeyman@research-works.com

Prologue: China and an Increasingly Disrupted World

Other than Stable Eras, all times are Chaotic Eras.... It is morning but the sun does not always rise in the morning. That is what a Chaotic Era is like.

Liu Cixin, *The Three-Body Problem,* 2006.

Before understanding China's change, it is necessary to appreciate the global context. Economic, political and social turmoil capture headlines every day. Voters' verdicts from Brexit to Trump, Philippines to India, suddenly indicate a desire for a break with recent decades, while the most polarized US politics in living memory and European introspection await their denouement.

Some 70 years after the end of World War II, 25 years after the collapse of the Soviet Union and 15 years after interventions in Afghanistan, Iraq and the Middle East, there is a sense of relative power shifts to an increasingly multipolar world. China is not about to replace the US, certainly not militarily. However it could be the world's largest economy by 2025. Already it is the world's largest in terms of purchasing power parity. In the absence of US leadership in the America First era, China is actively helping maintain multilateralism and open trade. It is now the top export market for 43 countries, the US only 32. A new world shape is forming.

When senior partners at McKinsey, high priests of globalization, pronounce we are living in *No Ordinary Disruption,* they define a new world. Disruption can be good in their eyes, as warm winds from China blow across the rest of Asia, Australasia, Latin America and Africa, not just in mining and agriculture but tourism, education and cheaper goods, rearranging world orders. Chinese consumers, companies, adoption of technology, increasing connectivity and participation in global rule-setting will be central to the world managing its way through this extraordinary disruption. In the West especially, the prospect sends a chill down many spines, but it need not. Indeed, if handled well, it should bring more benefits than problems.

Disruption and China's Great Change

The fastest change in world history is causing "near-constant discontinuity", in *No Ordinary Disruption's* words. Whereas the UK took 154 years to double industrial output per person while the US took 53 years, China and India have taken just 12 and 16 years respectively. The UK and US each did this with barely 10 million people; China and India have done it with about 100 times as many: one billion people each at incomparable speed, scale and, therefore, impact.

China's Great Change of 1978–2015 began when Deng Xiaoping and the economic reformers adopted reform and opening up to replace inward-looking central planning. Largely unnoticed in the West until after China joined the World Trade Organization (WTO) in 2001, this sparked more rapid globalization in manufacturing and services, followed by accelerating adoption of new technology and systems. Each builds on the other, making change faster, more unpredictable and difficult to manage. Geography and distance, history and social systems, urbanization and consumption, technology and competition, ageing and labour, all amplify each other, leaving people bewildered.

Distance is a barrier to understanding for Western leaders in government, commerce and academia as the Great Change occurred for most "on the other side of the earth". East Asian economic geography and societies evolve far faster than most Westerners and even many Asians can follow. For those familiar only with their own country, the concept of one world is perplexing, as Theresa May revealed. Often the Great Change is deemed a threat, leading to paralysis or mistakes. It flies in the face of the Great Moderation from 1992 to 2007, a golden era for Western firms and consumers, basking in the End of History's glow while reaping great benefit from the triumph of Western governance, firms and the post-Cold War peace dividend. Planet Earth would safely remain a Western world. Suddenly, after 2008, no more: such promise rapidly receded into history and a new reality dawns.

So much is happening all at once. Four global forces — shifting wealth, demographics, technology and connectivity — drive disruption and China's Great Change. The world's economic centre of gravity is moving east and south from North America and Western Europe to Asia and emerging economies. As Ronald Reagan said in his *Morning in America* speech, "You ain't seen nothing yet." It is now morning in Asia and the morning sun is rising again.

Consider what probably lies ahead, starting with wealth. China's 2020 e-tail market may total that of the US, Germany, UK, France and Japan combined, McKinsey calculates. By 2025, it estimates half the *Fortune Global 500 Companies*, once synonymous with being Western, will be headquartered in emerging economies: most in China. In 2000, only 5% were outside the West, a time in which many Western observers of China and Asia seem to be stuck. By 2025, the consultant sees more billion-dollar-sales companies in China than in the US or EU: muscle. By 2030, McKinsey estimates 60% of people with annual incomes over $20,000 will live in emerging economies, the largest number, again, in China: spending power. Nearly half the world's growth between 2010 and 2025 will occur in just 440 emerging-economy cities, again with China having the largest number: importance. Even if the forecasts are over-optimistic, few dispute the trend or outcome.

Transformative forces have spread rapidly from the West to the rest of the world, which has adopted new technology with alacrity, often faster, and on a greater scale. Instant data available to consumers and companies has ballooned. So has the power to collect and process it. All this shortens life cycles of products, companies and industrial structures. Decision-making has to be faster: all increasingly complex and difficult, with no let-up in sight.

Disruptive technologies are all around us. Dobbs, Manyika and Woetzel list four: beginning with the fundamental building blocks from the human genome to advanced materials. China has grasped their significance and acted swiftly. It now has the world's largest gene sequencing capacity: see Chapter 14. In the next wonder material, graphene, 200 times stronger than steel, China has forged strategic partnerships with world leaders. First with Manchester University, whose Nobel Prize-winning scientists pioneered the latest research, and then with leading producers. By 2012, China was registering more graphene patents than any other country. Manchester now has 4,000 Chinese students and 170 Chinese staff.

New machines will alter life further, ranging from much more sophisticated automation and robots to driverless vehicles on the ground and in the air: a truly new world. The first airborne solo taxi service is planned for Dubai's skies, carrying someone up to 50 kilometres on a single charge. Ehang makes the machines: a private Chinese company that did not exist four years ago but now leads in pilotless flight.

The Internet of Things uses sensors and actuators in machines to collect data to monitor operations, making decisions in everything from manufacturing and infrastructure to healthcare: all speed accuracy, information flow and action. Mobile computing devices are now much cheaper, more connected, spurring innovation and productivity, while cloud computing makes the digital world simpler, faster and more powerful. All help create new business models that are more flexible and rapidly scalable, requiring less capital.

Artificial intelligence will revolutionize work. Jobs once only humans could do are now done by machines that can learn, work with people and use artificial intelligence. All this accelerates the use of new technologies, amplifying trends, providing greater reach, better customer service and more efficient sales. New products are created at almost no marginal cost, empowering new entrants with lower costs and faster product times to market. Established players are often complacent, making them vulnerable to new, hungrier competitors who accept lower returns and work harder.

Changing demographics, as Western populations age and shrink, favour a younger Asia with China at its economic heart. Linking all this is the fourth trend, connectivity. China's Great Change is visible everywhere, in the flows of trade, capital, people and information. Made-in-China has become even more ubiquitous than did Made-in-Hong Kong, Made-in-Taiwan or Made-in-Japan. Road warriors flit around the world, from airport to airport, continent to continent. Global conference calls connect people, no matter the hour or location, in this 24/7 world. Yet it was only in 1987 that Professor Qianbai sent China's first email, "Crossing the Great Wall to Join the World". Now China has 900 million internet users, almost treble the US population.

Globally, all aspects of life are changing, sparking anxiety for the left-behind and those yearning for a simpler, more familiar past: Stop the World I Want to Get Off. Yet shifting wealth, technology, demographics and connectivity will not stop. Indeed, if handled properly, they should not. They just need to be managed so the "world is richer, more urbanized, more skilled and healthier" as *No Ordinary Disruption* anticipates. It adds that the big winners should be consumers, who may capture two-thirds of all cost reductions, reversing firms' growing pricing power of the 1990s and early 2000s.

China's Consumers

"Thunderbolt in the wine world" is how organizers of the *Revue du vin de France* World Championships described the 2016 victory of Chinese wine tasters. Beating over 20 other teams, including from France, Italy, Spain and the US, the winners diplomatically put winning down to 50% knowledge and 50% luck, a classic Chinese response with traditional self-effacing modesty. Hearing this, my mind went back to a vineyard in Ningxia where I helped with the harvest. Over dinner, with no fuss, the parents mentioned their daughter was going to Bordeaux in the morning to study viticulture for seven years: she was 15. Prepare the next generation early, otherwise how to compete?

Get used to thunderbolts from China. Think about this: Chinese made 50 times more mobile payments in 2016 than US consumers, trebling to $5.5 trillion in China while US payments only grew 39% to $112 billion. This confirms what is observed in other industries: Chinese consumers are much faster adopters of new technology than Europeans or Americans. How will that play out over the next five to 10 years? A Great Digital Divergence seems underway, a striking reversal of what held for two centuries.

"China's consumers are now so demanding and globally minded … you have to be world class to serve China," notes Gary Rieschel of Qiming Ventures. As Mike Morris explained over a quarter of a century ago, "The one thing you need know about Chinese consumers is they only care about two things: brand and value." Squaring that difficult circle is the China challenge: not easy but very rewarding for those who succeed. All this matters now China is the leading market for so many products and raw materials; by 2030 it could be for almost all. Chinese consumers not only create demand but keep manufacturers and service providers on their toes. Having lived through disruption all their lives, they have very low trust in claims made.

Famously well-informed, they spend longer researching purchases than consumers anywhere. Be it online or offline, they pay particular attention to the internet, social media and friends' advice. 61% of Chinese look for reviews online before buying a product: in the US only 39% do. After making a purchase, 52% of Chinese consumers write online reviews compared with 31% in the US. Chinese download 59% of all the world's smartphone apps, over treble their share of population. None of this seems remarkable in China with its palpable desire to engage the new, to experience the previously unknown or unattainable. Chinese consumers are making up for lost time, desiring exhilarating 21st-century change. This is not just confined to the rich. A young porter at Beijing's high-speed railway station arranges taxis with the latest iPhone. He is participating, living the life and is part of change. So are his high-speed train passengers.

China has long had the world's largest population but had minimal impact. Too poor for almost two centuries, China did not matter.

What now elevates its consumers to global importance is their purchasing power and curiosity. They in turn are changed by global exposure. From wine to autos, phones to fashion, Chinese have become a global force. Dairy products were not even part of their traditional diet. Indeed Chinese were said to be lactose intolerant, unable to digest milk or cheese, yet Pizza Hut has enjoyed great success in China.

Leisure and entertainment illustrate China's Scale. Shanghai Disneyland opened in 2016, making the Magic Kingdom easily accessible to the 300 million people living within three hours by expressway or high-speed rail. The $5.5 billion attraction, boasting Disney's biggest castle, exceeded its first-year visitor target of 10 million by over 10%. Box office success will increasingly be determined in China. Tencent in 2016 bought the *World of Warcraft* for $8.6 billion, shortly after its latest game-to-movie production grossed $156 million over the first five days in China, while the US opening weekend took in a lacklustre $24.4 million: no matter. Over half *Warcraft* players live in China where 15 new cinemas opened every day and ticket sales rose 50% in 2015. China could soon be the world's largest film market, leading to more Western films with Chinese flavour and storylines: TV too. The BBC introduced Chinese clues to its *Sherlock* detective series. Over six million in China viewed *Sherlock's* 2016 season opener on social media and internet within 24 hours of its TV showing.

For global companies to acquire or maintain world leadership, they have to win in China. Automaker Toyota lost the 2016 world sales crown to VW because it lagged behind in China. Despite its diesel scandal, VW sales in China climbed 12% to overtake Toyota, whose image is tarnished by the Japanese government's hardening attitude towards China.

This is not just about numbers. Chinese consumers have characteristics that will change world tastes and products. Upmarket hotels now have hot water at the ready, with thermos flasks and electric kettles in guests' rooms, along with China Global Television Network. Some Chinese restaurants in the West even serve good food because Chinese travellers now demand it. China influences design from electronics to clothing, regionally at first but globally later. Some only add to demand but others provide direct competition, and Chinese firms' great advantage is they naturally understand better than anyone the world's fastest-growing and often largest market, China.

"Darn right scary" is how McKinsey's Jonathan Woetzel describes cutting-edge surgical implants some Chinese undergo. China's Millennials are widely seen as being adventurous, often very experimental. It is all part of making up for lost time, trying the new, believing in it, something that China's middle class until recently has not been able to enjoy. Lei Jun of Xiaomi says that he sells not a product but "the opportunity to participate" in the 21st century and wider world. It is all part of life's new journey of modernization, new experience and participation.

China's Millennials

The single most important consumer group in the world is China's 15–29-year-olds, its Millennials. Some 318 million strong in 2015, they now outnumber the entire US population. Two-thirds are in China's highest income stratum, thanks to their greater education. *China Skinny* describes them as the "shoppers, travellers and hedonists who contribute most to China's retail sales growth". The average age of a BMW owner in China is 35; in Germany it is 53. Unlike their frugal Cultural Revolution parents, who experienced much uncertainty and so save rather than spend, China's Millennials have only known rising prosperity.

Combining pragmatism with opportunism, Millennials have a much more positive view of China than their parents. They have a confidence in the future. A global poll found 49% believe the world (presumably mostly their own) is becoming a better place. In the US and UK, the numbers were a mere 6% and 4% respectively. They have good reason to be optimistic: seven times more have a degree than those born in 1980. Comprising half of China's 120 million travellers overseas, their curiosity is powered by education and social media. Their incomes are seen doubling in the next decade.

Now China has real consumers of its own, hundreds of millions of them: at least 250 million in the middle class, by 2030 maybe 500 million. 70% of Chinese Millennials own their own home, with 81% of the remainder intending to buy within five years, compared with 35% who own in the US and 31% in the UK: double or more, according to a 2017 HSBC survey. Once a modern home is bought, the next priority is to fill the space with white goods and furnishings, whose growth in 2015 significantly outstripped property purchases. While filling the home, leisure, travel and entertainment spending have also taken off. Millennial China feels like 1950s or 1960s US and Europe, with the build out of suburbia and consumerism. As British Prime Minister Harold Macmillan said in 1959, "You've never had it so good." That is what the bulk of Millennials are experiencing, what Asia's young from Hong Kong and Singapore to Japan and South Korea felt in the 1980s and 1990s.

China's Millennials may be the world's most driven people, based on German research firm GfK's 22-country 2016 survey. In France, US, Australia, South Korea, UK, Japan and Hong Kong, the greatest concern was insufficient income "to live their lives". In China the top three concerns were pressure from self, inadequate sleep and not enough time to do what one wants — proving what many know: some Chinese work very hard, maybe too hard. On the plus side though, they do not generally max out their credit cards to support lifestyles beyond their means or run up bank debt, apart from mortgages. Only 25%–30% of new cars are bought with financing, the rest with cash, compared with 90% in the UK. Thrift and living within one's means for most are still a virtue in China.

The scale and importance of China are well known. Swatch makes 49% of its sales to Chinese, Ferragamo 39%; Apple sells 26% of its iPhones in China. The 19th-century wish of Manchester textile merchants for lasting fortunes by selling an extra inch of fabric to every Chinese never came true nor did Standard Oil's desire to fill the lamps of China, but 21st-century foreign firms are now realizing similar China dreams. The list could go on and on. The point is that China now matters, and it matters mostly because of its Millennials and the generation to follow, with even higher education and incomes. Apart from its markets setting trends and shaping products, as well as driving R&D and business models, this toughens Chinese firms. Previously they never enjoyed any advantage from the large population, now they benefit from its wealth and criticism, leveraging this growing strength abroad.

Chinese manufacturers have scale to exploit, driving down costs, justifying more spending on R&D, brand-building and marketing. This generates more demand: a virtuous circle. With 900 million internet users and one billion active users of WeChat's mobile text and voice messaging app, no wonder Chinese consumers are catching up rapidly with the rest of the world. In some cases, China is overtaking all others, as 2017's November 11 Singles' Day showed, ringing up 24-hour sales of $25.3 billion, far exceeding its US inspiration, Black Friday.

Private Companies

Foreign companies in China are up against not just reforming state enterprises but, even more threatening, dynamic private firms. Huawei, Alibaba and Tencent are the first of many. Here come China's whales, sharks and piranhas, in Michael Enright's graphic phrase. The private sector sharks pursue the state- or foreign-owned whales, while having to look out for the smaller Chinese piranhas, among the fiercest and most innovative competitors.

Dominating China's economy now are its private entrepreneurs who are increasingly regarded as equal to their global peers. Veteran US early-stage investor Gary Rieschel says they are no different in capacity, intellect or drive from those he backs in the US. Indeed, Chinese company founders "work incredibly hard, putting Silicon Valley entrepreneurs to shame. They have grit, determination and commitment" simply because there is no alternative to tenacity and hard work. Chinese markets are so competitive because of sheer numbers: intense. Rieschel describes an entrepreneur's life as daily combat sport. Having grown up in such a harsh environment, they are not intimidated, unlike many elsewhere.

On top of intense competition, there is uncertainty and ambiguity. Permanent transition creates fog. People do not know which laws or regulations will be enforced, so transition traps await the unwary. Entrepreneurs are therefore hypersensitive to the smallest shift in the official wind or industrial landscape, making them very nimble. All build systems to track change, process information and develop mechanisms to cope with it.

This is China's unwelcome competitive reality for the ill-prepared. Rapid transformation shapes product markets, the perfect Petri dish for change, not only because of China's size but also its evolving investment eco-cultures, each with unique characteristics. Beijing's venture capitalists visit Shenzhen more often, believing it creates business models faster than anywhere else. Neighbouring Dongguan overtook Shenzhen to produce the two largest-selling Chinese smartphone brands in 2016; and so it goes. If Chinese firms and cities need to keep ever-closer tabs on each other, everyone else from Asia to the West had better do the same. Otherwise they will not know what is heading for their shores until the *Jaws* theme music reaches a crescendo and it is too late.

Chapter 1

Change, The Chinese Principle and the Greatest Show on Earth

"*It is not the strongest of the species that survive or the most intelligent, but the one most responsive to change*," Charles Darwin

(1809–1882)

"*It is possible to see into the potential changes before they occur*,"

John Minford
Introduction p. xxvi
Sunzi's *The Art of War* 2002

China's Change is not about policy but process: not *what* but *how*. Each country or person is different, with their own history, characteristics and culture. Policy that works in China may not elsewhere. Anyway, plenty of opinion makers and policy institutes provide the what but not the how. China offers the how: a roadmap for thinking about renewal.

Chapter 1 explores the main themes of *China's Change,* many observed from my own experience and detailed, on-the-ground research. Starting with the essential background for context — China's history, philosophy, government and politics — the book then considers why China is so often misunderstood, particularly its economy, and how China's change will impact the rest of the world. With this complex mix revealed, China is a lot easier to understand. Essential Chinese ideas very largely exist in Western thought. Many have just been forgotten or disregarded, especially after the rise of short-term approaches to solve long-term problems.

Whenever I ask people in the West about long-term thinking, they laugh at its widespread but lamentable absence. The West has no *Book of Change* (*Yi Jing* or *I Ching*), which has analysed change for over 2,000 years. At least East Asia is familiar with its concepts and Confucianism, even if the younger generation is much less knowledgeable about them. Note, the traditional spelling of the *Book of Change* has been *I Ching*, but the current *hanyu pinyin* spelling is *Yi Jing*, just as Taoism has become Daoism. For consistency, *hanyu pinyin* is used throughout, except where this makes no sense. Also, I use Confucianism in a very broad sense to refer to the array of traditional Chinese schools of thought, including those of Confucius and his followers, Daoism and Buddhism.

All Confucian-based economies, bar China, Vietnam and North Korea, have become First World economies. A First World high-income China would be a complete global game changer, yet from 2016, if gross national income per person can grow annually by 6% within seven years it will reach the World Bank definition of a high income economy of $12,236. Even at 5% average growth, China would reach it by 2025. Prepare for major change before it is too late.

Applying Chinese Thinking

Given the many clouded views of China, it is necessary to state immediately that China does not have the best systems in the world. Furthermore, this is no Maoist or Confucian tract. It is an attempt to take from China ideas that create a process others can use to solve problems anywhere and to understand China's economy better.

Indeed the list of China's flaws has been long, be they in finance; from banks to stock markets, environment; from air to water and soil quality, society; from migrants to corruption or safety; from SARS to rail. Flaws though have been markedly reduced during the transition from central planning to a more market-based economy. Leaders in Beijing are generally very well aware of problems, often more so than their critics. They know everything takes time while experience teaches that change is more likely to succeed when approached gradually. Take safety, for example. Since 2000, China has had disasters in transport, health, food and fire because it lacked effective systems: babies died, epidemics only narrowly averted and passengers killed. Yet, China has developed a way to overcome problems, by understanding and implementing change. Its size creates complexity and much is intertwined. China is one enormous Rubik's Cube: change one thing and a myriad other things are altered. What China does have after setbacks is a process to regroup, to redesign systems and approaches so as to ensure disasters do not recur, at least not on the same scale.

Many outside China see one disaster or fault after another, presuming the same is true throughout. What many observers lack is extensive knowledge let alone the relevant perspective to appreciate context or scale. So much has to change that priorities have to be selected and followed strictly. Everything cannot be done at once. If China tried, it would be overwhelmed by administrative gridlock, poor implementation or unintended consequences: doomed to failure. Instead, it sets a clear sense of goals, guided by long-term thinking and gradualism to smooth the process. Change is supported by the often overlooked very strong assets of private sector dominance, education, R&D and new growth areas.

Chinese thinking about change is not some mysterious, opaque Oriental philosophy, but a very rational approach fully compatible with the 21st century. Managing change can be described in barely 70 words. For China, the main goals are harmony, stability and moderation: in other societies, goals will differ. They can though be crystallized using the same long-term, 360-degree thinking and vision, along with a good grasp of cycles and priorities. Implementation then follows with research and field work, pilot schemes and correct sequencing. Pragmatism, flexibility, gradualism, restraint and constant renewal are central to success. Educating people for politics and administration is essential. Such precepts may be ignored or contradicted, but they remain China's default thought position. Everything is work in progress, nothing is complete, but sufficient adoption of 20 essential ideas keeps China moving forward.

People everywhere have long-term goals and aspirations, ranging from work, incomes and identity to budgets, security and social stability. All have to be discussed and heard carefully, otherwise politics becomes a Tower of Babel with competing interests and ill-thought-out ideas collapsing the entire edifice. Many aspects of life must be considered, not as single issues, but as part of a connected whole. What will work look like in an age of artificial intelligence and robots? What skills, education and R&D will be needed to make the most of this major change and avoid the worst? How should foreign policy best be implemented? What are possible unintended consequences, such as waves of refugees resulting from armed intervention? How to alter global governance structures for economics and security to gain the most from rapid change while avoiding the worst? Sleep walking towards this misty future with the sound turned off is unwise.

New long-term approaches are hard but not impossible. When there is no obvious alternative, as in the late 1970s, minds can be focused as Margaret Thatcher's TINA (There Is No Alternative) did. Now, much of the West and parts of Asia have to acknowledge a similar point has been reached: their Stable Era is over. A new morning sun may await, but only if people reinvent themselves before a new Chaotic Era ensues. Muddling through with strident slogans and short-term tactics is no permanent solution. Nor is hoping something will turn up, as the ever-optimistic but impecunious Mr Micawber did in *David Copperfield.* Life's lottery is rarely that generous, usually quite the reverse.

How might Confucianism help Western and Asian democracies recover? Moderation and compromise are at the heart of Confucianism, as Arthur Waley, the leading 20th-century English translator of Chinese philosophy and literature, observed in 1938. In the shadow of the looming Second World War, he grieved for his liberalism after seeing totalitarianism rise in Spain, Portugal, Italy and Germany on the right and the Soviet Union on the left.

"That good lies between the two extremes has been very generally accepted by those who have tried to view the world rationally. As a political principle, it was the foundation of 19th-century Liberalism and in particular of English Liberalism...Unfortunately it is extremes and not compromises that most easily become associated with strong emotional impulse. The downfall of Liberalism has been due to the *failure to associate the middle way with a strong trend of emotion.* The success of Confucianism...was due in large measure to the fact that it contrived to *endow compromise with an emotional glamour,*" he wrote in his introduction to the *Analects of Confucius.*

Today, Waley would hope that Confucianism, well away from the extremes, could again inject rationality, moderation and emotional glamour into debate during a time of accelerating global disruption and a search for new political moorings.

When the World Looked to China

China's links with the rest of Asia go back thousands of years. To the east and south, they extend from Japan's Kyoto, which copied the Chinese capital's city plan and philosophy during the Tang Dynasty (618–907), to Indonesia, where Confucianism is one of the six state-recognized religions, reflecting three millennia of contact. To the west, the overland Silk Route, through central Asia to India and Pakistan, began more than two millennia ago.

More recently, Chinese traders settled in the main Southeast Asian cities of Manila, Jakarta, Bangkok and Yangon before a wave of labourers came to the tin mines and rubber plantations of 19th-century and early 20th-century Malaysia and the trading entrepôt of Singapore. Their influence, not just through descendants, has left an indelible impression on Southeast Asian thinking. Some of Chinese philosophy's main ideas are still familiar, though often much faded.

Increasingly removed from direct experience of the East Asian Miracle, today's Asia would do well to revisit it and the Chinese philosophy at its roots. After all, Asia did before. So did the much more distant West, borrowing ideas for government, technology and philosophy, from bureaucracy to porcelain and human rights; and now, even maths education and bike sharing.

To reform an ineffective and often venal civil service, Britain, in 1855, did not hesitate to embrace a seemingly thoroughly modern and

Western idea, meritocracy: an idea very much in tune with the times. Other European countries, the US, Canada, Australia and New Zealand all followed suit. Instead of senior administrative positions being awarded on the basis of patronage, favour, nepotism or bribery they were to be won by public examination: on merit. The result was a bureaucracy of greatly enhanced quality. Selecting only people of ability helped Britain manage the Industrial Revolution's problems and capitalise on its opportunities to become a leading global economy and power. Nowhere in Europe or America at the time had adopted such a "modern" idea, yet the practice was 1,250 years old.

Meritocracy came to Europe indirectly through empire. Struggling with its increasingly unwieldy and complex administration, the British East India Company sought solutions in the early 1800s. The answer, company officials in Guangzhou suggested, was to learn from Imperial China's system of public examinations that had started in 605. To their minds, this was the foundation of China's success. In 19th-century Westminster and Whitehall, meritocracy in the civil service came to be called the Chinese Principle: Britain's senior civil servants became known as Mandarins.

Like silk, tea, pheasants, rhubarb, umbrellas and much else, this British import came from China. There was nothing surprising about it. France's Sun King Louis XIV in the 17th century wanted to know more about China, especially its sciences, mathematics, philosophy, medicine and emperors. Voltaire, the very embodiment of 18th-century European Enlightenment, praised Chinese government and Confucian morality. Indeed, he wrote a play about it based on the 13th-century *Orphan of Zhao.*

Learning and copying from China had been going on for hundreds of years, if not a couple of millennia. Marco Polo brought knowledge of porcelain to Europe in 1291. While remarking that "nothing lovelier could be imagined", Edmund de Waal in *The White Road* noted that bowls and dishes were made from clay, "stacked in huge mounds and then left for 30 or 40 years exposed to wind, rain and sun...You must understand that when a man makes a mound of this earth he does so for his children." One thing the West learned was that long-term thinking was part of traditional Chinese thought and practice.

The United Nation's Universal Declaration of Human Rights drew heavily on the concept of the universality of ideas, influenced by a Lebanese diplomat Charles Malik and Chinese philosopher-cum-diplomat Chang Peng Chun, representatives of two of the world's oldest cultures. These were not just Western ideas. The first paragraph quotes Mencius saying the highest aim should be to rule through benevolence, *ren*. Chang told the United Nations in 1948, "In the 18th century, when progressive ideas with respect to human rights had been first put forward in Europe, translations of Chinese philosophers ...had inspired such thinkers as Voltaire, Quesnay and Diderot in their humanistic revolt against feudalism,": so much for human rights being a wholly Western concept.

What the World Needs Now

Ideas to overcome increasing global disruption are needed badly. States failing to meet public expectations disrupt Western politics, security and economies. Provision of basics like education, healthcare and infrastructure is wanting. All play out in the political arena, which is a large part of the problem. Increasingly, the same is happening in Asia, from insufficient affordable housing in Hong Kong to the need for a new approach in Singapore and harmony in Indonesia.

Broad goals (apart from re-election) are increasingly lost as special interests, cronies, lobbyists, identity politics, narrow pressure groups and a general sense of malaise take control, polarizing politics. Adversarial politics divide rather than advance society. Checks and balances to protect against tyrants and predators are abused or distorted, with deadlock resulting. Elections on their own are no guarantee of good government, as Thailand and the Philippines have shown, let alone the West. A sense of the long-term, integrity, the common good and compromise is needed, a spirit of moderation and not of winner-takes-all: all solid Confucian principles.

A failure of the political class and its advisers defines much of the West today. Gambles are taken on domestic, foreign and economic affairs, as the UK's Scottish referendum, Brexit and austerity have shown. The modern state is based on its bureaucracy, whose competence, autonomy and accountability are critical to its success, making David Cameron's failure to instruct his cabinet office to prepare contingency papers for a Brexit vote simply breath-taking. Brussels' inability to explain itself adequately to voters eroded support for the EU. The US is no different, only the details. Alexander Hamilton lost the argument for a sufficiently strong central government. Instead, Madisonian checks and balances restrain power, especially of the executive, while Jacksonian populism distrusts bureaucratic expertise for being elitist, preferring instead more political appointees in senior posts, quite the opposite of what a well-motivated, competent and autonomous civil service needs.

In contrast, China has been a "precociously modern state" for over two millennia, in US political scientist Francis Fukuyama's eyes. In the second century BC, Han Dynasty China had many of the attributes of what Max Weber in the late 19th century considered a modern state. Therefore, it should be no surprise that East Asian administration and statecraft, whose Confucian framework guided the East Asian Economic Miracle, has much to offer.

What China Offers

The two millennia old *Yi Jing*, the *Book of Change*, is called *the* Chinese book by Australian National University Professor John Minford. China "gets" change, today's West does not. After all, China has suffered so much from Chaotic Eras, including eight of the world's 12 bloodiest wars, forcing it to understand change in order to regain stability. Compared with what the West now faces, East Asia navigated through much greater uncertainty and change during its economic miracle of the last half century. This is modern Confucian-influenced Asia's great strength, transforming itself beyond recognition.

These are proven ideas. Three times, for about half of the last 1,400 years, China has been the world's leading economy. Three times it has stumbled, declined and then recovered. Fellow Confucian-based societies Japan, South Korea, Taiwan, Hong Kong and Singapore have been the greatest economic achievers of the last half century, climbing from Third to First World. Now China, knowing how to manage change, has again grabbed global attention by lifting 700 million people out of poverty, creating a middle class of over 250 million and jobs for 900 million.

This is in great contrast to the West or parts of Asia today that display no appreciation of the need to understand change let alone how to manage it. Societies have no clear set of common goals or priorities. Long-term thinking is lacking in the major political parties. So much is *ad hoc,* one-off, tactical moves, short-term games, as Brexit and US politics reveal so graphically. Decisions are reactive rather than pro-active. As Einstein said, if you keep doing what you have always done, you will continue to get what you always got. Therefore change but how?

The How of Change

Change in East Asia is traditionally managed through process. It is *not* primarily a blueprint or set of policies. Rather, it is a series of steps to discover what works to solve real challenges. This is not about policy and power, but about processes to solve problems, many inextricably intertwined. The West rarely thinks about process, only blindly about policy, as if policy is a panacea. Big issues, be they refugees, foreign relations, security, migration, globalization, unemployment or depressed areas are not connected in government policy, but they often are in real life. Unintended consequences buffet the West. Single-issue politics dominate. 360-degree thinking is missing, so is compromise. Moderation shrinks as societies are pulled to extremes.

Ideas about managing change can apply to everyone thinking about the future be they individuals, families, firms, government or society. To succeed, all, especially mainstream politicians, need to make their case by approaching long-term problems differently. Otherwise, politics becomes mired in short-term thinking, increasingly ineffective and dysfunctional. Reluctance to embrace long-term thinking is strong: deferred gratification is not appreciated or popular. New ideas are rarely easily sold, especially when coming from another culture. Many assert that democracies cannot copy post-1960s East Asia, which was authoritarian during its rapid development; and China is still nominally a communist state. All this misses the key point. Successful change comes through process, not solely policies or political systems.

Think of change as a three-part process: goals, means and people to identify priorities before devising and implementing policies. Successful methods are non-ideological: street-cleaning for instance, as 1930s New York Mayor Fiorello La Guardia remarked. Sometimes considered authoritarian, to Confucians, he was pragmatic. To them and La Guardia, managing change is not about shiny new ideological policies, hankering for a lost world or a new beacon gleaming on the hill, it is about process.

Accepting that China's experience is relevant requires a fundamental re-think about China. For almost two centuries since Voltaire and the British bureaucracy's reformers praised China, the West has had a largely negative perception of China, first as the Sick Man of the Orient, next as the Yellow Peril and then as Red China. Even two of China's leading writers, Mo Yan and Liu Cixin, respectively described the Cultural Revolution as "unprecedented fanaticism" and the "Madness Years", neither reassuring labels. There has been much alarm.

The West, not surprisingly, looks at China through Western eyes: a China of the observer, not the observed. Better to start with how China sees itself through its traditional philosophy, still largely China's default position. Compounding the problems of unfamiliarity, language, geography and history is what Oxford's Raymond Dawson wrote in 1967's *The Chinese Chameleon: An Analysis of European Conceptions of Chinese Civilization,* "Communism conceals China from us". Extreme Maoism was an aberration that still informs the West, leading to many misconceptions, particularly about its economy and society: ghost cities, shadowy banks and excessive debt will all be explained and demystified. Overlooked are China's dynamic and dominant private sector, education levels, R&D and new growth areas that promise to avert any impending collapse.

Universal Thinking

This is not about Chinese exceptionalism, let alone superiority, but merely a corrective to misconceptions. Indeed, many parts of Western thinking and language are imbued with similar aphorisms, folk sayings or writings. Ideas are frequently universal. In economics too, markets, innovation and the new economy all figure prominently in government thinking about the future.

Charles Darwin concluded it is not the strongest of the species or the most intelligent that survive, but those most responsive to change. The Victorians in their heyday knew this. So did the Greeks at the dawn of Western civilisation. Socrates, sounding uncannily like Confucius and born just 10 years after his death, said, "Remember, there is nothing stable in human affairs; therefore, avoid undue elation in prosperity or undue depression in adversity". Plato, echoing Heraclitus who died about the same time as Confucius, wrote, "Everything changes and nothing remains still...you cannot step twice into the same stream". Change is inevitable, prepare for and handle it.

Who might have written, "Assume nothing and never become too wrapped up in success or pleasure, because there is always something around the corner to cut you down to size"? Was it Confucius, Mencius or the *Book of Change*? In fact, it was "a small piece of advice" written in 2011 by the great Australian cricket captain and commentator Richie Benaud: be alert to the possibility of sudden, major change. Life is capricious. Cycles, reversion to the mean and equilibrium are fundamental to markets and economics in the West. People everywhere know this, but when it comes to politics, they all too often ignore it. Trapped in a rut, they are beguiled by short-term promises and the assumed inevitability of straight-line progress. The truth is that the recent trend may not be your friend, but your enemy.

Ironically, China has much more in common than today's West with earlier creative Western peaks, from Athens to Florence, Edinburgh and Vienna to Silicon Valley. Even though these were rooted in Western civilization, it is a world that many in the West have lost or ignore, not understanding what previously drove progress. Many are obstructed by an often self-serving, complacent and unrealistic view of how the world should be: always to their advantage. A reality check is needed not just in the West but in Asia too, as an older generation passes away, whose thinking was often rooted in traditional Chinese philosophy, which had known great turbulence and poverty before experiencing the transformation of East Asia's economic miracle. Its children and grandchildren largely assume continued peace and prosperity, though some are now starting to feel less sure.

History is relevant and useful, as the Scots, who invented modern historical fiction, appreciated. The past matters in order to understand the present and future. Those ignorant of history will "forever remain children in understanding", as the Scottish Enlightenment's foremost philosopher, David Hume, held in the 18th century. George Santayana wrote in 1905 that, "Those who cannot remember the past are condemned to repeat it." Emperor Taizong of Tang had said, "If I use history as a mirror, I shall know how to reverse adversity". All are similar ideas expressed thousands of miles apart, separated in time by over a millennium: value history.

Lessons from the East Asian Economic Miracle

The roots of the miracle may be hotly debated but the outcome is undeniable, East Asia has been transformed. Market-friendly policies, industrial policy, state intervention, thrift and hard work are thrown into the mix of interpretations. Fukuyama singled out one common denominator: all are "competent, high-capacity states".

Without new approaches, old formulae will not work any better than before, maybe even worse. As Einstein implied, progress requires change. Straight-line progress though is a myth. Cycles happen, as Asian philosophy, investors and sports fans everywhere know only too well. So do countries, empires and civilizations that have fallen. Only some at the top believe they are immune to cycles, natural hubris; and all in human history have been proven wrong. Cycles can, however, be prolonged and ameliorated by continual renewal of thinking, *weixin*. That is the incentive to change.

What the West lacks most is long-term thinking. Some Asian democracies are starting to suffer from the same failing. "One who fails to plan for 10 generations is incapable of planning for one time. One who fails to plan for the whole situation is incapable of planning for a partial area", wrote Chen Danran (1859–1930). Hardly an arresting sound bite or snappy election-winning slogan, but true nonetheless. Without long-term, 360-degree thinking, one cannot run effectively a family or firm, let alone a government. The competence bar is set high simply because it is informed by over 3,000 years of written history and philosophy: actual experience, good and bad, failure and success. Many lessons are learned from China's often harsh history, including of recent times.

Understanding Change: China's X-Factor

Over the millennia, China has developed the philosophical concept of *yi*, change; and how to adjust to it. To practitioners, this is a science. Reform is a process, knowing how to set goals and conceive ideas in a non-ideological, practical way.

Traditional Chinese philosophy has several advantages. First, it can look simultaneously at the long and short term, with the concept of *yin* and *yang* as the forces of *yin* (negative) and *yang* (positive) have both short and long-term dimensions. These complement, support and replace each other to give strength, in a continuous, unending process. Firms, individuals and politicians in the West are largely short-term focused, measured primarily by quarterly earnings, annual performance or the next election, which do not allow the full long-term forces of *yin* and *yang* to play out.

Chinese thinking sees the need to establish clear priorities. When a Dutch academic was asked pre-Brexit in 2016 to list the major challenges facing European security he mentioned five — refugees, borders, security, economy and financial issues. *China Central Television* interviewer Yang Rui enquired, "In which order should they be addressed?" The academic replied they were all so important they must be done "simultaneously". Yang's temporary silence expressed his amazement: desirable maybe, but practical? Surely not. Any system would buckle under such a load, not least the EU's. Some sequenced strategy, based on Europe's history and philosophy would not go amiss.

Accepting uncertainty being natural is another Chinese advantage. People deal with uncertainty rather than ignore it. Founder of China's leading white goods maker Haier, Zhang Ruimin, asserts that companies cannot say they are successful, even when they have been. The best they can say is they hope to move with the times, staying in the game to catch the next big wave. That is how to handle uncertainty and manage risk, by recognising the inevitability of change.

Constant renewal, *weixin*, encourages companies not to aim for defensible positions, but for continual transformation. That way they stay fit and nimble, ready to seize the next emerging opportunity. Furthermore, tolerate failure and re-group after a disaster: a much more Silicon Valley mindset than most Western companies possess. Chinese do not ignore or wish away uncertainty. Indeed, some relish it, as they do ambiguity. Both can provide escape from tight corners or develop new opportunities.

Chinese philosophy asks the hard questions and accepts incomplete answers. Taking a 360-degree view, it does not resort to unrealistic ideas like perfect markets or rational man to assume away difficulties. There are known unknowns and unknown unknowns to consider, even if they cannot be known very exactly. Better to be aware of the possibility than to ignore it altogether is the Chinese view.

Managing change is integral to handling life's capriciousness, complexities and uncertainties, especially matters of "fortune and calamity". Particular attention has to be paid to danger, caution, timing and cycles as well as the mechanics and dynamics of change. Behaviour should show restraint, avoid excess, prepare for adversity and demonstrate endurance. This has all been laid out, analysed and argued about endlessly for millennia. However, how could it be applied elsewhere?

Can Chinese Thinking Help Tackle Others' Problems?

China offers over 2,000 years' experience in managing change. Having learned from some very turbulent history, China has devised a process that is pragmatic and asks the right questions. In an increasingly disrupted world, such Chinese thinking can be adapted anywhere.

Take three major global issues, jobs, banking and inclusion. How would Chinese thinking approach them? With jobs, Chinese policy would not focus on those lost, as Donald Trump has done. They are largely gone, instead, consider where and how new jobs could grow most over the long term. Banking would search for a stable financial system that does not regularly plunge the economy and society into crisis. Exclusion is a drag on the economy, threatening conflict. Therefore inclusion, to achieve harmony, is China's top goal.

Jobs "One who fails to plan for 10 generations cannot plan for one time". Chen Danran (1859–1930)

Lesson: Identify the major long-term trends: then go with them, not against.

China's Approach: When I asked a senior Chinese technocrat in the mid-1990s what the government would do about falling rural real incomes, I expected a long list of policy measures. Instead, there was a short question. "What percentage of people in England farm today?", she asked. Somewhat surprised, I replied "3–5%", which she already knew, having studied in England. "Well, China one day will have the same percentage as England, not the 70% it has today," she answered. This would take many decades but acknowledged the long-term trend to respect. Some measures can ease transitional strains but policy makers should never lose sight of the main long-term trend: fighting it is futile and costly.

One decade is the basic unit of time for government in China. That was Neville Maxwell's observation over 40 years ago to David Batt, adding it is perfectly normal to look out two or three decades, even a century, to shape policy. The destination must be known before the journey begins. For example, to upgrade manufacturing China has outlined a strategy up to 2045, by which time it intends to be the world's leading manufacturer. The first decade has been detailed from 2016 to 2025. Then it will be reviewed, amended and detailed further. For the overall economy, China published with the World Bank in

2012 a report entitled *China 2030*, outlining the challenges China faces in becoming a high-income country; and their solutions. See Chapter 13 and Appendix.

Application: The future of work over the next few decades looks radically different. Robots and artificial intelligence may well mean far fewer of today's jobs exist. Furthermore, competition will increase as education rises worldwide. What all this means for employment and the economy is the challenge.

Chinese thinking does not start from today's problems. It begins with the likely end-reality or goal, before working backwards to figure out the transition. In transportation, imagine a world of automatically-driven and environmentally sustainable vehicles, on the road and in the air: encourage investment there. Many jobs were destroyed in the horse carriage and haulage industries in the early 20th century, but motor cars and trucks created far more jobs and much more wealth. The same can happen again.

Travel and tourism employ one in 11 workers worldwide, growing 30% faster than the global economy. Chinese have become the world's largest group of international tourists, over 120 million in 2016. They are increasingly adventurous, once they have visited the top tourist destinations. Tap into them. Isn't it obvious? Yet are villages or small towns ready? How many have signs let alone social media sites in Chinese? Even as Chinese tourists turbo-charge growth, few cater to this major emerging market. Jobs in hotels, home-stays, cafes, tea houses, bars, restaurants, shops, transport, tours and entertainment will multiply, just as they have in national capitals and other prime destinations. From this tourism (and education) comes familiarity, from which more trade, investment and spending can grow, long into the future.

Banking "The simpler, the better": China Banking Regulatory Commission Chairman Liu Mingkang 2006

Lesson: Do extensive research and fieldwork, *yanjiu,* to avoid a repeat of the West's 2008 financial crisis.

China's Approach: After the collapse of Soviet communism, China examined thoroughly the causes to prevent similar problems overwhelming China. Continuing with the same system, largely unchanged, would merely get what it has always got. New paths are needed. China identified almost 70 contributors to the collapse, studying them hard for a decade. As David Shambaugh noted in *China's Communist Party: Atrophy and Adaptation,* "It was not an idle exercise in academic research among some Marxist theoreticians". It was a non-ideological enquiry determined to address with realism, pragmatism and research, a matter of potential life and death for the Communist Party: see *yanjiu*, Chapter 3.

Application: China asks the big, fundamental questions and then does its in-depth research. What are the roots of the problem? What are banks for? China, even pre-1949, has viewed banks as serving the nation. Banking should help the real economy; and not be an end in itself. Long before the post-2008 Occupy movements focused on the 1%, traditional Chinese thinking believed society cannot be stable if only a small section prospers. Therefore, banking should be a utility to safeguard people's savings, facilitate payments and fund borrowers, not a profit-maximizing industry at others' expense, loaded with incalculable risk. What is good for banks may not necessarily be good for society — and not even for banks in the long run, only for its executives, as 2008 proved. Risk should be understood and controllable. The simpler the better is how Chinese banking regulator Liu Mingkang described derivatives before the 2008 financial crisis. The world cannot afford another major banking crisis, yet reforms globally since 2008 still do not ensure a sustainable banking system.

Banks are not manufacturers. They are fundamentally different. If a car maker's models continually crash, markets would quickly force it out of business. Not so banks, as events after 2008 and other financial crises have shown. Research has to identify the roots of the problem: too little equity, too much debt, bad risk assessment, disastrous management and systemic contagion among them. Banking is both local and global. This requires co-ordinated regulation and co-operation at both levels to reshape the world's financial architecture, otherwise even more punishing banking crises lie ahead from which escape will be even harder.

Inclusion: "Harmony is the most precious fruit": Confucius (551–479 BC)

Lesson: Harmony is the highest goal. Inclusion is integral to it.

China's Approach: China starts its thinking with long-term goals, which begin with harmony and the resulting stability. "The most precious fruit of ritual (social obligations that bind society together) is harmony… all matters great and small depend upon it," Confucius said. Social and economic disharmony threatens the foundations of stability, the other top Chinese goal. Having had more Chaotic Eras than Stable Eras, China is very alert to the danger.

Application: Harmony and inclusion require that economic disparities are addressed, when they become serious. Laggards, be they in rural areas or rust belts, inner cities or regions, always exist. Development is uneven. Therefore, more of the budget has gone to poorer areas and provinces, especially in central and western China since 2000.

Apart from recognising the need for greater equality between regions and individuals, China also prioritizes economic growth out of which to improve wealth distribution. That is why China opted for economic stimulus over austerity after the 2008 Western financial crisis. Economic growth is the solvent that should help adjustment. Austerity just makes recovery and change all the harder.

Social cohesion depends on an acceptance of fairness. China's education spending has doubled as a percentage of GDP since 1995. Healthcare has followed suit. Interventions in the property market have adjusted supply and demand so housing remains affordable, a global problem, including in the wealthiest Chinese cities. Elsewhere, in issues from religious tolerance to social inclusion of sexual minorities as well as the major definers of race, class and gender, Ho Kwon Ping in Singapore argues for a "cohesive diversity". This is as true for the West as for Asia. In China, it is interpreted as harmony, inclusiveness.

What Might China Look Like?

Speculating about the future did not appeal to Confucius, who said it was hard enough to understand the present. However, given the current great importance of China, inevitably, people want to know what China might look like in 10, 20 or 30 years' time. To answer that question, I turn to Singapore and two Singaporeans for clues.

Having lived in Singapore for 20 years before moving to Shanghai 15 years ago, I used to dismiss the idea that China would look like Singapore. The difference in scale was just too great, Singapore's history too short, China too complex. Gradually though, I realised China has consciously learned much from Singapore, from administration to corporate governance, provident funds and state-owned enterprise reform to skills upgrading. China has merely taken back what Singapore had learned from China: lessons from its Confucian roots, which Maoist China severed during the Cultural Revolution.

Two Singaporeans who run global businesses, in technology and hospitality respectively, have insights into China's change and future. Both know China well, after over 30 years of involvement. Before chairing both Singapore Telecoms and DBS, Singapore's leading bank, Koh Boon Hwee graduated from Harvard Business School after taking a first in mechanical engineering at Imperial College, London. He is now a successful investor in cutting edge technology companies. When asked about the quality of Chinese technology, he answers it is now far more reliable than Japanese products were when "Made-in-Japan" became the new standard in the 1970s.

China's great difference compared with only 10 years ago is a "no brainer", Boon Hwee asserts. Three forces in business, technology and government assure its future. Market penetration is still low for many products, with many of the 800 million plus people of central and western China only just joining China's rapid transformation. In technology, two world leading China-based companies illustrate the trend. DJI is the world-leading drone maker while AAC makes phone components. Boon Hwee has invested in AAC, which with over 2,000 patents has acquired a reputation for "designing the next solutions to problems producers have yet to discover." He puts Chinese technology successes down to not just hard work but also the fact that firms had no alternative, with nothing to lose, no downside. No legacy systems held them back. Tencent, now a Chinese giant, could afford to give away its services for free because it had no existing subscriber base to protect. China Mobile had no fixed line telecoms infrastructure to worry about disrupting. New models could emerge. The great enabler is that in Boon Hwee's words, "China's government is pragmatic, non-ideological and a world leader for pushing increasing economic openness."

The person who has taught me most about Asia over the years, apart from my wife Tse Oy, is my former colleague, Ho Kwon Ping, founder of Banyan Tree Resorts and chair of the trustees of Singapore Management University (SMU). The first I knew of him was in 1976, when in London I read a *Far Eastern Economic Review* article about the arrest of two of its journalists, detained without trial under Singapore's Internal Security Act for writing with a purportedly pro-communist slant (in a business magazine owned primarily by a leading bank, HSBC). Kwon Ping was held underground in solitary confinement and subjected to sensory deprivation for about two months.

Ahead of moving to Asia, I wondered what I might be getting into, though I comforted myself with the thought I was going to the British colony of Hong Kong over 1,000 miles away from Singapore and that I was only doing economic, business and financial journalism, not politics. Little did I know how closely they are intertwined with politics in Asia, or that in less than three years, Kwon Ping and I would sit opposite each other in the small economics and business corner of the *Far Eastern Economic Review*'s Wanchai office, overlooking Hong Kong harbour, talking Asia, trying to figure it out. In another three years, Kwon Ping gave up journalism, after his father had a stroke, to take care of his family's business in Singapore. Of his now 40-plus Banyan Tree and Angsana hotels, almost one-third are in China, the fastest growing source of luxury resort, spa and eco/adventure tourists in the world.

My friendship with Kwon Ping continued as I too switched careers in 1981 and moved to Singapore. There, through him, his wife Claire Chiang and many other friends, I began to learn much more about Asia and what lay at its heart in China. Also how it thought and differed from the West. I had already begun to learn in colonial Hong Kong about Chinese thinking, history, art and music from my wife Tse-oy, but living for the first time in the Chinese-dominated state of Singapore introduced me to new dimensions, including the importance of family, nation, government and role of the elite. All involve a series of relationships and mutual obligations (rituals). Kwon Ping stresses they are not superior, as some assert in the Asian values debate, but they are different, with both strengths and weaknesses.

The local word *kakis,* buddies, is at the root of a string of relationships. Four of us played squash every Saturday, when we *kakis* were in town, leaving plenty of time afterwards to discuss news and trends. Apart from friendship, sport and common interests, this was an informal information network comprising Kwon Ping with his various family businesses in Singapore and Thailand, Kim Yong who for over two decades headed trading at Wilmar, which became the world's largest edible oils group, Peck Ming a senior journalist at the *Business Times* and me contributing a foreign perspective. Beyond that was a larger group of families, who all became friends, as did their children. Without any relatives in Singapore, this became our surrogate family.

Family for most Asians, even those in dysfunctional families, is central to their lives. Families have friendship ties that are also very important. When Kwon Ping had a long-service award ceremony in Indonesia, he invited my sister Michal to go with him. He began his speech to Banyan Tree staff by introducing her and saying that he had known her parents for over 30 years: long-term relationships are important and to be regarded highly. His 2014 IPS-Nathan Lectures about Singapore in 50 years' time, *The Ocean In A Drop*, are dedicated to "my family", all four generations of it: parents, wife, children and grandchildren. None of them are named individually. When I asked Kwon Ping about it, he was surprised I found it unusual. After reflecting, he put it down to acknowledging their roles in what mattered to him in life. I doubt if any Westerner would think in quite such terms or express it so: individuals would be named.

Kwon Ping was born in Thailand, educated in Bangkok, the US and Taiwan, then went to live in Singapore. There, he became a citizen where his father was born, a fourth generation migrant from Guangdong. Singapore was a very young and small country of barely two million people in the 1970s, which needed to build its identity, forged out of four different racial groups and several religions, to develop its poor economy. Nation building was a conscious decision. Enabling this, Confucianism helped strengthen the state by arranging loyalties and obligations through mutually respected rituals.

Another Confucian approach relates to the elite's role. Government jobs carried the most prestige in independent Singapore's early years. The words of 11th-century Song Dynasty scholar Fan Zhongyan about the elite being, "the first to worry...and the last to enjoy," rung in its ears: see Chapter 3 Elite. As new opportunities opened up in the 1980s and 1990s, fewer top graduates went into government, but the sense of responsibility for the nation did not change nor were its best and brightest lost. A tradition of "national service" evolved, where the private sector, when needed, advises government, usually for free. A similar system exists in China.

Despite his 1976 detention, Singapore was happy to bring Kwon Ping into the elite, where he has served in several capacities. At first, he struggled with exactly how and how much he should be involved. Doubtless, Singapore's first Prime Minister, Lee Kuan Yew, too thought hard about how precisely to use his knowledge and ability. However, Kwon Ping had no problem with accepting the idea of working for the nation, not something that many in the West would have done after detention. Apart from chairing the trustees of SMU, Singapore's management university, he sat alongside Lee Kuan Yew as a director of the Government Investment Corporation. He has also been a director of government-controlled Singapore Airlines and chairman of Mediacorp, Singapore's main media group. Overseas, he was a main board director of Standard Chartered Bank for 10 years and is now on the board of UK drinks company, Diageo.

On the question of whether China in time could become like Singapore, Kwon Ping makes several points. Ideas like family, nation, the role of the state and the elite are common to both: they are Confucian, though far from being exclusively so. He feels that other common ideas such as vision, long-term thinking and priorities may have less to do with Confucianism and more to do with Singapore and modern China's origins — poverty. Both needed to get out of it fast.

These were instruments of escape, though admittedly included in the traditional Chinese philosophy tool box; and very practical.

"From Third World to First" was Lee Kuan Yew's title for Singapore's story. Singapore's per capita GDP of over $50,000 has reached US levels, ahead of the other Asian Tigers of South Korea, Taiwan and Hong Kong. It ranks just behind New Zealand and Scandinavia as the world's least corrupt country. These are Singapore's singular achievements in half a century, admired for its success, not because of Confucianism, ideology or any other "ism". The only ideology has been supreme pragmatism, very Confucian: to accept change and to go with it, not to resist, very Daoist.

Like China, Singapore learns from setbacks. After the 1985 Pan Electric crisis, when its out-of-control stock market had to close for three days, Singapore went through a national exercise to regroup. Then after the 1997 Asian financial crisis, some 200 private sector people met over several months with government officials in various working groups to make recommendations on Singapore's economic direction. Each time after regrouping, Singapore advanced to a higher level of economic development, becoming richer.

The longest-ruling elected government in the world, governing non-stop for over half a century since full independence in 1965, the People's Action Party's legitimacy comes from delivering on its promise to create a strong economy that could look after all its people, both in work and retirement. Apart from its highly strategic location, there was nothing exceptional about Singapore, other than political will, leadership and popular acceptance of the two. The only other characteristic was to understand and embrace change. Many economic policies came straight out of Western economic development thinking. The leading advisor from 1961 to 1984 was a Dutch United Nations economist Albert Winsemius. Harvard, especially its Kennedy School of Government, has been an influence in recent years, as it has been for China.

Could China emulate Singapore? Kwon Ping believes it can, if it overcomes corruption, as Singapore has long achieved. If it does, then China could have a long period of economic prosperity ahead: it may well boil down to one word — corruption. Singapore has built a culture of financially clean government, partly by paying officials good salaries and imposing high penalties to reduce dramatically the attraction of bribes. The private sector is happy to participate in "national service", but only if government keeps its part of the bargain: deliver on the economy and stay clean.

Xi Jinping sees the link between clean government, development and long-term survival. Corruption is an existential threat. If China conquers corruption, parts could go on to have some of the highest per capita incomes in the world by mid-century, just as Singapore and Hong Kong, two other predominantly Chinese societies, have done. If not, China could stagnate or even collapse. The different outcomes could not be greater.

Observing China Change

From the shores of Coloane Island, one of the closest vantage points to China, I could see in the far distance, across the featureless grey expanse of the Pearl River, the occasional vessel coming into view. Then a wooden junk appeared with a red flag and five yellow stars fluttering from its stern. I could just make out small figures scurrying around the deck, under the timeless junk's square sails, like something from an old sepia-tinted print. This was the summer of 1977, *Saturday Night Fever* boomed out over Macau's beaches but nearby post-Mao China was silent, still and remote.

The excitement felt 40 years ago by a 26-year old journalist, catching his first glimpse of people from the real China, may be hard to imagine today, but it was considerable. For over a quarter of a century, China had been turning inward, cutting itself off increasingly from the rest of the world in self-administered isolation. China had an air of intense mystery about it. Behind a bamboo curtain lay one-fifth of humanity, but so little was known about the people and so much was misunderstood. This seemed to be my best and maybe only chance to see Chinese who actually lived in the People's Republic of China. Quickly, I dug into my battered shoulder bag for a camera and telephoto lens as my previous attempts in 1974 to meet, let alone photograph, the Chinese had been rebuffed when China was building the Great Uhuru Railway from Tanzania to Zambia. This opportunity was not to be missed.

The aftermath of the Cultural Revolution was still playing out in 1977. The economy was in limbo, if not decline. Reform was not mentioned. China had reached rock bottom. Not only was a model broken, so were many lives, dashing the hopes of a whole generation and more. Chinese were amongst the poorest people on earth. North Koreans were richer. Many Chinese still wore patched, well-darned faded Mao jackets. Colour choice was very limited: dark blue, olive green or sometimes light grey, which could be mistaken for a faint blue. That was it. No imminent consumer boom was in sight. The days of Chinese buying 30% of the world's luxury goods, were over two decades away. So was the time when a greater percentage of Chinese would own their own homes than people do in the US or Europe. Poverty was shared.

While the rest of East and Southeast Asia filled the West's shelves and auto showrooms, China's exports were minimal. Not only did it not have banks in any recognizable sense of the word, but China could not even feed or clothe itself properly. Young men in Nanjing competed to see who could wrap a belt *twice* around the waist: some were that thin, Clinton Dines observed in 1979. Everyone was rationed to five metres of cloth a year. Industrial coupons were needed to buy even simple things like light bulbs. Rationing kept demand down in the "shortage economy". That is how it "worked".

These were the most basic of needs. Basic systems were not in place either. All transactions were in cash, there were no checking accounts, let alone credit cards. Many banks and businesses still used the abacus, accounts were handwritten in ledgers. At work, people faced regular power shortages: infrastructure was lacking. David Bonavia in 1980 wrote that factories had "over-manning, idling, smoke breaks and unproductive political meetings." The days of China becoming the Workshop of the World were unimaginable. The work unit, the *danwei*, was central to urban lives, controlling everything from allocating jobs to authorising marriages and travel. Local street committee members, often old aunties and grannies, watched all comings and goings from the gate of every residential compound.

Published data was in the dark ages. Bonavia noted the grain harvest was "given in vague terms", not even specifying which crop comprised how much of the total. Steel data was even more useless. Hubei's steel output in 1978 was detailed very precisely as 10,264.67 times as high as in 1949. No figure was given for 1949: false precision at its very best, a number to two decimal places but no base for comparison, Keynes would have loved it. Since then, there have been fundamental changes in China, not cosmetic or superficial. The remaining primacy of the Communist Party does not mean there has been no real change.

Little did I know in 1977, how fast and by how much China could change. Within 15 months, I found myself a guinea pig for China Travel Service, after word on the Hong Kong grapevine was that China had started experimental tours for ordinary foreigners, no longer just for VIPs and Friends of China. This opening crack in China's Great Wall was a pilot scheme, a clear sign that wider change was on the way. The schedule was packed. Given the money we were spending, China Travel presumed we wanted to see as much as possible. The holiday was therefore more like a China boot camp.

Days often started at 5a.m. and finished late. There were village visits, though no longer to communes; and industrial workshops but no really large-scale factories. At a school still sporting Down With The Gang of Four slogans, chalked on the black board with a particularly evil depiction of Mao's wife Jiang Qing, our guide shamefacedly, with a very nervous laugh, admitted to smashing up the science laboratory when a Red Guard. We visited a hospital, but only as an unscripted emergency stop: it was very basic and dingy. We also took in the recently reopened Guangzhou Conservatoire whose erstwhile "decadent bourgeois musicians" had returned from "learning from the masses" in the countryside.

At least we could visit the limestone *karst* wonderland of Guilin. As we travelled down the fabled Li River, black cormorants regurgitated fish for their white-haired owners on the banks. Grey cloud swirled in and out of craggy limestone mountains, with their irregular, conical peaks, like something out of a moody Song Dynasty painting, shrouded in mist. However, it was the people, their lives and ways, that most caught my attention, bombarding my mind with questions. They still do to this day.

Barely five years later in early 1984, I was visiting my wife's home village in rural Fujian, certainly not then one of the 19 cities officially open to foreigners, but no one seemed to bother with this small detail. China was opening up, officially and, in its inimitable way, unofficially. No one was going to miss this opportunity after two long, lost decades. It was just emerging from what Nobel Literature Laureate Mo Yan called, "One of modern China's most bizarre periods, an era of unprecedented fanaticism…It wasn't until the 1980s, when China opened its door to the outside world, that we finally began to face reality, as if waking from a dream".

Pragmatism was alive and well. So was confidence. Even though property rights were not clear, a nascent building boom was underway. Rice farmers in Fujian found a new use for rudimentary ploughs, hitching carts to their lurching, spluttering machines that lumbered along the road, hauling rough-hewn lengths of granite to build the new houses springing up. Enterprise and innovation were back in China. The first country in the world to invent so many things was awakening. The seemingly endless list of firsts includes; the iron plough, which helped launch Europe's Agricultural Revolution; printed books which spread knowledge centuries before Gutenberg's and Caxton's "inventions"; the suspension bridge; the "Siemens" steel process; lacquer; chess; the decimal system; the compass; the First Law of Motion; paper money; poison gas and gunpowder.

The further north we went, the fewer private roadside markets we saw: dwindling to just one or two solitary farmers by the time we reached Hangzhou. Reform and opening up was making a slow start, more than five years after the 1978 Four Modernizations. Immortalised over 900 years earlier by poet Su Dongpo, Hangzhou's famous West Lake was dispiritingly soulless. Where were the lyrical willows and fabled clear water, let alone the secluded lovers? No romance or ethereal atmosphere was alive in the cold spring of 1984 nor was warm hospitality.

Things got worse. Shanghai was "full", the "concierge" at Hangzhou's leading hotel pronounced firmly, without concern: so much for Mao's slogan Serve the People. All Shanghai's hotel rooms for foreigners were said to be taken as US President Ronald Reagan was in town with the international press corps in tow. Everything was in short supply, including hotel rooms for foreigners. In the spirit of the times and with no other options, we ignored the official information and took the train to Shanghai anyway, which only 35 years earlier had been a leading global metropolis, albeit a post-war one struggling to get back on its feet after the great destruction of the eight-year Japanese invasion and civil war.

When we arrived in Shanghai, many shops were almost empty of anything people wanted to buy, as befitted a shortage economy. The most memorable were two stores on Nanjing Road, Shanghai's Fifth Avenue, Oxford Street or Orchard Road. One sold just a few translations of Marx, Engels, Lenin and Mao in English and other foreign languages, scattered haphazardly around the store. The display window of another incongruously housed enormous pieces of industrial machinery where smart, fashionable clothing had been sold in another era. On a busy Shanghai street, these were not surprisingly deserted except for a curious foreigner, his wife and baby son. Only the Number One Department Store was packed, so full that this 14-month old foreign Eurasian baby caused a traffic-jam on the fourth floor as people crowded around to snatch a glimpse of such an unusual sight, causing "traffic police" to wade in to keep people moving. The curious had become the curiosity: opening up was giving Chinese a rare, if not first, close-up view of foreigners. Reform and Opening Up was a two-way street.

The once-great city was a world of dull grimy buildings under leaden, polluted skies. Nothing since 1949 apparently had changed. Time seemed to have stood still. Exactly 15 years later in 1999, I would enter the 54th floor lobby of the brand new government-built Jinmao Tower with its 6-star Grand Hyatt hotel, decorated with a none-too-subtle nod to the Art Deco of Shanghai's glory days of the 1920s and 1930s. It was a statement: Shanghai is back and never intends to go away again — even if vacancy in the new Pudong office towers was a rather unpromising 80%.

Change in China, when it happens, can come at great speed and with enormous force, as the recent adoption of mobile payments shows: 50 times more than in the US. Now everyone seems connected, happy to buy online from anywhere and on a far greater scale than in the US or Europe. My own work began to reflect China's change when in the early 1990s I began regularly visiting China for economic and investment research.

In 2002, I left Singapore after two decades to live in Shanghai. Indeed, we became property owners in what was still a very infant market. Many doubted foreigners were even allowed to own property where we had handed over our cash: not comfortable information to learn, after the event. In fact, the law had been changed, just one month before our purchase in 2001. Change can happen when least expected; and against the forecasts of overcautious or ideological "China experts".

Trying to work out what has kept China's economic express from jumping the rails has been for me the big question of the last two decades. There are few bigger questions in contemporary economics. Was it a set of pragmatic economic policies that China implemented, was it a new economic "unprecedented fanaticism" for a better material life that drove over one billion deprived consumers or was it the more basic muses of Mo Yan: hunger and loneliness? All have combined to motivate a nation to reverse the sharp relative decline. In 1800, China was the world's leading economy, according to economic historian Angus Maddison. Yet by 1913, China's economy ranked 64th out of 65; and in 1975, it was 65th, last. That is some decline, never forgotten in China, though often ignored or unknown elsewhere.

When asked in early 2002 why I was moving to Shanghai, I replied that for anyone interested in economics, business and social development, China was The Greatest Show on Earth. Shanghai would provide a front-row seat from which to watch China change: the ending of this drama no one knew, certainly not me.

The Greatest Show On Earth

"Waahhh" exclaimed Xiuyun, our normally quiet and undemonstrative niece, who after a short, sharp intake of breath fell silent. Suddenly and totally unexpectedly she had come face to face with what lay at her feet. Far below the 30th floor of Broadway Mansion, like a vast model in miniature, spread out Shanghai's historic Bund, Suzhou Creek and the majestic bend of the Huangpu River, as it swung to join the great Yangzi on its way to the East China Sea and the awaiting Pacific Ocean. Had the world shrunk? Perched on the edge, was there danger?

Xiuyun had just had one startlingly new experience, hurtling heavenward, squeezed in a tomb-like rattling old elevator. Now she stood at a full-length window, hundreds of feet above the ground. The highest Xiuyun had ever been before was atop her uncle's three-storey village house. We never thought to prepare her. Excited to see Shanghai's famous breath-taking Bund for the first time from such a height and from such an iconic 1930s building, I assumed Xiuyun would be too.

I was just as ignorant of Xiuyun's perspective on the world as she was of Shanghai, with its New York-style skyscrapers and their incredible views: unimaginable to her in the village. Once she had recovered, digested some of the new reality and considered what it might mean, this clearly was the Greatest Show on Earth. Even the enormous, to her, train station at the provincial capital of Fuzhou or the beauty and scale of Hangzhou's famous West Lake had not prepared her for this.

I often think of this Waahhh moment when foreigners first come face to face with China. Frequently, they are disoriented: things seem wrong, missing or bad, though a loud Wow of stupefaction and wonder is not uncommon. A long silence often ensues. It is all too overwhelming. I learned that from Xiuyun at the top of Broadway Mansion in 1984. Little did she know then how much China would change, let alone how rapidly. Nor did I.

Philosophers and Policy

Confucius This Shanghai temple declares that Confucius (551-479BC) can be known and true for thousands of generations: forever. His moral philosophy highlighting virtue is one of the three pillars of Chinese thinking, with Daoism and Buddhism.

Jia Yi Scholar-official Jia Yi, who died in 169BC, is still considered relevant reading two millennia later. In China, history is the raw material of philosophy. Mao Zedong had 11th-century Sima Guang's *Zizhi Tongjian* reproduced in modern script and language, all 294 volumes and 3 million characters of it, covering almost 1,400 years of history.

Mencius Mencius (372-289BC), like Confucius, was another scholar-official. He helped establish Confucianism at the heart of Chinese governance for millennia, by expanding its thinking with a heightened focus on benevolence.

Laozi Laozi founded Daoism in the 6th century BC, with nature and its forces at the root of philosophy. This, especially the idea of cycles, is central to interpretations of the *Book of Change*, which John Minford has called *the* Chinese book.

Lord Shang Lord Shang (390-338BC), the founder of Legalism, has greatly influenced Chinese rulers with his emphasis on the need for detailed laws and their strict enforcement.

Chapter 2

History, Philosophy, Strategy and Governance

"If I use history as a mirror, I shall know how to reverse adversity."

Tang Emperor Taizong (598–649)

"Thought grows out of environment."

Arthur Waley
The Analects of Confucius 1938

Even though the subject was principally economics and finance, Xi Jinping's speech at the 2017 Belt and Road Forum was largely about history and philosophy. History, along with the philosophy that springs from it, is an integral part of the language of politics and life in China. As the traditional Chinese saying goes, "Events of the past are teachers of the future," or as the model Tang Emperor Taizong said, history should be a mirror from which to learn how to manage problems.

Arthur Waley began his classic translation of *The Analects of Confucius* with the crucial insight that Chinese thought has grown out of its environment, whether triumphs or disasters. The link between China's earlier turbulence, with its seemingly endless wars and human misery over two millennia ago, still holds. Diplomatic and military strategies are quoted. Apart from instilling considerable pride, China's "5,000 years of history", almost 3,000 years recorded in great detail, teaches lessons to contemporary China, drawn from real Chinese history, such as the Silk Routes, that connected China with Europe over 2,000 years ago. So too does thinking about governance.

History: The Raw Material of Philosophy, Statecraft and Governance

Back in 174 BC, Jia Yi, a young 28-year-old Han Dynasty scholar-official, wrote about administration. Today, he is still read and considered relevant. Jia's proposals covered the whole gamut of questions about internal affairs, diplomacy, society, law and education: answers were very practical.

What if the emperor's relatives do not follow his laws or instructions? Break down their territories into smaller units so they cannot rival the central government. What if extravagance or lust for power sap national strength? Create a sense of shame by teaching Confucian good behaviour, benevolence, righteousness and upright living. Set a moral example: educate the prince, the future king, to be an exemplar for his people. To prevent revolts: reduce torture. In foreign affairs, take a tough stand against the "barbarians" on China's northern and western borders. Change mindset and stop fearing the marauding Xiongnu horsemen, who for centuries had swept down from the steppes into the plains to plunder.

Jia is just one of many former government advisers whose thoughts are still read. Parts echo in Xi Jinping's *The Governance of China*. Particular attention is paid to older history that Westerners would consider ancient and useless. Some incident 3,000 or even 4,000 years ago can be as important in China today as recent events: sometimes more so. Not just Chinese history. Currently they consider very seriously what Thucydides wrote in the 5th century BC about clashes between old and rising powers. History is part of one lengthy continuum from which to draw ideas, lessons, warnings and inspiration: like a long river, as Chinese say. When the Academia Sinica moved to Taiwan in 1949, the Institute of History and Philology was one of the first two departments re-established: there are 31 today. History was considered that important.

Three million words and 294 chapters long, the 11th-century *Zizhi Tongjian* took 19 years to complete. Covering history from 403 BC to

959 AD, it provides some 1,362 years from which to learn about governance and strategy: a lot. The Song emperor praised his senior minister Sima Guang's work, giving it a special title, *"Aiding Governance: A Comprehensive Historical Mirror"*. Historical figures were appraised, the rise and fall of dynasties explained. With this knowledge, governments can adopt good policy, structures and strategies whilst discarding and avoiding the bad. In 1956, a new version was published at Mao Zedong's behest, who said he had read it 17 times. A team of 21 specialists rewrote it in simplified characters, with modern idioms for wider comprehension. Such has been the importance of China's long history, including after 1949.

History in China has been and remains the raw material for philosophy and strategy. It is much more than just a story about a people. With three millennia of continuously recorded history, dated by confirmed sightings of eclipses and written in a still comprehensible language, China has a treasure trove of insight into human nature, folly, failure and great achievements. The ebb and flow of affairs, the nature of cycles and long-term perspective all come into sharp focus in 21st-century China as people and government work through their everyday lives and the nation's future, consciously and unconsciously guided by history. Important actions of emperors, prime ministers, advisers and generals are recalled, debated. So too are strategies, many tested over thousands of years.

Reaching back so far rarely happens in the West (apart from religion) certainly not in government. Indeed, if an event of several centuries ago, let alone millennia, were suggested as relevant today, it would probably be ridiculed. More likely, raising it would not even occur to anyone. The West has largely lost touch with its pre-industrial past at home, let alone far away in Greece, Rome and Mesopotamia. My first history textbook in 1959 was entitled *From Ur to Rome:* to understand British history then it was considered necessary to know its roots along the banks of two Iraqi rivers, the Tigris and Euphrates. The British educated elite in the late 19th and early 20th centuries learned Greek and Latin, partly because they provided lessons relevant for managing a complex empire as well as life. No more.

China's several millennia of history towers above the Roman Empire's five centuries. Nor has China lost an empire. As C.P. Fitzgerald noted in his landmark 1935 work *China: A Short Cultural History*, "No territory once fully subjected to this civilization has been wholly lost [unlike Western colonies], and no territory permanently incorporated has withstood the penetration of Chinese culture. The process of absorption has sometimes been slow, but always complete and final. The fluidity of frontiers is explained by the fact that the Chinese are less a nation than a fusion of people united by a common culture."

China's history is the record of an expanding culture, more than of a conquering empire, Fitzgerald concluded, one stretching from China's northern steppes to Indo-China. When it came to defining who is Chinese and who is not, culture, not race, was the identifier. Expansion was achieved more by settlement than by conquest, unlike the major Western empires of Rome, Spain and Britain.

Dynasties may wax and wane, heroes and villains come and go, war vies with peace, justice with injustice: everyone has history. The only difference with other countries is the sheer amount China has, how long it has lasted and what China has done with it. By any measure, it is epic. It is the starting point of so much. Former US Treasury Secretary Hank Paulson described his counterpart in finance, Wang Qishan, as "an avid historian, [who] enjoys philosophical debates." However, it is not just some politicians who are avid historians and philosophers. Most well-educated Chinese consider this to be perfectly normal.

History has always been a very serious business in China. "Historiography was not some scholarly pastime but a vital function of government", John Keay observed in his *History of China*. "Besides recording and organizing the past... there were lessons to be learned, mistakes to be corrected, reputations to be revised and wrongs to be righted," he noted. The Ministry of History supposedly recorded every imperial word since the Western Zhou Dynasty (1046–771 BC): see Appendix. The expression "the king has no joking words, even when a child", originated when Zhou King Cheng had to honour his childhood promise to give his brother a district in Shanxi because it was written down in the official records. These had the authority of the British parliament's *Hansard* or the *US Congressional Record*, only three millennia earlier.

Little escaped the official record. Diaries, anthologies and encyclopedias all added to the pile of history. Fragments of writing on animal bones, turtle shells and bronze ware date back to the Shang Dynasty (around 1600–1046 BC). Already it had an annual calendar of 365.25 days, broken down into 24 phases of the agricultural year, nearly four millennia ago. Before this recorded history, there were legends, just like those of Arthurian Britain or the Norse Sagas. These included the supposed founder of the Chinese people, the Yellow Emperor Huangdi as well as his adversary from the south in 2700–2600 BC. Today's great construction boom uncovers ever-earlier detail of China's past.

The Western Zhou practice of systematically noting history, decrees and policies spread to other states. Events from eclipses to floods, alliances to wars were recorded as well as rituals, poems, odes and songs. Confucius famously compiled the annals of his home state of Lu, in today's Shandong, and analyzed those of other major states. Like the Warring States period (475–221 BC) which followed, this was an era of intense insecurity, with civilization itself feared to be on the brink of collapse.

Out of Great Violence and Misery

The prolonged death throes of China's feudal system brought great violence and misery, yet this was the soil from which its greatest philosophical tradition flowered. It could not have been born without the unrelenting disruption that lasted from 771–221BC. The Hundred Schools of philosophy was the intellectual response to all this turmoil and death.

Out of the turbulence came wandering scholars like Confucius (551–479 BC), who sought rulers to advise wherever they could: see Confucianism later in this chapter. Confucianism has held China in its thrall for most of the last 2,500 years. Mao may have denounced Confucius, but Xi Jinping is not shy of putting him in the pantheon of philosophers he urges party and nation to study. Confucius Institutes are China's cultural centres abroad, started under President Hu Jintao in 2004.

China draws many lessons — particularly political, administrative and economic ones — out of this great body of history. Positive lessons come from Jia Yi's era, the Han Dynasty (206 BC–220 AD) that laid down stronger foundations of government. While opening it up to non-nobles, Han civil service reforms curbed bureaucratic nepotism, later inspiring the merit-based public examinations of the Sui Dynasty in 605. These laid foundations for the Tang Dynasty (618–907) to improve its bureaucracy to strengthen the state. The Tang, whom many Chinese regard as China's most cosmopolitan and greatest era, saw the arts flourish while foreign envoys and traders walked the streets of its capital, today's Xi'an. Ideas travelled back and forth along the Silk Route that connected China with Eurasia, all the way to India and Europe.

Negative lessons include Qin Shihuang, who in the third century BC burned books of the classics, had leading Confucianists buried alive and slaughtered like an earlier version of Genghis Khan. This violence proscribed history and ideas. It literally wiped out the written form, the very medium that upgrades oral tradition into documented evidence: an appalling heresy and crime in the eyes of the *literati.* This did not just happen once. The written word was destroyed by war, domestic unrest and invasions, not to mention fires and floods, even until the 20th century's civil war, Japanese invasion and Cultural Revolution. Restoring knowledge by finding people with memory of the content and history has gone on for over 2,000 years.

Warnings come from the dangers of vested interests, be they eunuchs in the Ming and Qing Dynasties or conservative resistance to Wang Anshi's new laws in the Song Dynasty. Xi Jinping and his advisers, including Hank Paulson's opposite number, Wang Qishan, who graduated in history after the Cultural Revolution, will doubtless have studied these hard so as to understand the causes of decline in popular support that ended 132 years of continuous peace under the Tang. A more recent lesson was the intellectual atrophy of rigid Confucianism, a major cause of the last dynasty's collapse in 1911.

History is the central weave of Chinese thinking and norms. Words and phrases themselves often refer or allude to history that infuses them with meaning. Everyday wisdom is rooted in history, learned at mother's knee or more likely grandmother's. Good behaviour is explained to young children, by telling stories about incidents or people in history.

Strategy: To Achieve Goals

Strategy, as much as history, has been beloved by China's literate classes for millennia. Indeed, as with philosophy, the two are intertwined, informing each other. Strategy is designed to achieve goals in the best, fastest, safest and most cost-effective way. Used in everything from government, agriculture, business and economics to politics, diplomacy and martial arts, strategy has to be practical and successful.

This combination of history, philosophy and strategy has spawned a whole genre of how-to-manuals. *The 36 Strategems* and *The 100 Unusual Strategies* are still read by officials, business people and the general public. There are seven military classics. Near-cult status surrounds legendary but real-life strategists such as Zhuge Liang, the third century AD prime minister of Su, immortalized in the *Romance of the Three Kingdoms*. Even further back in history, Jiang Ziya was the famed strategist for Lord West, the father of the founder of the Western Zhou Dynasty. Today they and many others are best known through film and television.

China's leaders since 1949 have been fascinated by strategy. Mao Zedong was a great *aficionado*. '"Know the enemy, know yourself, and victory is never in doubt". We must never underestimate the wisdom of this saying of Master Sun, the great military thinker of ancient China," Mao wrote. Zhu De, head of the People's Liberation Army, and Deng Xiaoping also studied the classics. Xi Jinping is trying to revive an interest in them through his China Dream, to provide knowledge and framework relevant for modern China.

Strategy is much more than just about warfare or brute force. As John Minford observes about Sunzi's fifth century BC *The Art of War*,

"The strategic advice it offers is much more than the conduct of war. It is an ancient book of proverbial wisdom, a book of life…the importance of mischief, cleverness and common sense in human conflict — as opposed to brute force." At the very start, *The Art of War* stresses the importance of avoiding war if possible, saying that the skillful strategist defeats the enemy without doing battle. The *taiji* master Yang Chengfu (1862–1935) advocated the "use of thought, not force". *The Romance of the Three Kingdoms* said, "It is best to attack minds not cities; psychological warfare is better than fighting with weapons," while the *Dao De Jing* held that, "The most skillful warrior is never warlike; the most skillful warrior is never angered; the most skilled at defeating the enemy never strives."

As the doyen of post-war US China scholars John Fairbanks wrote in the 1974 introduction to *Chinese Ways of Warfare*, "The aim of war is to subdue an opponent…change his attitude… induce his compliance. The most economical means is the best: to get him through deception, surprise, and his own ill-conceived pursuit of infeasible goals — to realize his own inferiority, so that he surrenders or at least retreats without your having to fight him." That is how China today approaches the US.

All this comes from traditional observation of nature and the cosmos. Central to strategy is *Shi,* "positional or situational energy: … the inherent power or dynamic of a situation or moment," Minford noted. "It is at the heart of the Taoist attitude to nature and life, which teaches that rather than struggle blindly against obstacles, we should understand the true dynamics of the situation… and act accordingly, in harmony with it." For China's rulers today, this shapes the approach and timing of their actions, as much as the form: go with the flow, but first understand the flow.

Government: Strong Centralized States

As long ago as 1600 BC, political organization created East Asia's "first great civilization", as Robert Bagley described Erligang in the *Cambridge History of Ancient China.* Centred along the Yellow River in today's Zhengzhou in Henan, it is famous for monumental bronze vessels and jade. This wealth did not come through conquest, technological breakthroughs or agricultural advances. Economic growth came solely from the more efficient mobilization of resources: using land and labour better.

Strong government through effective administration has since been the goal of Chinese governance. Reform was often about strengthening central authority, as it is today. Liberalism, let alone anarchism, never found much support in China, as there has always been a strong sense that someone must be in charge. Otherwise there will be great chaos or *da luan*, the biggest fear throughout China's history. Till this day, it continues to drive an acceptance of the *status quo*.

By defeating six other main warring kingdoms, Qin Shihuang first unified China into one strong centralized state in 221 BC, ending hundreds of years of near-continuous fighting and turmoil. Apart from unifying China, Qin changed the course of Chinese history in mundane, but very innovative ways. The transformative powers of administrative measures such as standardizing weights, measures, the written language, coins and cart axles should not be underestimated. Much was achieved through unity and standardization. Trade was greatly facilitated by a common language, currency and measures: distance could be conquered. All strengthened the economy, making government more powerful and enabling its bureaucracy to be more effective: a virtuous circle, for a time.

After its founder's death, the Qin Dynasty was soon destroyed by its brutality and despotism. The centralized state's first administrative reforms quickly followed during the four century-long Han Dynasty, especially under the seventh Han Emperor Wu who ruled for 54 years from 141-87 BC. Whilst favouring legalist advisers who advocated strict enforcement of laws and harsh punishment for offenders, Wu also strongly promoted Confucian principles in government and education as a source of morality. By 5 BC, there were 130,000 bureaucrats in national and local government, organized by hierarchy and departments. These were checked by a system of censors, auditors and inspectors, reporting not only bad performance and malfeasance, but good work as well.

The bureaucracy's fortunes waxed and waned along with the dynasties, but it remained the bedrock to which China could always return. Bureaucracy was China's antidote to anarchy, its bulwark against extreme tyranny. Rulers and bureaucrats could look to history and the philosophy that came from it, no matter if books were burned or scholar officials buried. What was retained or recovered could sustain an administered state for over 2,000 years.

After the next period of division and turbulence between 220 and 589 AD, the second major wave of administrative change saw the Tang Dynasty (618–907 AD) introduce provinces as the basic unit of government, with the emperor advised centrally by a council of high officials. Under them were departments responsible for specific tasks, as in modern government. There were six: the civil service ministry supervised administration; finance was responsible for agriculture, transporting grain, the main form of tax payment, and administering the census; defence; law; rites (moral education); and public works, especially roads, irrigation and flood control. Long before phones, telegraph, railways or planes, China ruled an estimated 52 million people in 754, the world's largest population. Its writ ran far and wide, helped by the census that collected details on every household. Not just family members and servants, but their cattle, crops, land and property, enabling the state to levy taxes and mobilize labour for public works.

The third wave of government reorganization was not so much about structure, but the role and policies of the state itself. The Song Dynasty (960–1279) introduced a more activist government, particularly through policy. In economics, Prime Minister Wang Anshi designed laws to boost farmers' incomes and cut their financing burden. In foreign affairs, it was wary of war. The Song strengthened the state by consent rather than force: everyone was yet again tired of war. By restoring the bureaucracy's pre-eminence, it reduced the military's power, helping avoid rebellions that had brought down the Tang and Han dynasties. It did, however, lose territory in northeast China, tarnishing its reputation among some Chinese.

C.P. Fitzgerald, however, considered Song emperors to be, "The most enlightened sovereigns who ever ruled China…tolerant, humane, artistic, and intellectual, free from the vices which have so disgraced Oriental monarchs". Chinese intellectuals have regarded the Song Dynasty as one of the peaks of Chinese governance and culture. The Song rulers greatly encouraged the arts, indeed the third Song Emperor Huizong was a noted painter, its porcelain outstanding. By 1124, the Song kingdom had grown to 100 million people, testimony to a prosperity based on effective administration, economic policy and good governance. The most recent history on which modern China focuses is the last dynasty, the Qing Dynasty (1644–1911) that took China to its zenith and then nadir, in terms of area and reputation. In the 17th and 18th centuries Jesuit missionaries considered China to be France's equivalent or even superior, except in religion, but by 1911, over 2,000 years of centralized government had collapsed.

The Qing emperors paid the ultimate compliment to Chinese culture. From China's northern border, this foreign Manchu dynasty adopted Chinese culture and administration, lock, stock and barrel, becoming its greatest proponents. The dynasty was very much a period of two halves. Under the first China-born Qing Emperor Kangxi (1654–1722), the Qing re-conquered former territories in Mongolia, Tibet and Turkestan while expanding to Burma, Korea and Annam (part of Vietnam). At home, China enjoyed 120 years of peace. In the dynasty's second half, in the 19th century, Qing fortunes suffered a complete reversal. Instead of Western admiration, China was, in Fitzgerald's words, "treated as a decrepit and backward absolutism destined to be carved up by the predatory imperialism of half a dozen foreign powers."

While technology and science took Europe to new heights, China stagnated, especially intellectually and in governance. China stuck to the most rigid Confucian traditions, dismissed European scientific advances as mere technical skills and succumbed to widespread corruption. It resisted change. Rebellions threatened the dynasty, divisions weakened the court. After the Empress Dowager Cixi finally died, the dynasty in Fitzgerald's words, "swiftly collapsed in the face of an incoherent national rising led by idealistic republicans, but backed by self-seeking generals." This incoherence and decline into warlordism led to the Communist Party taking power in 1949 when another military strategist-cum-philosopher, Mao Zedong, came to the helm.

Confucianism

China's ideal, even if rarely approached by most rulers, has been Confucianism, whose roots were in the Western Zhou dynasty that began about 1046 BC. When other states challenged Zhou, destroying peace in the Spring and Autumn and Warring States periods (771-221 BC), philosophers looked for ways to end incessant violence by establishing moral principles to unite people harmoniously.

Most rulers took Confucianism as their creed simply because they believed it worked: pure pragmatism. Few were interested in Confucian ideas about *ren*, benevolence (treating people humanely) or compassion. They saw a system that five times had instilled order for an average of 300 years in the Han, Tang, Song, Ming and Qing dynasties. Filial piety, loyalty to one's superiors, be they children to parents, wives to husbands, heads of households to government or lords to kings created a pyramid of loyalty and subjugation.

Confucianism transformed China from a spiritual culture to a humanist one. Although the emperor was the Son of Heaven, government was by the high-minded rather than the high-born. Meritocracy evolved and the wise man replaced the holy man, David Hinton wrote in *The Four Chinese Classics*. Daoism secularized the sacred and invested the secular with sacred dimensions. Rulers would succeed if filial piety and rituals, the "web of social responsibilities that bind society together", were supported by good agriculture, the basis of the economy; a strong military, providing security; and laws, restraining wrong doing. So why did dynasties that followed these prescriptions fall? They either failed to follow them sufficiently, were too weak or their emperors too young to rule, becoming victims of the machinations and corruption of relatives, in-laws and eunuchs.

In one of those striking oddities about China, Confucius was not the originator of Confucianism, merely its greatest sage. The forerunner and real founder of the philosophy that came to be associated with

Confucius was Zhou Gong, who was born over five centuries before Confucius. Zhou Gong was a military strategist, politician, educator and philosopher who established the importance of *li*, rituals (social responsibilities that bind people). The fact that the Zhou Dynasty lasted longer than any other owed something to the wisdom Zhou Gong provided as regent to his nephew, King Cheng.

Confucius (551–479BC), Kongzi in Chinese, built on these traditions of the Western Zhou Dynasty, which had already been challenged by the founder of Daoism, Laozi, who probably was 30–50 years older than Confucius. Laozi was much more interested in the cosmos and nature, along with humanity's place in it rather than in ritual and the like. Confucius emphasized the importance of virtue and education. These, to him, were the basis of good rulers and good government.

What mattered to Confucianists were the four books, five scriptures and six arts: namely the *Great Learning, Analects, Golden Mean* and Mencius; *Book of Songs, Book of History, Book of Manners and Rituals, Zhou Book of Change* and Confucius's *Spring and Autumn*; and ritual and manners, music, horse and chariot riding, archery and calligraphy and literary ability. All taught rulers how to behave and manage people. In the official history of the Spring and Autumn period (771–476 BC), Confucius selected exemplary rulers and passed moral judgment on others. He supposedly had some 3,000 students, who after his death collected his thoughts. Most were short sayings, one reason why they are usually very straightforward and comprehensible.

Mencius, in the fourth century BC, was another wandering scholar, who became a high official. His longer philosophical discourses, still easily accessible, built on Confucius and Zhou Gong, filling in more of their framework. Many were very practical, reinforcing the notion that Chinese are very pragmatic. Mencius wrote that "getting something done is like digging a well." There is no point in digging down 70 feet unless water is reached. Very practical, results-oriented in today's management-speak. In another instance, he said that rulers have three treasures — land, people and government. Mencius reduced important ideas to simple basics, providing focus on the essentials and avoiding getting bogged down in detail.

With any problem, Mencius advised a return to fundamentals. Apart from results, rulers' legitimacy rested on their behaviour. "Heaven sees through the eyes of people. Heaven hears through the ears of people," Mencius wrote. This is a key question for Xi Jinping. In his book, *The Governance of China,* Xi quotes from two Han Dynasty scholars in a similar vein. Liu Xiang (77-6 BC) wrote, "Decrees may be followed if they are in accord with the aspirations of the people; they will be ineffective if they are against the aspirations of the people". Weng Chong (27–97) said, "It is the people who know if a decree is good or not". There is no doubting Xi's train of thought. When Xi was a young official in Fujian, he was known for listening and gaining others' insights. He would not ask a businessman to do something, he would relate a problem and ask what would work best, an Indonesian Fujianese, who knew Xi, related to Bill Kazer.

Whereas Confucius concerned himself more with rituals (social obligations), Mencius concerned himself more with ethics and education as well as benevolent government. He did not believe in the principle of hereditary rulers, which would have appalled Confucius. Mencius said government was only justified if it protected people's interests. If not, it could be overthrown and the Mandate of Heaven withdrawn from a despot.

Confucianists continued to dispute and discuss the finer points of philosophy and governance long after Confucius and Mencius. The next major evolution in thinking came over 1,000 years later during the Song Dynasty (960–1279). This was more than 2,000 years after the foundations of Zhou, by which time, the classics were somewhat dated. The Neo-Confucianists re-interpreted Confucian poetry, literature and ritual. They were more concerned about the universe and human nature, including the heart. Confucius had said little about such feelings, but the Buddhists, including the Zen Buddhists, and Daoists had.

Confucianism was losing ground. In order to counter the Buddhists and Daoists, the Song Neo-Confucianists incorporated ideas from both, as well as from the four books. Wanting peace not war, they "sought truth through thorough analysis", while looking to self-education and ethics as the basis of individual virtue. This was the last major development in Confucianism, though there were constant renewals. In the Republican era, Chiang Kai-shek tried to revive interest in it, just as Xi Jinping is doing with his China Dream.

Communism

Now that Confucianism has survived Mao and is spoken of favourably by Xi Jinping, while Communism remains largely in name only, what influence has Communism left on policy formulation and execution? In terms of economic ideas, there are none that Marx or Lenin would recognize as their own. Central planning has certainly gone, the five-year plans are now called programmes.

Three things though have remained: a sense of needing a strong state, lessons from the Communist Party's history and the importance of change. All had echoes in traditional philosophy. How to respond to setbacks and correct mistakes is the greatest lesson drawn from party history. From its 1930 near wipe-out in Shanghai to the Jiangxi Soviet and the Long March in 1934–1935, the party had to rethink strategy repeatedly, just to survive.

After beginning with guerrilla warfare, towards the end of the civil war, the party fought major fixed-piece battles where it mobilized large resources, co-ordinating multiple fronts and extended supply lines. Getting one million armed men across the Yangzi River to capture the Kuomintang's capital of Nanjing, with all the enemy's firepower trained on them, was no small task: Deng's most famous military achievement. The party drew on lessons learned from such battles, as well as strategies recalled from its own and China's history.

The wartime experience became ingrained in decision-making. The first thing to do after a setback is to re-group. The process then follows a pattern. First, assess the situation, gather information: in wartime, intelligence. Probe further through *yanjiu*, research and field work. Then process and assimilate knowledge through seemingly endless discussions. This raw material can be tested through pilot schemes, adapted to local conditions. Understanding reality leads to innovation. When fully tested, such experiments can be applied on a large scale.

This process is still followed today, though largely in times of crisis or great need, for only these create major priorities to address.

Diverse and Time-Tested Ideas

Diverse approaches and ideas have enriched China. Just north of where Ming, Qing and even some Communist leaders have lived, lies the Tower of Orderly Administration. This is the name Yuan Emperor Kublai Khan gave Beijing's new bell tower in 1272, expressing the ideal objective of government. Orderly administration remained a fervent wish as well as a lofty aspiration for all rulers.

Unlike many countries that are dominated by a single belief system such as Christianity, Islam, Hinduism, Buddhism or Judaism, Chinese traditional philosophy is based on more than one dominant belief or thought system: a hybrid largely of Confucianism, Daoism and Buddhism. Differing from most belief systems, Confucius had little time for speculating about religion, the supernatural or an afterlife. He said he still had not figured out life. Indeed, Confucianism is not a religion involving a God or divinely-inspired scripture, it is man-made.

Today, China is an amalgam of several long-tested indigenous philosophies that ranged across a wide spectrum of thought but died out as Confucianism and Daoism became dominant. Later, they were joined by Buddhism from India in the first century AD to provide the third pillar of traditional Chinese thinking. Fitzgerald considered the survival of the two main local philosophies as "singular proof of the Chinese preference for compromise and the middle course." Even within the mainstream though, there were different approaches, further enriching Chinese philosophy. Daoists emphasized inactivity, being guided by nature: so much for an activist state. Confucius and Mencius believed in the goodness of people, while the Legalists like Lord Sang (390-338 BC) and Han Fei (280-233 BC) believed the opposite, advocating strict enforcement of laws to curb man's perceived evil nature. Much variety has gone into China's rich mix.

Confucius and Mencius are remarkably clear in their meaning, contrary to untutored perceptions of Chinese philosophers. They have none of the abstruse obfuscations often associated with philosophy. Admittedly, Daoism is more elliptical and harder to comprehend for those brought up on Descartes and Western logic. Laozi, Daoism's founder, held that there is the Way. However, it "cannot be named by human beings", hence cannot be fully described though it can be felt and observed, so people should yield to it. Brookings Institution's Kenneth Lieberthal calls its conception of heaven a combination of history and fate, a useful starting point for comprehension.

The Dao, the great way, is "open and smooth" yet unfortunately, people love "twisty paths". Hence, philosophy has to deal with real human beings: difficult creatures. Its concept of the world sees "complexity in simplicity and finds the vast in the minute". This becomes very apparent in the way China approaches and implements government policy. "Too much simplicity though breeds too much complexity," the Dao warns, just when novices think they understand.

"Knowing not knowing is lofty. Not knowing not-knowing is an affliction": this sounds like US Defense Secretary Donald Rumsfeld musing about known unknowns and unknown unknowns, but in fact, comes from the *Dao De Jing* that was probably compiled in the third century BC. Daoist Zhuangzi helps put things in perspective. Everything is relative. Even big things can be small in the cosmos, which is where Daoists place life, with their emphasis on the natural world and universe.

Western political philosophy focuses largely on what to do — from Jean-Jacques Rousseau's *Social Contract* to Thomas Paine's *Rights of Man* and Vladimir Ilyich Lenin's *What Is To Be Done?* Rarely does it focus on how this should be done. Just Do It is the implication. Britain's Brexit vote followed in this tradition. In China, implementation is an integral part of philosophy. Strategy, linked with philosophy, is the other by-product of Chinese history. This is the practical, pragmatic strain that runs through much of it, guided by the importance of effective strategy to implement policy.

Some traditional Confucian ideas though are irrelevant or unacceptable in the 21st century. In this egalitarian age, Confucius's words stating, "Unless you have been appointed to office, don't fuss or fret over the business of government", are elitist. Similarly, Mencius said, "Those who use their minds govern, and those who use their muscles are governed. Those who are governed provide for those who govern... Inequality is natural. If you tried to make everything of equal value, confusion would reign. If elegant shoes and workaday shoes brought the same price who would bother to make elegant shoes?" The comments of Confucius about women and "little people" are equally unacceptable.

Much though is still perfectly valid. When asked for one word to guide someone through life, Confucius gave *shu.* This means that you should never impose on others what you would not choose for yourself: a perfectly modern idea, while resonating with Christianity of 2,000 years ago.

How Relevant is Traditional Philosophy Today?

Does every Chinese walk around, quoting from her little book of Confucian thoughts? Hardly. Does everyone know in detail the strategies of Zhuge Liang or even Sunzi? No. Are the majority of people of the Buddhist faith? Not quite. So what is the importance of traditional philosophy and all the history that underpins it?

Out of it has come a common body of thought: what Hu Jintao in 2006 called China's traditional culture, derived from Confucianism, Buddhism and Daoism. Confucianism stresses humility, moderation, respect for elders, teachers and powers that be. Buddhism began to localize an Indian religion two millennia ago, bending it to suit Chinese characteristics, but retaining its essence of acceptance and fatalism. Daoism values harmony while providing a concept of the cosmos and strategy derived from that.

How widespread is each of the three traditions? Those educated in the classics would generally respect Confucianism, with its filial piety, hard work and frugality, but after 1949, it was not taught. Almost all Chinese today therefore have only a cursory knowledge of Confucianism, which is why it is taught again in schools. Maybe one-third to one-half of Chinese consider themselves Buddhists, while Daoists are a smaller number. How many would have deep knowledge of all three philosophies and apply them equally? Maybe 100-200 is the answer of Reuters China special correspondent, Benjamin Lim. How can that be in a country of 1.4 billion people?

Many people only know their own beliefs, though not often in great detail. Very rarely would they be familiar with other traditions. Buddhists might not even know all Buddhist scriptures and teachings or be able to differentiate between Buddha and associated gods, let alone details of Daoism. Daoists would most likely know a historical figure like Zhuge Liang, but not necessarily that some of his strategy was inspired by Daoism. Even many scholars do not have a broad and deep knowledge of all three traditions. Like academics everywhere, tunnel vision is a common failing. Very few people have the whole picture in Lim's analysis.

Power is a jigsaw puzzle. Many can see parts of it, very few see the whole, let alone appreciate how to fit all the pieces together. That leaves ruling very largely to the rulers; and the rulers at the very top. It would include Xi Jinping and Wang Qishan, just as it did Mao Zedong, Zhou Enlai and Deng Xiaoping in the past, but not every single member of the central committee, let alone every one of the 89 million party members. Some would know more than others, but very few need to have the entire picture, in the Confucian view.

Throughout Chinese history, traditional culture provided a common set of beliefs that enable rulers to rule. Confucianism controls officials and the military, stressing loyalty to the ruler, lest they think of rebelling. Buddhism is for the masses. Its fatalism may contain laid off workers, victims of illegal land seizures or those unable to pay for healthcare or education. It is their karma, do not fight it, the reasons for misfortune lie in a previous life, nothing can be done. Daoism is mainly for the scholar elite, providing strategy to manage war or peace, as in Sunzi's *The Art of War*.

Traditional thought, therefore, is still very relevant in China, even in the 21st century and under communist rule. Without understanding it, politics and economics cannot be fathomed nor diplomacy or warfare. The next chapter looks at 20 essential ideas that lie behind Chinese thinking and change.

Chapter 3

20 Essential Ideas for Life, Family, Business and Government

However often their role has been ignored or subverted by ruling interests, China has essentially been a nation governed by philosophers.

David Hinton, *The Four Chinese Classics,* 2014

Philosophers have ruled or influenced China throughout time, whatever the discontinuities or deviations: not just philosophers but very practical ones. Those in commerce, government and politics were, in C.P. Fitzgerald's (1935) view, "essentially a practical race of men of the world": pragmatic, an essentially Chinese idea.

"Their civilization is based on the most forthrightly materialist value system in the history of mankind…. The trick is to find how things work and manipulate them for a better life for oneself, family or social group," David Bonavia in 1980 asserted in *The Chinese*. Chinese still agree with this description, considering urban Chinese in particular to be acutely aware of the function of things and accepting of life. Many are utilitarian, others more philosophical.

A Framework for Thinking and Change

To modernize thoroughly, China needs to change so much. The process is complex, the scope wide and the time needed long. Only a methodical approach, within a framework for thinking, will address successfully the numerous challenges. There are no 10 Commandments or even one principal text, no holy bible of change, just ideas scattered over numerous writings. Many are drawn from traditional Confucianism, but not all, though most are compatible with it.

This wisdom is almost holy writ. "Whatever follows our Zhou Dynasty, even if it comes a hundred generations from now, we can know it in the same way," Confucius said: for these are eternal truths. Not just moral truths but practical truths while building Fan Zhongyan's "tower of orderly administration".

There is no strict hierarchy of ideas to organize thinking in China as there might be in the West; all are interconnected in 3D thinking. However they do come under three headings: goals, means and people. Goals are the starting point of traditional thought. Means are practical ways to conceive and implement ideas, followed by people who have to use them.

The Process for China's Change: "How" Not "What"

GOALS			
Harmony	Stability	Moderation	
MEANS			
Crystallizing Ideas			
Long-term thinking	360-degree view	Vision	Cycles
Priorities	Research (*yanjiu*)		
Implementing Policy			
Pilot schemes	Sequencing	Pragmatism	Flexibility
Gradualism	Restraint	Continual renewal (*weixin*)	
PEOPLE			
Elite	Education	Integrity	Self-criticism

Goals

With clear goals, it is easier to see priorities and paths. When the need is greatest, as in post-Brexit Europe and culture wars–divided US, change may seem impossible, but it is precisely when new goals are most required. Problems differ and so will approaches, but everywhere goals are the start to finding solutions.

UK voters, after the 1930s economic depression and having gone together through World War II, set full employment, education, healthcare and adequate welfare as the goals to maintain national unity. People wanted change. Feeling was so strong they even threw out wartime leader Winston Churchill at the 1945 election. This consensus among the main parties held for almost three decades until new challenges required different goals. In the US, major changes were also wrought by wartime's "Greatest Generation".

Harmony: "The most precious fruit".

President Hu Jintao reminded China of the importance of social harmony. The economy was doing well in GDP growth terms in the early 2000s but the widening wealth gap and urban–rural divide could undermine it. This was not only unfair but threatened social stability as harmony requires the inclusion of all.

A mid-course correction began in 2003, adjusting for the often harsh but necessary market reforms since 1978. The Gini coefficient, measuring income distribution, entered the political vocabulary. China had become one of the world's most unequal countries in terms of income distribution, though little different from 19th-century Europe or US.

To promote harmony and inclusion, spending on health and education rose sharply. Education's share of GDP almost doubled after 1995, while a social welfare safety net is being woven by insurance schemes and government funding. Operations for life-threatening conditions are now heavily subsidized, otherwise the majority of families in China would face a financial emergency. There is also an economic rationale. China needs consumption, not savings. If people worry about retirement or large hospital bills, they will save. If they feel secure, not needing to save so much for a rainy day, they will consume more.

Stability: "The economy cannot be strong without it."

Whether from war, social unrest, poverty or unemployment, all of society is threatened by instability. China's history and past is living proof, so stability has been a primary goal for millennia. Ignoring or failing to achieve it can cause chaos on a grand scale. In history, Chaotic Era states' populations have shrunk by one third or even a half through war, disease, exodus and disintegration.

China has experienced much instability, suffering two-thirds of the world's dozen deadliest wars. These are not confined to two or three millennia ago. The Taiping Rebellion from 1850–1864 killed 20–30 million people, displacing many more from their homes. In the 20th century, 12–20 million civilians died during the Japanese invasion of 1937–1945, while another 2–3 million Chinese soldiers were killed or wounded. Over 80 million became refugees, about 15–20% of China's population. Then, in the famines following the Great Leap Forward, an estimated 30–40 million died in the 1960s. Many were persecuted and killed during the Cultural Revolution; unknown numbers died or committed suicide. Disastrous instability is not just a fact of ancient history, it is vividly recent.

Wending is to be stable, not shaky. Creating a *wending* environment is much desired, whether in economics, politics or international affairs. The implication is that peace and prosperity flow from it, enabling China to develop further. Deng Xiaoping referred to having two iron fists: the first, the economy; the other, stability. With the second, China can advance the first. Without stability, the economy cannot become strong like an iron fist and China cannot prosper. Both are interconnected.

Moderation: "Hold fast to the middle way."

"Hold fast to the middle way and the Golden Mean," Confucius advised, positioning himself firmly in the middle ground, not someone on the conservative fringes, where Mao put him. From this followed the Confucian priority for harmony and stability. Both reflect the need for moderation.

Moderation in all things, Confucius might have said. Indeed Mencius did say that "Confucius was one who abstained from extremes." The *Dao De Jing* recorded, "The sage steers clear of extremes, clear of extravagance and clear of exaltation." The *Analects* said, "The root of ritual… [is] simplicity rather than extravagance: in mourning, grief rather than repose." Appropriate behaviour is correct: again moderation.

Means

Reaching goals requires understanding all the means available. First, ideas have to be crystallized then implemented, whilst recognizing that workable ideas take time to emerge and bed down.

Long-Term Thinking: "One who fails to plan for 10 generations cannot plan for one time."

"We should take the long-term view," Xi Jinping wrote. The long-term is the starting point of policy thinking, the only practical way to approach successful change. Then work backwards, filling in with ever-increasing detail. Focusing principally on immediate problems may only create more and much larger problems later, as China's scale overwhelms policy lacking long-term thinking.

Neville Maxwell held that the basic unit of time for government in modern China is a decade: not literally, but roughly. He derived this in the 1970s from China's foreign policy, the ultimate long-term area where so much is outside a nation's control. Domestically, given China's size, policy formulation and implementation need at least one decade as challenges take that long to be addressed effectively. Some take several decades, as have poverty reduction and urbanization, two of China's greatest long-term successes.

When sustainable development was first included in the 10th five-year plan (2001–2005), I asked a senior official how long its full implementation would take. "Well, it appears in this plan to put officials on notice. Some experiments may begin. If these are promising, it may move up the priority list in the next plan, and half-way through that, people will know that implementation will begin in earnest. In the third plan it could become a high priority, putting further pressure on officials to enforce regulations," I was told. I could not believe it would take that long for effective action, especially as I asked the question in the middle of a pitch-black Beijing afternoon, but it did.

There were competing priorities. Fast economic growth was still the top priority in 2001 in order to fund other priorities like poverty reduction and urbanization. Nor had I reckoned with the scale of the problem, not so much technological or scientific, though there are plenty of these challenges too. The real problem is administrative. Officials, from Beijing to provincial capitals and the smallest counties, need to understand this is a top priority. Local vested interests have to be assuaged or punished before policies can be fully implemented. This all takes time. Forcing the issue might lead to insurmountable resistance, which could endanger numerous other reforms: very complex and full of risk. China is like a Rubik's Cube — change one thing and all is altered, possibly negatively: everything is connected.

Careful planning was emphasized by Confucius. The concept was alive and well long before the Soviets. "A man who attacks tigers unarmed and crosses rivers without boats, willing to die without the least regret — that is a man I would *never* take with me. The man I would *always* take approaches difficulties with due caution and always succeeds by planning carefully," the *Analects* recorded. The unprepared are reckless and will fail, the well-prepared succeed.

Placing great importance on the long-term, China makes detailed analyses of future challenges and solutions, be they to become a high-income economy by 2030 or to transform manufacturing by 2045: see Chapter 13. There is nothing more long-term than planning for future generations of a family, as many in Asia still do. Not just for one generation but for several. Hence the pertinence of Chen Danran's remarks about not being able to plan even for one occasion if a person cannot plan for 10 generations. This does not rule out short-term strategies but expects them to fit within a long-term perspective.

360-Degree View: "Combine all the elements."

"To continue reform comprehensively, we should strengthen planning at the top level and adopt a holistic approach," Xi said. This acknowledges that policy benefits from a well-rounded 360-degree view. Also, it prevents policy capture by vested interests or becoming stuck in narrow thought silos. Traditional Chinese philosophy has two insights into these problems: recognizing the need for holistic thinking, it "combines all the elements". Similarly, "an ocean accepts water from all rivers" means that things from different sources enlarge and strengthen the whole, while also diluting vested interests.

Chinese medicine too combines all the elements, in and out of the body. It cannot simply be broken down into fragmented, unconnected parts. A heart or liver cannot be separated from the nervous system, diet or environment. All are interconnected as they are in philosophy and government. The elements cannot be oversimplified otherwise they lose their essence. The Western mind often wants manageable structure and short sound bites. Chinese philosophy is happier with a grander all-encompassing system. From this flows the approach of many Chinese companies to problems: first locate the systemic weakness.

Long-term thinking started this section, but so could have a 360-degree view, pragmatism, priorities, harmony, education or the elite's role. All are important components of the same body of thought. As in Chinese medicine, they are all linked.

Vision: "Do not think of small gains."

Think big: China has long had the "vision thing", as US President George Bush called it pejoratively. Vision in China is a tool for rulers, firms or families to transmit messages clearly. This is particularly important in a multicultural continent with different regions, religions, traditions and education levels. Vision is the key to communication. Details can wait but communication of vision must first get everyone "on board".

The world's imagination has been caught by China's high-speed rail system, the 2008 Beijing Olympics opening ceremony and the Belt and Road Initiative. All represent China Vision in handling scale. Their inspiration and confidence comes from earlier millennia when China's Great Wall, the Dujiangyan irrigation system and the Grand Canal were built, testifying to vision and the ability to manage great scale.

Even though the Great Wall of China cannot be seen from space or claim to be continuous, "it sure is a Great Wall", to quote US President Richard Nixon; and a great inspiration for large-scale endeavors such as today's potentially world-changing Belt and Road Initiative. The Dujiangyan irrigation system began in the third century BC when the waters of the Min River were diverted into the central Sichuan plain, creating China's major rice bowl. This still exists and has become, like the Grand Canal, a UNESCO World Heritage Site for its outstanding feat of civil engineering. Strategically, it enabled Qin Shihuang to defeat the state of Chu and so, in 221 BC, unite China.

The world's longest man-made waterway, the Grand Canal connects Hangzhou in central China, once the commercial heart of its agriculture, with the Yellow River in the north. Produce and goods still flow from south to north. Much of its 1,100-mile length was joined up in just six years from 605–611, during the Sui Dynasty. Supposedly five million people worked on it, illustrating China's ability to mobilize vast resources and at speed: China Speed.

The latest big vision is the Jing–Jin–Ji scheme in northern China, creating a megalopolis of 150 million people. The Jing–Jin–Ji region of Beijing, Tianjin and Hebei will emphasize new industries and sustainable development; and could address Beijing's smog problem as the central government previously had no real control over surrounding areas where pollution originates, particularly in coal-burning steel plants.

This is China Scale and vision. Jing–Jin–Ji's population exceeds Japan's by 20 million, is treble that of South Korea's and equal to Germany's and France's combined. Reviving the Middle Yangzi River area around Wuhan will affect more people than live in the average European country or US state.

Cycles: "Be mindful of possible danger in time of peace... chaos in times of stability."

China's best-loved novel opens with a basic Chinese idea. "The empire, long divided, must unite; long united, must divide," observed the *Romance of the Three Kingdoms.* Cycles of stability are followed by periods of instability as early Ming Dynasty author Luo Guanzhong wrote in the 14th–15th-century novel about the decline of the Han Dynasty and the emergence of three competing kingdoms in the second and third centuries AD: cycles recur and recur.

When a peak or trough approaches, a reversal should be expected. This is as true in economics as in politics or social trends: repetition, repetition. Dynasties rise and fall. What waxes will wane, from empires to sports teams. Understanding cycles or rhythms can alert people to danger and opportunity. Prosperity can spring from calamity, as it did in China in 1978, while calamity can lurk in prosperity as the West found 30 years later. Vigilance is the message, complacency the enemy, but also *nil desperandum,* never despair just act.

Priorities: "They devoted themselves to essentials first."

Clear priorities must be established. The traditional Chinese way is to distinguish between the trunk and branches, the critically central from the merely important. Otherwise everything gets jumbled up, policies collide with each other and little is achieved.

Mencius advised to attend first to the essentials. These identify where to focus attention, time, resources and energy. There are so many problems to solve: some from the past, others that arise out of change. A great deal of discipline is needed in implementation, otherwise effort is wasted without clear direction and problems overwhelm.

The five-year plans, now called programmes, guide China towards its top economic priorities. A wide variety, they have included rebalancing the economy towards consumption, financial liberalization, the environment and western China. Local government can then figure out where to prioritize spending, while companies will know where the money is to be spent.

Over time, issues rise up the pole of priorities as earlier problems are solved and disappear, freeing up government time and resources. In the process, experience is acquired from experiments, providing better solutions: pure gradualism. This can seem maddeningly slow compared with the West's apparent immediate addressing of problems. All too often though, these "solutions" come to nothing due to lack of careful preparation, experimentation, sustained attention or resources: "unintended consequences" occur. China is slower, more deliberate but makes steady progress. After a decade or so (that basic unit of time in China) the steady, incremental approach is often on the way to solving problems. Like Aesop's fable of the tortoise and the hare, the painfully slow tortoise wins the race, and may even be the only finisher.

Research and field work: Yanjiu.

Chinese education has always drummed into students the need for study and continuous learning. Faced with a new task or problem, studying the issue in-depth through research and field work, *yanjiu,* comes as second nature. China's history may hold some clues, but lessons from abroad may be even more relevant, especially in technical matters. Chinese have been great absorbers of foreign experience. A recent case is instructive.

After the turbulent years of 1989 and 1990 in China, the Soviet Union and Eastern Europe, China's communist party faced a threat to its existence. So it conducted in-depth research into the causes of communism's collapse elsewhere. This was no whitewash. It was a far-reaching investigation, through intensive research and debate for over a decade. Despite the length of time involved, there was a sense of urgency. Reforms flowed from it, some to build the party's capacity to govern. Economic reforms, sparked by Deng's 1992 Southern Tour, arose out of this intense introspection about China's future.

Reform could not have happened without the *yanjiu.* The research identified almost 70 causes of Soviet communism's collapse. They gave China a strong idea of what to look for, a list of potential dangers — just as the *Yi Jing* would have advised. In economics, research highlighted many problems. The Soviet Union had stagnated and its consumers deprived as excessive military spending drained resources, while shortages created black markets. The Soviet economy lacked integration into world trade, financial systems or markets. There was little inbound foreign investment to make it more efficient. Inflation resulted, while backward agriculture and vested interests arrested change. By 2008, China scored well in the economic comparison, and even, to some extent, in politics.

The clearest warnings came from where China was most similar to the Soviet Union: in the social, cultural, coercive and international realms. Causes of the Soviet collapse included the rise of civil society, sporadic social protest, a moral vacuum, cynicism towards government and ideology, the impact of globalization, religion's growing appeal, unlawful tax collection, ethnic tensions and separatist forces. The internal party study did not shrink from detailing all these problems. China studied them, then shaped policy.

Unlike most Western analysis of the Soviet Union's collapse, which focused on Mikhail Gorbachev's role (done very much in the tradition of the great or flawed leaders school of history, as opposed to the school of great social and economic forces), China's research took a "much broader and historical view and offered a more systemic analysis of the multiple reasons for the collapse," George Washington University's David Shambaugh wrote. China possesses the capacity to analyse dispassionately.

Shambaugh concluded:

> One thing is certain: the CCP is definitely *not* awaiting the inevitable collapse of its power … [this] can be avoided by such introspection, adaptation, and implementation of pre-emptive reform and policy…a sober reminder of the CCP's vulnerabilities. Yet it is precisely these vulnerabilities of which the CCP is so conscious and has sought to address.

This was classic *yanjiu,* not a quick copy-and-paste version of a how-to manual but a very rigorous, warts-and-all analysis of the problems China could face. With the main goals identified, the right questions considered, China is ready to formulate policy so as to avoid collapsing like the Soviet Union.

Pilot Schemes: "Crossing the river by feeling the stones."

After *yanjiu,* one of the most practical features of China's approach to change is policy experiments. The phrase "crossing the river by feeling the stones" combines pragmatism with flexibility in the search for reality and certainty: an accurate description of China's economic and political journey in uncharted territory.

With 1.4 billion people, one size cannot fit all in government policy, business or life. All regions and cities are at different stages of development, with varying histories, geographies and cultures. Therefore policies are first tested in different parts of the country. Limited pilot schemes can reveal problems without causing much damage. Risk-averse officials are more willing to adopt new ideas if they know the policies have been well tested and the main bugs removed.

Even errors, though, have merit. As Mencius wrote, "We can change and grow *only* when we make mistakes. We realize what to do only when we work through worry and confusion. And we gain people's trust and understanding when our inner thoughts are revealed clearly in our faces and words", thus making a virtue out of necessity. Officials and entrepreneurs alike know this well.

The most famous pilot schemes in China's Great Change were four special economic zones, first proposed by Xi Jinping's father, Xi Zhongxun, when he was Guangdong's governor. Shenzhen, right opposite Hong Kong, was the most successful, even though it was originally little more than a fishing village surrounded by rice fields. That was its great strength, an almost blank piece of paper where new ideas could be tried and implemented, with few legacy systems or old officials to inhibit new thinking. Even the people were largely new, and young. This city of pioneering migrants from all over China has become home to world-leading telecommunication equipment makers and many other technology companies. Three decades later, Shenzhen's population exceeds Hong Kong's and now ranks number one for innovation in China, above Hong Kong.

The latest major experiment is the Shanghai Free Trade Zone. This began in 2013 to open further the economy to global market forces and opportunities, especially in finance and trade. Liberalization of interest and exchange rates has been trialed there. Once the bugs are found and removed, further financial liberalization can spread nationwide.

Customs procedures too are liberalized, speeding up trade and lowering costs: not ideological, but key to greater economic efficiency and investment. Mayor La Guardia would have approved.

Pilot schemes largely address major long-term fundamental policy change, designed to catch mistakes before a much larger roll-out. In this way, disasters with the magnitude of the Great Leap Forward and subsequent famine should be avoidable.

Sequencing: "Get the order right."

Mature economies lack the concept of sequencing. In the West, governments come to power with an election mandate, then, immediately after the election, a mad rush begins to implement as much as possible before the honeymoon with the legislature or electorate fades. China is different, with its emphasis on long-term thinking, clear priorities and one-party rule. Almost everything has had to change since 1978, big and small. The danger is not legislative gridlock but implementation overload leading to paralysis. The solution is sequencing.

The problem often in pursuing priorities is that other policies, regulations, institutions or even whole systems need to be in place first. Otherwise, new ideas may not work. Usually, in mature economies, the main building blocks have long been in place: not in developing China. Before interest rates could be liberalized, numerous reforms were required, ranging from basic bank audit and risk management systems to new departments and products. Without them well bedded down, interest rate liberalization would fail. If China wants to "make markets decisive", as the 2013 Third Plenum mandated, many things first have to change, not least establishing the rule of law and its acceptance. Similarly if corruption is to be brought under control, institutions not only have to be created, but so too a culture of the rule of law as opposed to rule by man. Cultures take a long time to evolve. Passing new laws is relatively easy but insufficient. An idea may be excellent, but successful implementation depends on other factors, which will have to be working well first. That is why sequencing is so important.

As Mencius said, "Though you may have a fine hoe, awaiting the season works better." Supreme strategist Sunzi's advice was more direct, "Do things in order. Get the order right." Xi Jinping quoted the proverb that in order to put on a shirt properly the first two or three buttons must be done up correctly. It is not just about having the best ideas, it is about doing them in the right order. Best wait for the necessary supporting structure or enabling means to become sufficiently strong and for experience to be acquired.

Pragmatism: "It does not matter if the cat is black or white as long as it catches mice."

Deng Xiaoping's phrase about the cat's colour is supremely pragmatic. When first used in the early 1980s, people instantly knew what was happening, what might be possible. Such pragmatism spoke to moderation and flexibility, hallmarks of traditional philosophy, not to the rigidly ideological 1960s and early 1970s. China was searching for what worked: practical methods.

After the ideological storms of the Cultural Revolution, politics reverted to what Bismarck called the art of the possible. This released Deng's cats. They were not after small mice but large change. Two examples showed this. In 1980, China opened the first special economic zone in Shenzhen, outside the socialist economic system but within China. Before 1997 it devised the formula of "one country, two systems" as an acceptable way for Hong Kong to return to Chinese sovereignty. This 50-year transition was certainly novel, pragmatic, gradual and remarkably flexible.

Pragmatism in China has long been regarded as one of the main principles of change. Its roots lay in education, whose original purpose was to prepare people for government. This brought the educated elite face-to-face with the turbulence of politics and war. Many resorted to pragmatism to save their positions, even their very skins. A strong strain of pragmatism has informed Chinese life ever since, the lubricant of both survival and change.

Economic reform quickly encountered the need for pragmatism. A group of overseas investors wanted to invest in China but would only do so through someone they knew well and trusted. To solve this problem they chose Rong Yiren, their old college friend from Shanghai's leading English language university, St John's. Rong was well regarded in China as a "Red Capitalist", becoming a vice mayor of Shanghai, a key adviser in the early stages of reform and later China's Vice President. To their relief, to overcome the initial problem, Rong was allowed to set up China International Trust and Investment Corporation (CITIC), China's very first credit trust.

However all parties then realized an even greater problem faced them: private enterprise had been abolished in China. So the option of overseas investors funding new Chinese ventures by working through known and trusted individuals was not possible. Still keen to invest, the foreign investors suggested a structure built around trust that had been invented in the UK and developed further in the US. This was translated into Chinese as *Xintuo*, meaning that someone entrusts funds to another person to be used for a specific purpose. Such pragmatism proved adequate in the reform's infancy, when progress was made not by ideology or blueprint but through "crossing the river by feeling the stones".

Flexibility: "If you are learned, you are never inflexible."

Pragmatism naturally assumes flexibility. The *Analects* start by saying, "If you are learned, you are never inflexible. When you are wrong, do not be afraid to change." In a similar vein, Huan Kuan during the Western Han Dynasty (206 BC–25 AD) in his economics study *On Salt and Iron* wrote, "A wise man changes his way as circumstances change, a knowledgeable person alters his means as times evolve." Both sentiments would be echoed in the early 20th century by Keynes who said, "When the facts change, I change my opinion. What do you do, sir?"

Confucius elaborated in the *Analects*, "The noble-minded are all-encompassing, not stuck in doctrines. Little people are stuck in doctrines", underlining the need for flexibility and tolerance rather than rigid ideology. A traditional saying expresses this as "100 torrents eventually turn events into gold". Tolerance and patience pay off.

Be flexible, not rigid. Premier Zhou Enlai was deemed a bamboo, bending with the wind but not breaking: a commendable quality in China. Thus he survived all Mao's twists, turns and plots. His successor as premier, Liu Shaoqi, was a pine who could not bend: he broke and died.

Gradualism: "Do not rush things."

Following Daoist thinking, China does not do "Big Bangs". Involving undue force and considering China's Scale, they greatly increase the likelihood of chaos and failure. "Gradually progressing forward", is the Chinese way. Gradual, incremental change, one step at a time, is more manageable. When wrong, less harmful, easier to correct: small gains are the basis for larger gains.

Confucius advised, "Do not rush things.... If you rush around, your efforts will lead nowhere, your great endeavors will go unrealized." Again this reflects the reality of China Scale, as well as the experience of governing and implementing change. Gradualism was a hallmark of much Western political reform. Achieving universal suffrage in Britain took 97 years from 1832 when only 3% of the male adult population had the vote. Full effective voting rights in the US took even longer, from 1820 until the Voters' Rights Act fully enfranchised all African Americans in 1965.

The more recent US concept of Big Bang may work in mature systems, such as in UK finance in the 1980s (though that is debatable) but not in less developed transitional economies and societies, such as in Eastern Europe and Russia in the 1990s, which lacked sufficient shock absorbers. Even if achieved, the price may be high in terms of social cohesion and long-term stability. Gradualism should be more effective and less costly in the long run.

Xi's careful, gradual approach is seen in the three-year drafting of the new norms on political life and internal supervision regulations. *China Political Weekly* described it as "a highly structured, iterative process that solicited opinions from various stakeholders. Xi did not force these changes through, but rather made sure to embed them in a process that allowed participation by a large group of Party members. In a word, he made sure to garner support for the new rules".

Restraint: "Angry words cannot be taken back."

Behaviour should be restrained, including speech. Confucius held that three things cannot be taken back—"a shot arrow, a missed opportunity or angry words." Such restraint goes along with moderation, gradualism and flexibility.

Continual Renewal: Weixin; Renew every day.

China's rulers for almost 4,000 years have been warned against resting on their laurels. Through the idea of *weixin,* constant renewal, they are exhorted to renew themselves and their thinking: the same with governments and people.

The concept dates back to at least the 17th century BC when King Tang of Tsang had *weixin* inscribed on his bronze washing basin, "Renew yourself everyday and all the days thereafter." The Zhou Dynasty (1046–256 BC) took *weixin* as its motto. The *Book of Poems* recorded that although Zhou was an old state, its way of life was continuously renewed. The *Great Learning* strongly commended Tang's verse to all *junzi* (gentlemen), central to Confucian education ever since.

People

While the traditional governing system was elitist, entry to it was supposedly meritocratic. The elite was meant to be the conscience of society. Human frailty is the Achilles heel of any system, so Confucius and Mencius placed great importance on the quality of people, education, integrity and self-criticism.

Elite: "They transform like rain coming in the season."

Chinese traditional philosophy is frankly elitist. The *shi,* the intellectual elite feels responsible for society. There is an element of European *noblesse oblige* in all this. However in China, it was not so much those of noble birth but those of the highest education who were the *shi*, the governing elite. They had a clear sense of duty as Confucius said, "The noble-minded are clear about duty. Little people are clear about profit."

"Be the first to worry about the world's worries and the last to share its joys," Fan Zhongyan, the 11th-century Song scholar told the elite *junzi* in his *Memorial to Yueyang Tower.* No one epitomized this more in late 20th-century Asia than Singapore's Lee Kuan Yew. Even after a year of almost double-digit GDP growth, his New Year speech would be full of gloomy predictions and exhortations to do better. He never seemed to take a break nor expected other colleagues to do so. That is their lot. Elite life is a continuous grind: much as in China today.

Those returnees from education abroad, who decide to work in government, have a similar sense of social responsibility. Salaries and accommodation are not grand at the lower levels, certainly not compared with the private sector; and the hours are long. Yet the scholar–official ideal to serve the country is still alive. A young IMF staffer confirmed some turn down the rewards of Wall Street or foreign universities to return to this life. After 20–25 years they may be among China's financial leaders, as Liu He and Yi Gang became, providing an inner core for the technocracy.

Mencius could have been writing with such returnee scholars in mind when he said, "Heaven appointed the wise to awaken those who will be wise, appointed the awakened to awaken those who would be awakened. I am one of the awakened, so I should use this Way to awaken the people, otherwise who will awaken them?" A very strong sense of national duty infused Mencius' thinking. A sense of responsibility is not just confined to the governing elite, it extends to the business elite too: see Chapter 12.

Mencius, as ever, best summarized Confucius on the subject of this very Chinese elite. "The noble-minded teach in five ways. They transform like rain coming in the season. They realize integrity. They perfect talents. They answer questions. They cultivate themselves and so stand apart as examples," Mencius said. They are teachers and enablers.

China is very conscious of the elite's quality and differences within it. When I was planning some research in central China, a senior Beijing official commented that Anhui and Jiangxi were forging ahead because of new government leaders with good reform records in Shanghai and Jiangsu. Banks look favourably on projects in areas where leadership is well regarded: the people at the top. They can indeed transform like the coming of rain.

Education: "Study as if you will never know enough, afraid of losing it all."

The basis of good government for Confucius lay in people and their self-cultivation through education in knowledge, morality and behaviour. "My life is limited but my learning is unlimited," Confucius said, implying that learning never ends. Knowledge can be acquired anywhere. Continuous learning is captured in the phrase, "When I see three people walking I should be able to learn something from them", either positive or negative.

A common phrase is, "study so you will not be ignorant". For without study and knowledge you will not be able to handle real life. Few seem to leave that to chance. China values education greatly. "Broad learning with resolute purpose, earnest enquiry with attentive reflection on things at hand — therein lies humanity [selfless concern for others]," Confucius said about learning's purpose.

Education today has become more about career than self-cultivation, but once the ladder has been climbed there is increasing interest in the latter. As Confucius said, "Cultivate yourself with a serious, respectful attitude. This brings peace and security." Lectures abound, teaching everything from strategy, history and philosophy to economics and investment. This thriving industry fills a gap in formal education. Lecturers are accessible through digital media and expensive conferences, cashing in on this latest Chinese boom. Tele-lecturer Yu Dan has sold over 20 million copies of *Confucius From The Heart: Ancient Wisdom For Today's World.*

Continual learning is a feature of officials' lives. McKinsey's Jonathan Woetzel, who works principally with government officials, believes that China's government stands out in its commitment to learning. At the apex of the system are several national academies: for agriculture, science, social science, engineering, medicine and governance. Full of academics, like a Chinese equivalent of the graduates-only All Souls College at Oxford, they work mainly on specialized national issues. Then there are the universities, below which are a myriad of single-subject institutes.

Senior officials make study trips within China and overseas to learn about other realities, issues and policy options. Then there are multilateral links with similar entities. For example, the People's Bank of China and Ministry of Finance are linked with the IMF and World Bank; the National Development and Reform Commission, responsible for energy among many other things, with the Paris-based International Energy Agency; advanced and prosperous cities like Shanghai with economically poor Xinjiang or as a port with Liverpool; and so on.

China has developed a very uniform and cohesive system of government, given the country's size, breeding a high level of familiarity and trust among officials. The party is supreme but non-party members can rise to the upper ranks of government, even occasionally up to minister, especially in technical areas like science, technology and healthcare. All officials have shared similar experiences, using common language and ways of thinking. Study trips or personnel transfers frequently succeed because officials, who have never met before, feel they know each other's ways. All have helped build cities, dealt with common problems, sought investment and followed similar systems.

Integrity: "Many worms will disintegrate wood."

Confucians believed that the root of good government is good people. Therefore corruption has concerned them throughout history."Worms can only grow in something rotten," wrote poet Su Dongpo (1036–1101). The *Book of Lord Shang* (390–338 BC) warned that, "Many worms will disintegrate wood, and a big enough crack will lead to the collapse of a wall." Worms, and in Xi Jinping's warning, tigers and flies, meaning very large beasts as well as minnows, all threaten integrity today.

"In government the secret is integrity. Use it, and you will be like the pole star: always dwelling in its right place, the other stars reverently turning around it," Confucius said. The *junzi* were the noble-minded, the basis of good government. They were modest, quiet and oozed integrity; "The ancients spoke little. They were too ashamed when their actions fell short of their words."

The *Analects* also record that compared with "lesser mortals, the noble-minded cherish integrity, little people cherish territory. And while the noble-minded cherish laws, little people cherish privilege.... *Junzi* understand what is moral, the petty what is profitable.... *Junzi* agree with others without being an echo. Petty people echo without being in agreement." Mencius summarized the ideal *junzi* or scholar–official as, "Never being corrupted by riches and honours, never departing from principle despite poverty or humble origins and never submitting to force or threat." Britain hoped for the same high standards after the 1855 civil service entrance reforms and the 2009 MPs' expenses scandal.

Self-Criticism: "Correct small mistakes, before they become more serious."

Although the West often sees self-criticism as a totalitarian weapon, in China it evolved as the way a *junzi* could improve and correct. "Straightening one's clothes and hat" is an old expression to correct small mistakes before they become serious: a tactic to gain forgiveness for some but a genuine means to change for others.

Some 89 Chinese rulers made public self-criticisms, according to Xiao Han of China's University of Politics and Law. Supposedly, the practice dates back to the Xia Dynasty around 2200 BC. Zhou King Cheng, whose regent Zhou Gong was the original source of Confucianism, made 260 self-criticisms, doubtless under his uncle's influence. The model emperor Taizong made 28. Even Wu, the martial emperor of Han, in his old age, apologized for over-taxing people to pay for his military expansion: he stopped doing so.

These 20 ideas comprise the main parts of Chinese philosophy relevant to change for individuals, firms and government alike. The next five chapters look at how change is conceptualized and theory put into practice in economics, social policy and politics.

Chapter 4

Pivots of Change

You must understand change: if you only know what is regular, what is unchanging, and do not know change, you will be like the man who dropped his sword in the water and tried to find it again by making a mark on the side of his boat — wasting your time.

Ming Dynasty scholar Liu Yin

What do you want to learn? Everything!

Huimin Borrower Group Goat Rearer, Yanchi, Ningxia, 2014

Change is an unexceptional, commonplace word in English: plain, dull and uncomplicated, something taken for granted. Its colour is grey. The word implies little more than differences over time, which tend to get smaller and smaller, often coalescing altogether: not very interesting.

In Chinese, the word is very different: much more profound, complex and dynamic. *Yi* may be a small, short word but it is not simple. Very sophisticated, with many related meanings and much nuance, *yi* has a depth which explains much in life, embodying a much stronger idea than its English translation.

To understand change is to know how to manage life, from family and commerce to government. As Confucius said, after studying change for five decades, one would surely be free of serious flaws. That says it all. A lifetime's experience managing and responding to change exposes people to just about everything that matters. This idea is deeply rooted in the thinking of individuals, firms and officials. Change is their dynamic, even if it is not always thought of in such precise terms.

By pointing to change, the prime minister of Eastern Zhou in the Warring States period famously dismissed the feudal oligarchs' objections to his reform proposals. Su Qin (380–284 BC) pointed out that for 3,000 years the character for change, *bian*, had covered everything in history, all its ups and downs, all the winds and clouds under heaven: war, social change, diplomacy, strategy and economy. Everything involved change. Proving that change worked, he quoted the evidence of five successful emperors who took new paths and three kings who followed different methods. All had risen up to replace the existing Son of Heaven whose dynasty had decayed into tyranny or weakness: the Shang had removed the Xia, the Zhou changed and replaced the Shang, while the Eastern Zhou renewed the Western Zhou.

From the Western Zhou Dynasty, the *Zhou Book of Change*, one of the five Confucian scripts, draws on ideas of philosophy and history probably already then two millennia old, passed down orally and inscribed on bronze ware, bone and turtle shell. After another 900 years or so of commentary, it evolved from a work of divination to one of philosophy and how to manage life. This is today's *Book of Change*, the *Yi Jing*, which was written in 136 BC, educating people about change and the pivots that drive it.

The Meaning of Yi

Yi, which is the noun for change as opposed to *bian* that is the verb, conveys many meanings: mutation, multiplication, deviation from the norm, rising up and falling down, tumbling and rolling. It reconfigures and transforms, implying fluidity: it can be a liquid, gas or cloud. *Yi* brings challenges, uncertainty. Balance and equilibrium can be lost or restored. Unless rebalanced, *yi* eventually brings crisis.

A new normal has to be accepted, as Xi Jinping describes the new economic reality. People have to adjust, so too markets and society. There can be opportunities and dead ends, golden moments and dangers. *Yi* has many forms and meanings, which in China are seen as part of one very powerful concept: *yi* is how society, individuals and firms evolve.

Lives can change dramatically. The founder of the 17th-century Ming Dynasty was a beggar who, to get food, became a monk. In the opposite direction, China's most revered poet, Li Bai, in the eighth century advised the emperor one moment but was condemned to distant exile the next. People still remember such examples to shape their view of life. That is the point. Such extreme change is possible. They do not even have to look at the distant past. The fates of Politburo members Zhou Yongkang and Bo Xilai, who in 2013 and 2015 respectively were sentenced to life imprisonment for corruption, bribery and abuse of power, are very recent reminders. In the West, change in the fortunes of the powerful may be dramatic in tabloid terms but do not have the extreme consequences of a fall from grace in China.

The West's concept of change lacks profundity in Chinese minds. It fails to join all the dots from history in "the great tunnel of time", which combines the economy, politics, society and context. The Industrial Revolution stands on its own in the West, largely separate from today. It does not prominently serve as a direct lesson for the present, let alone the future. Its heroes are confined to a distant past or forgotten: fleeting celebrity has replaced them as role models. Much is lost in the Western assumption of straight-line progress being automatic, where the past can be improved upon and largely forgotten.

Many in the West believe they are changing when in fact they are not or, at least, not significantly. In politics, the left is often stuck with an unchanging, outdated view of the working class, role of the state and inevitability of progress, while the right can yearn for a simpler past, while ignoring the need for effective regulation as well as the reality and threat from inequality. Few grasp the potential full extent of current disruptions. Even fewer see the need for new approaches to manage them.

There is much noise but little sign of fundamental change. Implementation can be painfully slow, diluted, even lost in the mire of conflicted concepts. Who knows what Brexit means: just a word until the final details. Speed is not the West's *forte* anymore. The UK still has not decided on whether to have a "fourth" London airport over half a century after government first proposed it, and already has six. In New York, it took over three decades to decide to build a Second Avenue subway line.

More seriously, permanent solutions to financial instability and low economic growth have not been implemented, even after the great disruption and cost of the 2008 global financial crisis. The largest US bank, Wells Fargo, seemed in 2016 to have learned nothing, persisting with practices severely questioned by the Senate.

Change is no longer the West's main dynamic as it was in the 19th and much of the 20th century. It is, though, again in China. The G7 is ineffective, which is why China pushes for a greater role and capacity in global governance for the G20. The 2016 Hangzhou summit was the first formal step in this direction.

The Chinese Book

The *Book of Change*, the *Yi Jing*, is not a book to be read from cover to cover. Rather, it is an anthology to be consulted and contemplated, educating people about life and decision-making, along with change's central role. The *Yi Jing* is an "encyclopedia of proverb, imagery and symbolism.... It is *the* Chinese book, daunting though that may seem", John Minford asserted in his 2014 study *I Ching*.

Societies and people need to renew themselves constantly, as *weixin* advocates. Renewal must be continuous, creating new life. Adaptation, extent, speed or goals may vary but there should be no limits. Nothing is out of the question. Consumers, entrepreneurs and technocrats aim for boundless achievements, not driven just by profit, but also by pride and purpose.

The *Yi Jing* originated in divining the future. As this was elaborated and analysed further, it came to be valued more for its wisdom than for its predictive powers. Through *yin* and *yang*, people learned that what waxed will wane and vice versa, teaching them to prepare for and understand changing times. *Yin* and *yang* are interconnected, complementary polarities that reinforce each other. Ideally they should be in balance. When they are badly out of kilter they will reverse and crisis may occur. Things should be seen in this light and from all sides to achieve harmonious balance, taking a holistic 360-degree view. From these basic principles comes acceptance of the *Yi Jing* as a book of wisdom.

A central point of the *Book of Change* is that the future can be anticipated, in broad terms, removing some of life's uncertainties. "It is possible to see into the potential changes before they occur, to grasp the subtle configurations of *yin* and *yang* and thus attune oneself to the energy in the world around us," Minford wrote in his introduction to the *The Art of War*. "Confucius said, 'To know the pivots is divine.... The pivots are the first, imperceptible beginnings of movement, the first trace of good or bad fortune that shows itself. The superior man perceives the pivot and immediately acts.'"

The original ideas are close to the world view of early Daoism, almost five centuries BC, but its classical expression came in the Neo-Confucian synthesis of the 11th-century Song Dynasty. As Minford said in his introduction to the *I Ching*, the Song scholar Cheng Yi wrote,

> The *Book of Change* is transformation. It is the transformation necessary ... to be in tune with the movement of time, if we are to follow the flow of the Dao.... The book is grand in its scope: it is all-encompassing. It is attuned to the very principle of human nature and life-destiny; it penetrates the underlying causes of both the occult and the evident ... the principles governing fortune and calamity, the process of waxing and waning, the Dao of progress and retreat, of survival and extinction.

The *Yi Jing* considers what determines "fortune and calamity", particularly danger, caution, timing and cycles. It examines change's nature, mechanics and dynamics so people can adapt to them calmly and thoughtfully. Much is common sense, which often is not so common. Handling danger is a top priority. "Crossing a great stream", as the *Yi Jing* termed it, goes outside one's "comfort zone", exposing people to danger. In planning be cautious, patient and restrained; in unexpected difficulty be very careful, allow nature to take its course. When hemmed in, be steady and persevere, remain optimistic. Recklessness will only worsen matters. Better to wait for conditions to change favourably. Do not be over-optimistic however: danger still lurks.

Danger should be faced: it can be overcome with perseverance and good faith. It lies not just in forests, wide open spaces, weather and enemies but within oneself from pride, self-importance, boasting and guile. There are many dangers in life to handle and overcome. Caution is the key, whether it is danger or complacency to avoid.

Take good care.
Imagine yourself,
On the brink of a great abyss,
Imagine yourself,
Treading on thin ice.

Everything depends on timing. Things should be done in a timely fashion: this is repeatedly mentioned. Bide one's time, wait calmly for the right moment to act; knowing when to stop is equally important. A period of instability is a transition. Before acting, establish carefully what is true or false. When "small people" prevail, it is better to retreat. When opposition arises, address minor rather than major issues. In adversity, find the right combination of action and inaction.

Actions have their own dynamics and mechanisms. Less action can contain anger and restrain desire, restore equilibrium, overcome obstacles or enable change. Even its opposite, increased action, can in bad times speed up the arrival of beneficial change. Ideally, any rise should be steady and not too rapid. The same goes for economic or corporate growth. Progress should be gentle and slow, so it can be absorbed and put down strong roots. Decisions should be made carefully in the light of reality. Movement should be gradual, in stages. Change should not be hasty, otherwise it may be unsustainable.

Sequencing is important. When objectives can only be met through a series of measures or actions, the right order has to be followed, progress gradual. Anything else will disrupt, potentially leading to failure. The idealized image of progress is the flight of geese crossing the sky in perfect order before descending smoothly. This was the idea that Japan, another country that studied the *Yi Jing*, used from the 1950s to the 1970s for Asian economic development, with Japan as the leading goose and economy, followed by all others from South Korea to Southeast Asia.

Cycles are a basic concept of the *Yi Jing*. Things can change suddenly, especially when they have been going on for a long time. The *Yi Jing* warns that "wealth and poverty, finery and rags, can change places with alarming unpredictability and rapidity". These cycles can be daily, monthly, seasonal or annual, even lasting a lifetime.

The *Yi Jing* can be the basis of business strategy or, as Professor Mun Chin Kok of Hong Kong University calls it, "Chinese leadership wisdom". Mun defined six stages of a firm's development whilst advising how to adapt its precepts to change. He draws 10 ideas very relevant to business from the *Yi Jing*. They are immediately recognizable to those in business but only reached widespread academic notice through Minford's *I Ching*.

10 Ideas for Business

Starting-Up:	Take a humble, gradual approach. Consider all risk factors.
Advice:	Seek and take advice from capable people.
Goals:	Avoid excess, be modest. Do not soar too high or go too far. Know when to stop.
Delusion:	Nothing lasts forever. Expansion has its limits, as does contraction. Beware of grandeur and hubris.
Aggression:	Do not be overconfident, especially against a strong market leader who may well strike back.
People:	Give capable people their heads, freedom to do their best.
Values:	Share in order to build mutual trust.
Danger:	Prepare for danger by making a firm more adaptable.
Balance:	Find a middle way between restraint and freedom; balance corporate and social responsibility.
Leadership:	Be calm, avoid being rash or impulsive. Outwardly be "flexible and adaptable like water, internally strong and dynamic like thunder". Finally, see point one.

In addition, leaders should remember:

— Adopt a low profile, restrain emotions and conserve energy for a better time.
— Be tolerant and open-minded.
— Let go, allow people to follow their own ideas. Forcing them to follow is futile.
— Accept others' opinions. Lower one's self; be flexible.
— Actions should speak much louder than words.
— Do not compete with others. There is no need to show off power or ability.
— Be concerned with others' problems, not with one's desires.
— Behaviour should be balanced, neither extravagant nor restricted.
— Recognize one's limits.
— Know the difference between courage and folly: do not step on the tiger's tail.

Three recurring *Yi Jing* themes draw on Confucianism and Daoism — restraint, excess and endurance. Restraint should be exercised, holding strength in check. Natural forces should be harnessed and inner strength nurtured. Physical might must be used only after careful deliberation. Danger lurks in a lack of restraint.

Excess, be it flaunting strength or wealth, is inappropriate and could be costly. As Minford describes it, "Progress comes, not fiercely, but like a gentle breeze. It will be harmonious, slow, accomplished by moderation. By being too arrogant and impulsive, [it] alienates others and isolates self.... Any excess will be harmful."

Endurance is one answer to adversity. C.P. Fitzgerald in 1935 highlighted it as an important Chinese characteristic. Events before and since have only confirmed that. Zhang Libang, a doctor whose life spans that of Communist China including the Cultural Revolution, emphasizes endurance as the most important Chinese characteristic. Indeed the return of official approval for Confucianism over recent decades, outlasting Mao's denunciation, proved the endurance of China's longest-lasting philosophy itself.

China's Change in Practice

When I mentioned the book's original working title of *Managing China's Change* to a senior official whom I have known well for over two decades, she stopped for a few seconds, thought intensely, and then, with real Mandarin understatement and agreement, pronounced it a good title: as if she suddenly saw in those three words a summary of an official's life's work in a way she had never considered.

Change is generally welcome in China, given in 2016 the World Bank ranked it only 66th in GDP per capita terms; hundreds of millions live on low incomes, some 40 million below the official poverty line. A positive attitude to change makes sense, explaining China's economic endurance, resilience and record-breaking growth. This differs greatly from developed Western economies where change is much slower and often feared, with proportionally far more losers than in China, without the benefits of a fast-growing economy to offset the uncertainty, trials and tribulations of change.

China has speed and scale. It is used to making major, often tough, decisions, simply because there are so many more to make if China is to end its near 200-year relative decline: doing nothing is not an option, given its desire for high-income status. China's officials, and now businessmen, are used to managing large scale, fast pace and rapid mobilization of considerable resources to create change in a country whose defining symbol is the Great Wall. Whole streets can disappear in a matter of days to make way for redevelopment to relieve intense overcrowding and often poverty by providing much more living space, indoor sanitation and all the modern conveniences most in the West take for granted. Less than 40 years ago this was not the case in China. Then China faced urban decay, economic stagnation, much uncertainty and extensive poverty.

Whenever asked about China's change, I reach for a host of mental images: flashbacks acquired in travel and meetings around China from 1978 onwards, especially since moving to Shanghai in 2002. The extent, pace and profundity of change plus the sheer energy, resilience and endurance of some people, places and companies is so striking.

The snapshots are much more about individuals than just about China or a system. Their ability to change, determination and often courage, frequently against the odds, is what has carried China forward. They range from migrant workers to those who have helped shape government policy, from reformed state-owned companies becoming global players to privately-owned firms that did not exist when Deng made his 1992 Southern Tour. Chinese traditional thinking has what Chinese–American psychologist Angela Lee Duckworth believes is an essential ingredient of success: grit. This requires long-term thinking and vision. Setting a long-term goal and sticking to it is key to success: perseverance. Life is a marathon, not a sprint. Some have strong resilience to hardship, adversity and setbacks, others optimism. China has not been short of either in recent decades.

Companies

An immaculately-suited Hong Kong financial adviser looked down at the plunging stock price chart on his smartphone as we walked around a Shenzhen factory in 2008. The only thing investors needed to know about the firm we were visiting, he pronounced, was when it would go bust. It didn't.

Instead it became China's largest domestic automaker, selling over half a million vehicles by 2013, and the world's largest electric light-duty plug-in vehicle maker by 2015. In 2016, signalling how far its technology had developed, South Korea's Samsung bought a stake in it so as to be among the leaders in the race to build the Next Big Thing in autos: electrical and self-driving cars. One decade ago it may well have been a Korean company at the forefront of such path-breaking technology.

Only two days after the factory visit the same adviser sent a fax reporting that Warren Buffet's Berkshire Hathaway, the most admired US investor, had just bought over 10% of the Shenzhen company's stock, which it still holds nine years later. Since then BYD has defied naysayers and rewarded Buffet's long-term judgment. BYD stands for Build Your Dreams. Founded in 1995, its history summarizes the hopes of China's entrepreneurs and consumers, long before Xi Jinping in 2013 outlined his China Dream. BYD is an apt metaphor for China's whole economy. Starting with very few immediate advantages and experiencing many headaches along the way, it has reached a critical mass that now gives BYD global scale, presence and recognition.

Former government chemist and researcher Wang Chuanfu started BYD to make batteries, becoming the world's second largest maker. Only in 2003 did it even begin making cars, with an eye to developing electric vehicles in the potentially large China market, then still one to two decades away. BYD devised its own business model, breaking down job functions to reduce unnecessary dependence on expensive capital equipment by using cheaper manual labour where possible. I later saw seven people working on one car, three of them with both feet off the ground: one crouched in the front, another kneeling in the back and a third on the roof. Considering China's looming labour shortage and rising wages, I was not impressed, but no one explained the innovative business model and capital savings. Anyway, there were other approaches in China's auto industry, illustrating its diversity, far from the image of a copycat economy.

When I first visited the original Geely plant in 2004, it was already using robots. Not just any robots but ABB robots: world quality, not cheap imitations. Having acquired the Volvo Car Group from Ford in 2010, it is now exporting S90 Made-in-China Volvos to the US, the world's most demanding market. Geely is scheduled to manufacture in England the new generation of iconic London Taxis, which it now owns, with world-leading emission standards. Grabbing world headlines, Volvo announced it will become in 2019 the first to produce only hybrid or electric vehicles; no longer will Volvo cars be solely powered by the internal combustion engine: a turning-point in industrial history, made by its Chinese owners with their long-term vision.

Geely has invested $9 billion in Volvo product and engine development, as well as new platforms. These will not only make Geely by far the most advanced Chinese automaker, but it also claims the production platforms will put it ahead of other Asian makers. Only VW, Audi, BMW and Daimler will have such sophisticated platforms. The first new Volvo models developed under Geely ownership all received good reviews. No longer loss-making, Volvo's profit margins are close to those of its main German competitors.

Neither BYD's nor Geely's achievements were imaginable to me in 2002 when I arrived to live in China, especially the ability to reach demanding US engineering standards. To founding Geely's Chairman Li Shufu, with the unique perspective on life the Cultural Revolution imprinted on his generation, it may have been less of a surprise. Ambition was not lacking in his generation when Li founded Geely in 1986 to make refrigerator compressors. The exact path forward, though, was unclear, very much a case of "crossing the river by feeling the stones".

Bao Steel I first met at a 2003 private sector workshop Research-Works organized in Shanghai. Bao, Shanghai's leading state-owned enterprise (SOE), provided a deliberate contrast to all the private sector companies we had invited. This was no high tech young company but a representative of the old order. Yet after two-and-a-half days of meetings with mainly young, private companies, it was state-owned "behemoth" Bao that proved to be the star, helped by the fact that in a room bristling with the latest phones, it was the Bao executive who first announced that US-led forces had just begun their shock and awe bombing of Baghdad. Information about the invasion of Iraq came to us in Shanghai courtesy of a SOE. Clearly it was much more familiar with the world and comfortable with the latest technology than many imagined.

Such modernity was not expected from a state-owned metal basher. Indeed less than 15 years before, my colleague Chuck Bradford, the top-rated US steel analyst, told me he had just visited the best and the worst steel companies in Asia. South Korea's Pohang Iron and Steel (POSCO), with its state-of-the-art facilities was the best: everything was meticulous with hardly any workers in sight at its super efficient, highly automated plant. The worst was Bao Steel, full of excess labour, poorly organized, littered with waste and about to triple its capacity: a typical SOE. What a difference three decades has made. Now the global industry talks of Bao as the world's second or third best steel maker: POSCO has become number one.

Often it is not the senior executives that make the impression. At Vanke, it was line managers in 2003 that impressed, talking with great understanding about how property markets work. Other developers paid little heed to markets. Most thought *guanxi*, official connections, were the key to success. Vanke was different, as befits a company whose founder Wang Shi twice scaled Mount Everest. It learned the hard way in the 1990s Hainan property crash. With annual sales over $52 billion in 2016, it is now the world's second largest residential property developer.

At Sany, which has become China's leading construction equipment maker, it was the "buzz" that my colleague Anna Kieryk noticed when visiting the inland province of Hunan. This was in great contrast to the quiet, sleepy feeling of its neighbouring state-owned competitor with its "green tea culture" of a then typical state entity with its slower pace, where "workers" enjoyed reading newspapers, chatting with colleagues and sipping green tea out of glass jars, all in company time. Sany, she judged, felt like Silicon Valley. This had not escaped the notice of the world's number two construction equipment maker Komatsu that has updated its Sany data monthly for over a decade.

Hunan also boasted other innovators: Yuan Longping, the father of China's famine-averting hybrid rice, as well as the innovative state broadcaster Hunan TV that gave China its own version of Pop Idol in 2004, with a peak audience of 400 million. There was starting to be more to China than its rapidly richer coast. An industry for which China used to have no special global reputation was rail. Yet, even before the development of high-speed rail in China, Zhuzhou CSR in Hunan clearly had something. Before being corporatized it was the research division of one of China's two state locomotive makers. At our first meeting, its transition from an academic and bureaucratic mindset to a commercial one was evident. Applied research and management, not mere output numbers, were the focus of conversation: a great transformation for an SOE.

Huawei and ZTE stood out in the new city of Shenzhen in 2002, where less than 25 years earlier, bent figures could be seen harnessed to the plough as human cattle, literally. I was drawn to visit Huawei by a CISCO consultant calling Huawei the Chinese CISCO. Though China had yet to make a name for itself in telecommunications, clearly there was both talent and ambition in the early 2000s. Barely a decade later, Huawei overtook Ericsson in 2014 to become the world's largest telecommunications equipment maker. By 2016, Huawei and ZTE registered more patents in North America, Europe and Japan than any other firm. All this testifies to China's growing R&D capabilities and future presence in new cutting-edge technologies.

Places

Sometimes the place itself is the phenomenon. Chongqing, Zhejiang province and its capital Hangzhou are examples. Often I am asked to take investors somewhere with the "wow" factor. I used to demur, saying "wow" lies in the eye of the beholder, unsure exactly what would instantly make people I did not know say "wow". To me, China's change is more long-term and subtle — an ancient land, often best seen between mist and mountains, like in some 1,000-year-old Song Dynasty painting.

Then, in 2010, I took a group of investors to the former war-time capital Chongqing, growing at a pace that even staggered the rest of China. As the group got down from the bus after an unusually swift 30-minute journey to the hotel — new roads and tunnels had just opened — a normally staid fund manager exclaimed involuntarily, "Wow!" "Wow" indeed. I had visited Chongqing many times since the 1990s, before the Yangzi's Three Gorges were flooded to create the dam to generate 7% of China's electricity, and had lost the sense of awe China can have on a new pair of eyes. My interest had moved on to the software. What were people saying, doing and thinking? What was different from my last visit?

On the return bus journey to the airport, just 15 minutes after leaving the hotel, a South African economist stood up to announce we had just passed more cranes in that time than operated in all of South Africa. The count continued as Chongqing's crane-dotted skyline changed little for another 40 minutes. This was just one city in China, though a quite extraordinary one even by China's standards. Wow!

Close to Shanghai lies China's private sector dynamo and third largest exporter, Zhejiang province. Research-Works spent much time tracking Zhejiang after the 2008 global financial crisis as China was the world's largest exporter, making it, in many eyes, the most vulnerable economy to collapse. Things turned out quite differently from consensus expectations. China pre-empted a contagious crisis with its bank-led stimulus to spark a recovery. Companies and households in Zhejiang's small and not-so-small towns benefitted from the 2009 and 2010 flood of money. This then seeped down into the province's informal capital market from which non-bankable private companies can borrow at much higher interest rates.

There was nothing at all wrong with the informal market. For long it played a very useful role. However, it was not designed for large volumes, especially those directed by outsiders who neither knew nor cared about its centuries-old delicate mechanisms, information networks or workings. They had no interest in sustainable long-term lending, only in short-term gain. A sudden surge of misdirected liquidity inevitably came to an abrupt and painful end after the flood reversed sharply when monetary policy tightened. The timing for Wenzhou could not have been worse, for tightening occurred just as repayment of expensively high-cost debt came due. There was carnage. Suicides cast a dark shadow over the business community. Company after company faced bankruptcy, unable to repay loans, many of them priced at 20% annual interest or more. Many others secretly thanked their lucky stars, thinking that there but for the grace of God....

Courage had been the one quality that many entrepreneurs possessed in the first two decades of Zhejiang's boom: often just the courage to take on more risk than their rivals, as Professor He Sijiang of Zhejiang University puts it. This all unraveled after 2008 when business fundamentals reasserted themselves and entrepreneurs had to manage their way through unnerving, opaque volatility. Some failed, but what we found from 2011 onwards was surprising, far more dramatic than even the stories of bankruptcy told.

Companies were surviving, contrary to the incessantly negative consensus narrative. Firms were adapting, using their knowledge of traditional philosophy about the inevitability of cycles, the need for flexibility and vision plus short-term strategies. Indeed some emerged stronger than ever, having learned many painful lessons. In the previous decade, we had unearthed and watched new leaders emerge in large sectors from autos to steel, property to rail, now we saw the next generation of leaders emerge in numerous sub-sectors. They were a lot more prosaic and smaller — pumps, wheel hubs, garden furniture, buttons, zippers, even a port, though one of the world's largest, founded in 738 during the Tang Dynasty — but all revealed what was really going on in the province dominated by private small and medium enterprises (SMEs) that were becoming China's new backbone.

When we asked about promising Zhejiang companies, the name that kept cropping up was the provincial capital's Alibaba. This was four years before its 2014 record $21.8 billion New York stock market fundraising. People talked with envy and admiration about the e-commerce giant's stunning growth and success. They also highlighted the low bad loan records and traditional credit assessment methods of Zhejiang's two leading private banks, Taizhou and Tailong. These beat their state counterparts hands down in terms of low loan defaults and better service. Some mentioned Alibaba's initial stumbles in online financing but then watched its second attempt that could help recast entire parts of China's financial services. In Beijing we met champions of change promoting Alibaba and other IT-savvy non-financial companies to shake up the large state banks. This, though, was no David and Goliath struggle. Alibaba's new campus could be in Silicon Valley or Hsinchu Science Park, Taiwan rather than in Hangzhou, which had felt so soulless on my first visit in 1984. By 2017, Hangzhou has its own very 21st-century investment ecoculture. This Chinese David has the technology, the necessary work culture and, increasingly, the capital to succeed, all built with plenty of grit, on its way to becoming a global Goliath.

Disruptive technologies capture reformers' imaginations in Beijing, be they home grown like Alibaba or foreign like carmaker Tesla. These they hope could spur efficiency in China, help reshape the economy and reach new markets. China could leapfrog old technologies and soon line up with world leaders. There may be an element of hubris in all this but China does have a couple of aces up its sleeve. Scale is the most obvious. That can make up for quite a lot. China is now the world's largest market in more and more products. Other industries of tomorrow are not far behind.

R&D is the second advantage: see Chapter 12. The government's two decade-long encouragement of R&D is paying off. Shenzhen's Tencent combined the two to create a domestic market of a growing one billion users for its WeChat communication service, helping revolutionize mobile e-commerce in the process. This it could leverage overseas. Alibaba could too and was doing similar things in the new economy. As well as buying into China's leading white goods retailer Suning and Shanghai's largest department store, it also developed a foothold in the US, enabling foreign consumers to access China's manufacturers and traders. Now Alibaba promises Donald Trump it will create American jobs. Change just never seems to stop.

Zhejiang's capital Hangzhou is becoming one of the next major global investment destinations, some 700 years after it amazed Marco Polo. Historian Michael Wood called Song Dynasty Hangzhou the most civilized place on earth four centuries before the European Renaissance. As host of the 2016 G20 leaders' meeting, it showcased its increasingly dynamic investment ecoculture, epitomized by Alibaba. The first generation of modern China's entrepreneurs is now providing the capital, management skills and guidance for the next. Along with Shenzhen and Beijing, Hangzhou is creating China's own smaller Silicon Valleys and firms. None are global household names yet, though some are gaining increasing recognition, just as the Japanese did in the 1970s and South Koreans in the 2000s.

People

Behind all these places and companies are the hundreds of millions of ordinary people who have made change and growth possible. Knowing their individual stories is to understand China's change.

"80% of the people who were in my department when I joined just over two years ago have left," Wu reflected as he described what change means in practical terms. "They left, either because they were not adaptable enough (many are like that) or the nature of the job changed and they now have the wrong skills. They are no longer needed," this mid-thirties Shanghai executive at a high profile private company explained dispassionately.

"Each year, I can see the change. In fact every year is so different from the last. From the people who work here to the job itself. The KPIs (key performance indicators) and what my bosses want change, so does our work's focus. To keep advancing, the company's strategy changes. That alters our business models and even the corporate culture. I can feel it every day," Wu says, realizing that it is not just every year that things change, it is felt literally every day. "Not just the work I do has changed fundamentally a couple of times in the last two years but even where I work. The geography has changed too. As the easy opportunities in China are exhausted, so we have to look abroad. I go to places and countries I would never have imagined visiting, let alone going there for a living — Brazil, Europe, Russia and the Middle East," he explains, rolling off the list of places like some corporate road warrior recalling his relentless travel schedule.

Reaching for his smart phone Wu says, "I showed this photo of a small town in Europe to a friend who visited there seven years ago. He said it hadn't changed one bit. It was exactly the same as in my photo." After a pause for reflection, Wu captures his thoughts in a statement, framed as a question, "Europe doesn't change, does it?" He was probably thinking that hardly anywhere in China, at least in the urban China he inhabits, would *not* have changed. Whole streets could have disappeared in seven years, even entire neighbourhoods, as new buildings sprouted skywards and complete areas transformed: peoples' lives too.

As I get up to leave, Wu adds another statement dressed up as a question. "The theme of our last annual dinner was Evolution. Our company is now over 20 years old, founded in the early '90s just as politics were receding and the economy was being freed up for entrepreneurs. So we were celebrating that. I suppose that evolution is change isn't it?" Wu concluded. Charles Darwin certainly thought so. After a moment's pause Wu added, "In fact, everything *is* about change." He could have said "in China now" but that was a given. So was the assumption that it is not like this everywhere in the world nor was it when he was growing up in 1980s China.

"Chinese people are adaptable to change, they have to be, but they have become quite good at it," Wu believes. "Not everyone welcomes change. Taxi drivers are being hurt by new rivals like Didi Chuxing. Those quick on their feet can join these new companies to earn more. Those left behind in the old traditional taxis see their takings fall by 20–30%. The new companies may hit reality soon but the drivers that moved there are adaptable. They will anticipate further change and have their eyes wide open," like the rest of us, he could have added.

Some never even get to be licensed taxi drivers. Wang plied his trade as a "pirate" taxi driver for over a decade until he fell foul of change. He was caught, as many are, when China moved along in its transition. It could be called the Transition Trap. Rules and new regulations, long ignored, start to be enforced more often and people find themselves on the wrong side of the law: companies and global multinationals included.

Wang came from a very poor part of Anhui to work in a major city where taxi licenses usually went to people with *hukou*, full residence rights belonging normally to people born in the city. After state firms laid off many in the 1990s reforms, the local government gave them priority, certainly over out-of-province migrants. So Wang never received a proper taxi license and when it came for another crackdown on illegal taxi drivers, he was stopped, his car impounded. Wang knew this could happen and was prepared. He took up a job offer from a rich industrialist whose main need was to have his daughter ferried to school and back: very undemanding work at double Wang's average income. Money was guaranteed and without the long hours let alone the uncertainty of living outside the law.

How long Wang will chauffeur this young princess and her family is unclear. With savings from his long years of migrant city work, he has already built a modern home in his old Anhui "village", which in reality is a sizable town. Moving back home is in his mind. His son, the first from the village to do so, is in university with a scholarship.

Wang's family has lived change for over three decades with no complaint: it was the political turmoil and lack of useful change before that was the problem. Wang's father was the first from his village to *xia hai*, to jump into the sea, meaning to go into private business. This was in the 1980s when he gave up his state electricity company job to start the village's first shop selling basic electrical machinery. These included everything from table fans for homes that baked in central China's legendary hot summers to rice processing equipment for the farmers who were beginning to get rich and could profitably use some machinery. Wang's father understood the full force of what change could bring. While working for the government, he helped bring electricity to the village.

However, in his mind he knew it was not just he and his colleagues who had brought electricity to his very poor village. Therefore his long-held wish was to visit Beijing to pay his respects to the man he credited with bringing the electricity. So a few years ago Wang took his elderly father to Beijing to pay respects to Mao Zedong in his mausoleum at one end of Tiananmen Square and his giant portrait at the other end above the entrance to the Forbidden City, the home of Ming and Qing emperors. His father may have been the first post-1949 entrepreneur in the village but he was no ideologue. He had a clear view of what had driven the change and who he thought had to be thanked. His own role in it had been rewarded by the opportunities it had given him and his family in the private sector to improve their lives. Change on balance had been good, if bumpy and uncertain.

Further west, 500 Goats Aunt heads her local Huimin borrower group in Yanchi, Ningxia. Huimin gets its name from the character for benefit *hui* while *min* means people, hence "to benefit people", and is a unique entity that began in 1996 as an NGO before becoming a microfinance company in 2008, lending mainly to rural women.

Never accept a drinking challenge from a woman who owns 500 goats. That was the most surprising finding from microfinance research I did in two of rural China's poorest counties. Years of after-rugby training had not prepared me for such a test. The challenge was in white liquid, to be polite, white lightning to be more accurate, probably over 60% proof. Dinner's neat rice wine was at least warming and the crowded all-female borrower group was noisy, as copious quantities of local meat and vegetables were demolished. This was late September in Ningxia; the nights were already shorter and decidedly nippy.

My challenger exuded the self-confidence and determination of the successful. Bundled up against the cold in a blue down jacket, she circulated round the tables like the consummate hostess, only with much more vigour and physicality. This was her way of welcoming me and getting the attention of everyone in the room at the same time. She succeeded. The scene could have been out of a Thomas Hardy novel set in mid-19th-century England: except for the line dancing afterwards, which was the high point of the evening, the modern and imported equivalent of boisterous dancing at the Dorset county fair. There was, though, one very big difference. The lives of the 40 or more women who had come to their regular twice-weekly social evening had seen their lives transformed.

Before Huimin, Yanchi women did not dare borrow money. They did without. Often they fended for themselves as their men migrated to towns or other provinces for work, leaving them to eke out a bare subsistence. On the edge of Ningxia's desert, which runs into the great Gobi Desert, they were among the poorest of China's poor, totally excluded from credit and therefore the modern economy. Now the better off earn Rmb 30,000–50,000 ($4,545–7,575) a year, after all expenses. The average is more like Rmb 20,000–30,000 ($3,030–4,545). Not an enormous amount by global standards but well above what they were earning 10 years before, if they were earning anything at all, and more than most farmers earn in the rest of China today. As one woman put it, "Previously we ate meat twice a year, now we eat it whenever we like."

However, it is not just about food and dance. The Huimin borrower group provides some education, especially in basic finance and business: everything from budgeting to bargaining, as well as animal husbandry. With a nervous, embarrassed laugh, 500 Goats Aunt admitted how she learned to use an ATM machine from the group. When I asked another, younger, woman, the star line-dancer, what she wanted to learn from the borrowing group, she threw her arms in the air and declared triumphantly, "Everything!".

The lives of these 40 or more women, along with about another 5,000 in Yanchi, have been rapidly transformed by a combination of Huimin credit and grass. To be more precise Huimin has taken the Grameen Bank model that Nobel Laureate Muhammad Yunus devised and modified it for China. Realizing what farmers needed most was capital, Long Zhipu, previously an agricultural official, founded Huimin. In 2016 it had 17,000 borrowers. The local Ningxia grass on which animals graze has over 100 varieties spiced up by two naturally occurring herbs, *kudos* and *ganzhou*, which the animals wash down with some fine natural minerals in the water, giving the meat great flavour and quality.

In the poorer part of Ningxia lies Tongxin county with a population of 380,000 living in widely scattered villages. Many of the women in their 40s and 50s are illiterate. Now all their children finish secondary school, while 30% in Ningxia go to university or for technical education. Shrinking villages are not yet a problem in rural Tongxin, but in Yanchi they are. In some cases they have disappeared altogether as China's relentless urbanization rolls on. The founding leader of the local Huimin borrowing group reflects this. Her ambitions are no longer rural. With the help of Huimin loans, she has a vehicle repair shop in town, having already developed some properties for the aged, many of whose children have left the region.

Rural China is relentlessly becoming urban China, just as happened in the West. Women's opportunities and many lives are transformed. The first manufacturing jobs for women came to Guanqiao Se Zhuang village in Nan'an county when Nanfung Textiles moved production there from Hong Kong. Before the 1980s the only cash work locally for women was picking tea at 50 US cents a day, and this was seasonal, not permanent, work. Nanfung paid two dollars a day, all year round. Among Nanfung's workers in Fujian was my niece, Xiulin.

Xiulin was ambitious to break out of the dull rural poverty of her youth. She had a strong tradition on which to draw. The village founders, the Yangs, came from the north, migrating after the Huang Chao rebellion in 874 scattered many leading Tang to the far provinces of southern China. The Yangs claim descent from Han General Yang Zhen, who was famously incorrupt. The Han Dynasty official history records that when he was assured by someone who tried to bribe him that no one would know, Yang Zhen countered that "heaven, earth, you and I will know", for which his family was given the honorary name of Four Knows Yangs.

Prominent among the early Yang generation in the village was a herbalist, Yang Sugong, who earned the title *Taiyi Zhenren* after curing the Tang Empress of breast tumors. He then returned to his new home in the south where the family memorial hall lists his name along with all the other Yang ancestors since arriving in the late 9th century. More immediately relevant to Xiulin was that many of her recent forebears had migrated both within China and outside. Most had gone to Southeast Asia in the 19th and first half of the 20th centuries where Fujianese became the dominant Chinese in Indonesia, Philippines, Singapore and parts of Malaysia. Many succeeded and quite a few became rich, inspiring others to try their luck.

Guanqiao Se Zhuang's neighbouring village is the Ong village whose son gave its name to the main street in Manila's Chinatown, Ongpin Street. Philippine President Corazon Aquino's family was from nearby. Tongan, the neighbouring county to Nanan, was where Kwek Hong Png was born. At the age of 16, Kwek left to seek his fortune in the South Seas where he founded, with his three brothers, Hong Leong, which became Singapore's largest property and hotel group. When the young Kwek arrived in Singapore, Tan Kah Kee from nearby Xiamen was already well on his way to becoming Southeast Asia's richest man in the 1930s. These were the Alibaba Jack Ma's of their day, inspiring many others to try their luck in new ventures: role models.

Xiulin's road to migration began with learning basic textile skills. Her energy, wits and ambition led her to become a factory supervisor, which after years of saving brought her a new Suzuki motorbike. Not a local brand, they didn't last, she had told me emphatically. The extra wait, so as to afford a foreign brand, was well worth the effort, she insisted. As a teenager she was a determined tomboy, wearing blue jeans, somewhat out of place in still conformist, conservative 1990s village life. So she found work in a textile factory in far-away Shanghai that was running out of labour and could pay above Fujian wages, while offering far more attractions to ambitious young women hungry for something outside rural China.

The long hours and much pressure, though, steadily drained Xiulin of her energy. Once-ruddy cheeks turned grey, her face became drawn and she lost weight. Her health suffered from the long hours, stress and bad employers over the years. Finally she returned to the village. Maybe she had hoped to marry someone in Shanghai who could give her a Shanghai *hukou*, the much treasured urban residence status, but that did not happen. Her hopes faded with her health. Whatever it was, Shanghai exhausted and disappointed her.

By the time Xiulin went home, the village was more like a small town. Much more work was available than when she had left a decade earlier. The skills learned in Shanghai stood her in good stead, not just the technical skills, but knowledge of the outside world, the pace of urban life, the tastes and ways of its people. She easily found work as a bookkeeper in a factory, married and had a child. The stress was a lot less; she had more time for herself and family. Original plans had not worked out as the once young bundle of energy had hoped but this was not necessarily for the worse. She was better off than her parents who still worked the land. Xiulin has an office job, air conditioning and a child, whose prospects are much greater than her own when she left school.

Migration has been a constant theme and fact of life in much of China throughout history. Despite the often strict residence laws after 1949, it continued, though at a much slower rate than happened after the reform and opening up of 1978. In the 1950s and 1960s, when technical skills were short, the government posted those with scarce skills all over the country. Often husband and wife were separated by hundreds or even thousands of miles for years, except during the annual Spring Festival holiday when, if they could, they made the long, tiring marathon journey home for the traditional family reunion. One of Xiulin's great uncles, a 100 metre sprinter, had the good fortune to be selected by Fujian to run in Shanghai where he set a record time which, he recalls with pride, was not beaten for seven years. This fame brought work as a leading sports coach in Shanghai, including in the 1970s a two-year contract training athletes in Saudi Arabia, and he did manage to get the much-prized Shanghai *hukou.*

Xiulin's sister, Xiuyun, she who exclaimed "Waahhh" above the Bund in Shanghai, married a young soldier from neighbouring Jiangxi province because he literally had the hunger of someone from a poor rural area that throughout history had known poverty, plagued as it was by both floods and drought. Well-watered coastal Fujian was the attraction to him, whereas to the family that let him marry its eldest daughter, he had the drive and straight-forwardness that was already starting to wane as coastal China became increasingly money-conscious as it lifted itself out of poverty. Furthermore, the parents were sure he would settle down in the village, which he did, whereas local men might seek new pastures further afield as past generations had and found new wives.

The nearest major town, some 45 minutes away, is Quanzhou, which in the seventh century was the world's busiest port after Alexandria. Arab ships and merchants came on the monsoon winds to buy tea, porcelain and silk for the Middle East and beyond. Muslim, Christian and Hindu tombstones stand in its graveyard as a reminder of Quanzhou's prosperous past and global links. Fujianese claim 40,000 Arabs lived there in its heyday. Quanzhou was the main port for the southern Silk Route. Now it is the start of the new maritime Silk Route in the Belt and Road Initiative that aims to revive the old communication links between China, the Middle East and Europe: see Chapter 14. The cycles of trade and movement of people continue. The wheel turns.

Norman Tebbit famously admonished the stay-at-home unemployed of distressed 1980s northern England to "get on their bikes" to find work when the old 19th-century industries like coal mining were collapsing. That was never necessary in China as hundreds of millions of mainly poor, young rural migrants left home in a rite of passage to follow their dreams in the 1990s and 2000s to the factories and boom towns of coastal China. Not all were realized but at the very least the experience taught skills, especially to women who managed to break out of the humdrum life of home, children, family and village. Many accumulated enough capital for a small business or savings to start a family, giving them new status, much more than their mothers, grandmothers and others had in traditional China. Hundreds of millions returned not just with skills but with new aspirations, not only for themselves but especially for their children: their greatest achievement.

Gold Mouth Aunt was usually the first to enter the family courtyard to greet us when we arrived in the village. Understanding the ways of the world and the "pivots of change", she came from an earlier generation of migrants. From her sturdy but quick-moving frame came the warmest of welcomes, topped off by the broadest of smiles revealing her four or five fine gold teeth, which is why I affectionately called her Gold Mouth Aunt, though only in English.

The ready smile of gold teeth radiated her forceful personality and commanding presence. Everyone noticed when she came into the room, often because they heard her strong, fast voice precede her. Bright eyes were always glancing around, logging every change, whilst focused hard on what was said. Rapid greetings and questions were those of someone comfortable with the wider world, someone accustomed to a more frantic pace than existed in a slow-moving village. Gold Mouth Aunt always had her wits about her and a high emotional intelligence to match. Married to the son of my father-in-law's elder uncle, she was a Yang by marriage and so related to everyone else in the village. In Se Zhuang they are all Yangs, several hundred or even thousands of them.

By the late 1980s she had built a large red brick mansion, decorated with green tiles from nearby kilns, which had sprung up since 1978 to feed China's new building boom. Its entrance, like Gold Mouth Aunt herself, was imposing. Complete with granite Roman columns and a balcony above, her home overlooked the village's rapidly shrinking rice fields. This red mansion was the culmination of her life's work, her vision and long-term goal. To build her village mansion she made enough money in Hong Kong by dividing a four-room rented apartment. Gold Mouth Aunt sublet to three other families, keeping the smallest space for herself, to maximize her income. She did all this without being able to read or write, let alone speak a foreign language.

On arrival in Hong Kong in the late 1950s, she shared a room with my mother-in-law Woo Mingfeng, her mother-in-law and daughter, my future wife, who in 1956 had preceded Gold Mouth Aunt out of China. After three decades she had made enough money to return to the village with her objective met. The left-behind wife of a husband who had gone to Zamboanga in the southern Philippines, where he married again and raised another family, she had earned the respect of the whole village and the means to support herself for the rest of her life.

A clear sense of long-term priorities enabled Gold Mouth Aunt to focus on what really mattered: her survival along with the welfare and prosperity of her family. This channeled all her energy into the prime purpose, as migrants the world over so often do. She did not waste a moment or opportunity to advance her goal. If it meant travelling to Zamboanga with no command of English or Tagalog to settle matters with her husband, while terrifying his Filipino second wife in the process, as senior first wives from China often did, so be it. She would find people who could handle the official paperwork and help her get there. If it meant renting out individual rooms to Guangdong tenants in Hong Kong, who could not readily understand her Fujian tongue, again so be it. She could do that. Her wits were focused completely on her prime objectives as she navigated life's challenges and changes. Gold Mouth Aunt had grit, guile and a radiant smile.

Managing Change

Regrouping Regrouping after disaster to solve crises was a valuable early lesson from guerrilla warfare for the Communist Party: it is still done very effectively today. From the verge of a SARS pandemic, in which 770 people died, China has managed since 2003 to avoid a repetition: disasters are the catalyst for change, from food and transport to finance.

Great Wall The Great Wall symbolizes key elements in Chinese philosophy — long-term thinking, vision, managing large scale, mobilizing substantial resources and endurance.

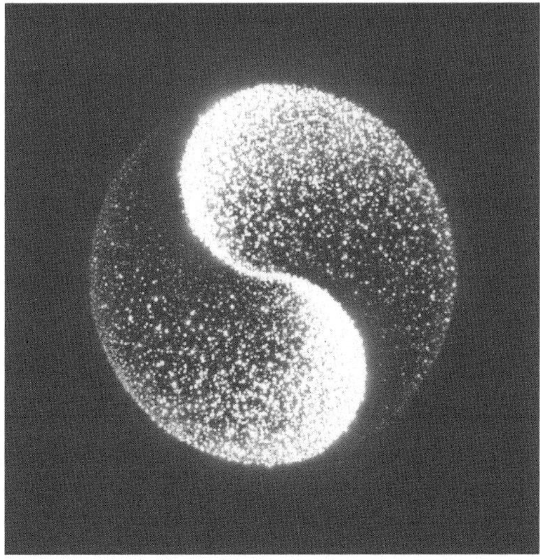

Yin and Yang Chinese philosophy may appear baffling to some Westerners but Niels Bohr, founder of quantum physics, illustrated the cover of his ground-breaking paper with the Yin and Yang symbol.

Ideas Common to China and the West

Evolution "*It is not the strongest of the species that survive or the most intelligent, but the one most responsive to change.*" Charles Darwin

Importance of Change "*If you always do what you always did, you will always get what you always got.*" Albert Einstein

Vision "*China ... is the world's largest technocracy ... ruled by scientists and engineers who believe in the power of new technologies to deliver social and economic progress ... in the most ambitious programme of research investment since John F. Kennedy embarked on the moon race.*" James Wilson, director of the Royal Society 2007

Total Transformation

Shanghai Skyline 1980s Pudong on the eastern bank of Shanghai's Huangpu River was sparsely populated and under-developed in the 1980s.

Shanghai Modern Skyline Within 30 years Shanghai has been transformed. Over five million people live in Pudong with its 21st century skyline and the world's busiest port, where once there were only swamps and small farms. Shanghai is again a global metropolitan city and commercial centre, now with 24 million people and a hinterland of 400 million.

Chapter 5

Managing Change — China's X-Factor

China has always done something when necessary in the past. Why would you think it will not do so again?

Michael Enright, Hong Kong University, 2012

Almost four decades after economic reform began, why, if China understands the importance and dynamics of change, do so many problems remain unresolved? The answer is simple. Almost everything had to change. Not just old problems, but new ones arising out of rapid growth and unfinished reform.

It all takes time. There is no precise economic blueprint to copy. China has to find its own way, "crossing the river by feeling the stones". It had a sense of the destination (modernization) but not the precise path. Often, much was unknown about the journey. Setbacks were handled along the way, priorities established and action sequenced. All this can take a very long time.

Background

Hong Kong University and former Harvard Professor Michael Enright immediately interrupts anyone who states that disaster will strike unless China does something about a particular problem. He interjects, "Well, China always has done something when necessary in the past. Why would you think it will not do so again?" *That* is the right question.

China is not unaware of its problems or the need for change. Officials are often more acutely aware than their critics. Wang Qishan heads the anti-corruption campaign. Like his mentor, Premier Zhu Rongji, Wang is known for his frank talk and ready admission of problems, before buckling down to solve them. When foreign bankers praised China's banks for getting through the 2008 financial crisis, Wang replied that if they had seen inside Chinese banks, they would know how much more needed to change. When he called a meeting with academics and others outside government in 2013 to discuss approaches to combat corruption, he told them to criticize fully, saying China's leaders had all read the very unflattering comments about themselves on *Weibo* (which now has more active accounts than Twitter) so nothing could upset them.

This is not Chinese exceptionalism. The difference in China is that people are highly conscious of what needs to be done to overcome all the mounting challenges and problems since the 19th century. Almost everything has to change or the economy would collapse. Consider the list: feed adequately the entire population, wipe out illiteracy, ensure everyone has a job, end acute overcrowding, provide better education and health care, and do it in a country of 1.4 billion people. Addressing these problems creates new ones: pollution, congestion and industrial accidents, among them.

China's overlooked X-factor, or more precisely, that of modern Confucian societies, is the ability to work with, organize and respond to change. Government and individuals have to be able to anticipate, handle and sustain it. As Daoists believe, fighting change by going against the flow is futile. Often, change happens when people least expect it, as the 2008 global financial crisis and Britain's Brexit proved, as Chinese philosophy had warned for millennia.

What the Confucian states of East Asia have in common is a culture derived largely from Chinese traditional thinking, much based on China's history. The concept of a Confucian state is an oversimplification, but it gives the essence of common ideas. These begin with the state being involved in the nation's welfare, including economic welfare. People cannot be well off if the state does not prosper in the long-term: neither is it right. This is a fundamental Chinese belief. In the West, for some, it is alright that a few people are very well off even if the country is faring poorly.

Such traditional thinking has not meant a state-dominated economy in China. Only after 1949 did state ownership become a primary idea. Confucians assumed private ownership and advised bearable taxation, only about one-ninth or one-tenth of income. They had learned, often from direct experience, about predatory rulers who taxed far too heavily so as to fund their repeated wars. That said, and the fact that the era of Northeast Asian development states passed more than three decades ago, the role of the state is far from dead: in the West too. The US government bailed out the financial and auto industries in 2008, while in the UK, the free market party of Margaret Thatcher talks about the need for long-term planning while Theresa May has a Department of Business, Energy and Industrial Strategy. These ideas would not have shocked centrist politicians like John. F. Kennedy and Edward Heath half a century ago but went out of fashion in the Reagan–Thatcher era.

Managing Change: Identify Top Priorities, Focus on Systems Not Ideology

Doing everything at once would be doomed to failure. China knows better than to do Big Bangs. Given its scale, China addresses only the top priorities first, usually over the very long term. In less critical but still important areas, China generally waits for crises to occur before handling each individually. This shortens considerably the otherwise limitless list of problems, making key priorities more manageable. Otherwise only gridlock would ensue. Government could not cope; it would be overwhelmed.

When problems appear individually, each requiring a great deal of focus from Beijing and plenty of provincial follow-through, they can be handled much more effectively. This is how progress occurs in many countries. It is how US airport security improved greatly after September 11, 2001. Similarly, the US Environmental Protection Agency was founded in 1970 after the Cuyahoga River in Cleveland caught fire in 1969, and not for the first time. That had happened 101 years before. I saw the Han River in Seoul, South Korea on fire in 1978. Disaster and death are seemingly development's inevitable, if regrettable, rite of passage. Preventing repetition, at least on the same scale, is the real progress.

Much of China's change is about systems, not ideology. As New York Mayor Fiorello La Guardia said in the 1930s, "there is no Democratic or Republican way of cleaning the streets," there are only good systems and bad systems. After the turbulent 1960s and 1970s, China knows this is universally true.

Air safety in China leapt to the top of priorities in the early 2000s when its planes, some of them old Soviet aircraft, seemed to be regularly crashing or falling out of the skies. Air safety was a new problem, or at least the scale was. More people were flying, and safety was unacceptably poor. The solution was to go around the world to do some *yanjiu*, research and field work, as Chinese officials have done for thousands of years, first to understand the root causes and then how to address them. New aircraft were not the only solution. Air traffic control specialists came from the US to advise on overhauling Chinese systems with the latest equipment and thinking. Since introducing a new air traffic management system in 2004, air safety has been good.

SARS (Severe Acute Respiratory Syndrome) in 2003 took China to the very brink of a pandemic. Over 8,000 cases were reported and 774 people died. The world largely did not want to know China: hardly desirable for a leading exporter. The country closed down for almost three months. City streets were deserted at night for fear of contracting the unknown virus that could mutate rapidly and for which there was no known antidote.

When it was all over, China then looked in-depth at SARS to learn lessons and avoid a repeat by understanding much more about communicable diseases and epidemics. China still has overcrowded and unsanitary conditions, especially in areas like sub-tropical Guangdong where SARS originated and people live in close contact with fowl and animals: a breeding ground for viruses to mutate rapidly. However, a start was made. Ever pragmatic, China lobbied for Hong Kong's health chief Margaret Chan to become the World Health Organization's (WHO) Assistant Director of Communicable Diseases, then WHO Director-General responsible for global health overall. The knowledge gained helped mitigate the severity of H1N2 bird flu outbreaks and doubtless prevented others. In 2015, China began working on Ebola with the US, having created its own vaccine against the disease. Epidemic control and prevention has advanced.

Food safety instantly shot up the list of priorities when China's melamine milk scandal broke in 2008: six infants died, 54,000 needed hospital treatment and some 300,000 babies and their anxious families were affected. Once all the facts were established, one of the next steps was to invite US government agencies to come to teach Chinese customs officials about US food import rules, standards and inspection. The real purpose, though, was to learn as much as possible to bring China's lax food safety systems up to scratch, based on world best practices.

Overnight solutions do not exist but a start was made. Food safety is much more than just about exports. Government legitimacy is on the line, as in every major crisis. Public criticism has become increasingly widespread and vocal over the past decade. Indeed it seems as if Beijing tolerates some public demonstrations, especially over the environment and safety, in order to understand what is happening and to force solutions. This provides feedback, enabling central government to keep tabs on local officials while allowing people affected by bad decisions and, often, corruption to express their anger. The purpose is not simply to fix problems but to reform systems to minimize the chances of them happening again.

This is how the 2015 Tianjin fire was approached when a great chemical fireball incinerated over 160 people. Finding the causes was only the start of the process. Given China's safety environment this was a forlorn hope unless prevention became a top government priority, which it did. By the end of the month, nearly 1,000 local governments had submitted to Beijing plans to upgrade or remove chemical plants throughout China. New buildings, including Shanghai's latest skyscraper icon, were delayed by much more intensive fire safety permit procedures. That was the real start of change.

Waiting for disasters to happen may seem rough and ready, with lives left at risk, but it is the only practical way in China, given that policy implementation gridlock is the alternative. So far it has worked, notwithstanding that crises continue to happen, causing lives to be lost. Such cases of negligence are not confined to China, nor are solutions. In 1966, 116 school children and 28 adults died when a colliery tip of mining debris collapsed, engulfing a primary school in Aberfan, South Wales. The official inquiry blamed the National Coal Board for extreme negligence: parliament passed legislation on mine-tip safety. Out of that came change and progress in the UK, just as worldwide improvement in airport safety came out of 9/11.

Only weeks before the Tianjin fire, a freak hurricane was said to have hit a ferry on the Yangzi River. Over 400 people drowned, many elderly holidaymakers, in China's worst marine disaster for over 70 years. Certainly there was very heavy rain at the time, but was there more to it? Many questions remain unanswered about safety systems, their implementation and monitoring, the companies and personnel involved. People will hope that, like SARS, it is a wake-up call to adopt new systems to prevent such accidents.

As long as the trend improves, public tolerance will not be stretched too far, but the 2008 Wenchuan earthquake and the 2011 Wenzhou high-speed rail crash, which killed 40 passengers, showed there are limits. The rail ministry had long been considered especially corrupt, leading social media to claim corruption contributed to the crash. Earthquakes may be unavoidable natural disasters but much can be done to limit fatalities and destruction. Social media exploded after the Wenchuan earthquake in Sichuan killed over 5,000 school children in what it assumed was substandard school construction due to corrupt avoidance of basic safety standards. Altogether, 90,000 died in the quake. Often, in China, it is not a case of lacking laws, rules and regulations, it is poor enforcement that causes the problems. Presumably after each specific crisis, these are more strictly enforced. Officials know next time there will be no excuses to prevent their dismissal or worse punishment.

China has had floods for millennia. In response, early warning, evacuation and rescue systems have been developed, so, while floods are still frequent, human casualties are far fewer. In the 1931 Yellow River flood, up to four million people drowned. China now lends its rescue and reconstruction experience after natural disasters to other countries, including to nearby Nepal after its two major 2015 earthquakes.

China has become expert in crisis management. Wang Qishan, built a career principally on crisis management and the ability to manage change. Wang gathered provincial crisis experience ranging from the early 1990s mega-bust of the Hainan property market to the first financial crisis involving foreign banks with the 1999 Guangdong International Trust and Investment Corporation (GITIC) default. Then when attempts to cover up the national SARS epidemic failed, Wang was drafted as Beijing's mayor to manage that, a real crisis with potentially national and global repercussions. He was then able to ensure the 2008 Olympics were not a disaster but a success: not so easy, as Salt Lake City and Athens discovered. *En route*, he had been vice governor of the People's Bank of China and headed the China Construction Bank, learning about the true condition of unreformed banks. When Xi Jinping needed someone to head the anti-corruption campaign, he turned to Wang who is not called the Fire Chief for nothing. Wang Qishan's CV is compelling. He is a proven assembler of effective teams who know how and where to find the bodies. Furthermore he has a spotless reputation: clearly the man for an existential crisis like corruption, having learned all this in the heat of crises.

The Role of the State, Policy and Time

The aim of all Chinese governments has been a strong state, quite the opposite of the Founding Fathers in the US. The purpose of reform in China is always to strengthen the central state never to minimize it. Government policy, though, no longer adheres to any strict ideology or preset grand plan. That overly rigid approach went out of the window after the disruptions of the Great Leap Forward, the Cultural Revolution and the failed Soviet central planning model.

"Seeking truth from facts" and "crossing the river by feeling the stones" might not sound very profound or precise, but turn out to be a lot more realistic and practical than many Western approaches created in ivory towers, think tanks or by industry lobbying groups. This pragmatic policy formulation has many elements, pilot schemes and sequencing among them, as described in Chapter 3.

Decision-making has to be methodical. China aids this with its "planning" system and the elevated role of its senior technocrats. It is not about having a Leninist top-down system with the party deciding everything, let alone decision-makers being "red" rather than "expert", as in the 1960s and the 1970s. Institutions like the State Council, the National Development and Reform Commission, the Ministry of Finance and the People's Bank of China, along with the Leading Small Groups of the party, constantly search for diverse inputs to thinking, co-opting talent and developing consensus beforehand so ideas are broadly accepted before implementation. When all these elements are combined, the chances of policy success improve.

All countries constantly need to restructure. Many in the West forget this, blinded by assuming markets and political pluralism do the job automatically. Whether it is the US having to scale back healthcare costs after they doubled as a share of GDP or the EU having to rethink its structure or migration policies, all societies must be aware of the continual need to restructure, otherwise trends become unsustainable or sclerosis sets in, along with economic decline. Markets and democracy alone are insufficient to ensure this happens seamlessly.

Awareness may come more easily in Asia where the *Yi Jing* has taught for thousands of years that the one constant in life, apart from death and taxes, is change. Long-term thinking is needed, some of it in outline going out several decades. Far in advance of implementation, much study, consultation and discussion is done. Then when one journey is completed, traditional Chinese thinking assumes another begins or suggests itself. Neither construction nor reform can be switched on like a light bulb, where one Big Bang can change everything instantly and forever. If only it were that easy, China's mandarins must wish. China is a continent, not a small laboratory where everything can be controlled and executed quickly. After record-breaking rail construction, China's network is still only half the length of the USA's, yet China has almost four times the population and fewer car owners. Only 22 out of China's 150 cities with over one million people have subways or rapid transit systems. There is still much to do.

Never to be forgotten is Premier Zhou Enlai's possibly apocryphal reply to the French ambassador at his Bastille Day reception. Fishing for compliments, the ambassador supposedly asked Zhou what impact the 1789 French Revolution had on the development of China's politics. "Too early to tell" was Zhou Enlai's diplomatic reply, avoiding offending the other ambassadors. Things can take a long time in a continent of now 1.4 billion people.

Implementing Change: Five Case Studies

There is no one way to approach change. Every situation is different. However there are common factors to consider as five areas of public policy — economy, stock market, healthcare, environment and children — illustrate.

Economy

An outstanding example of managing change was China's response to the 2008 global financial crisis. After US Treasury Secretary Hank Paulson laid out in Washington to visiting President Hu Jintao that the US, and hence the world, was staring into a financial and economic abyss in late September 2008, Hu and his senior technocrats went to work.

First, identify the top priority. Answer: limit the damage to China so as to maintain domestic stability. How? Launch a powerful economic stimulus to support Chinese demand. This would help prevent a global depression that would hit the world's largest exporter hard. China's top goal was achieved. The stimulus worked. Slowing some reform to achieve the number one priority was an acceptable price to pay as China's 2016 GDP doubled from 2007, up 107%, while the US and austere Britain rose anaemically, only 12% and 9% respectively, over the nine years.

The stimulus was not, as many assumed, hastily cobbled together in a few weeks after Lehman Brothers closed. It had been prepared since early 2008 as China's semi-annual economic review anticipated a sharp US slowdown or even recession in 2009, one of China's two major export markets. This regular exercise by the central bank, finance ministry and economic overseer (NDRC) checks to see if China's economic, fiscal and monetary policies are on track, while thinking what could blow them off course.

Policy can then be adjusted and communicated, first to political leaders for approval and then to the main economic players, starting with the banks. This was no state secret. A senior economic adviser Professor Fan Gang told the CLSA China Forum in Shanghai in May 2008 a stimulus was being prepared, four months before Lehman Brothers' closure triggered the global financial crisis. Behind the economic review process lie five-year programmes and individual annual outlines that can be adjusted. Many stimulus projects had already been screened and approved or were in advanced stages of both. Bringing them forward by a year or two was easy. Many were the next stages in projects already under way, therefore well thought out and tested: not rushed, ill-prepared or a waste of money.

Beijing quickly combined central and local government funding with bank lending to support the economy. Initially, it was mainly to the largest state-owned enterprises (SOEs), which in turn lent to their suppliers whose businesses, cash flows and repayment ability SOEs often knew better than banks. When Asian financial systems were underdeveloped, this was common during liquidity shortages, for example using *chaebol* in South Korea or private sector giants like the Tatas and Birlas in India. It was not perfect but it was far better than doing nothing.

"Shovel ready", generally well-considered, viable activity resulted. Later in 2009, when the damage was better understood and a property recovery under way, banks disbursed funds directly to companies for existing or new projects. China knew it would have to close the liquidity spigot one day but that could be left for when the economy was largely recovered, which indeed it was in 2011 when monetary tightening began.

Stock market

The main thesis of *China's Change* is not that China has the world's best systems: clearly it doesn't. What China does very well, though, is to regroup after setbacks reveal major defects. Then it usually swiftly understands the problem and adapts to correct deficiencies, finding lasting practical solutions.

To many sceptics China's stock markets in 2015 and early 2016 illustrated that things could still go very badly wrong. To experienced observers of change, what was telling was the relatively speedy response to the revealed incompetence of China's stock market regulators and their faulty systems. This was already known in the broader financial and government system, but by tradition could not be changed until a very evident problem appeared. Before then, the entrenched silo system kept other officials out of each tightly defined area of responsibility or fiefdom.

Beijing's response followed a familiar pattern. First, a key technocrat and others were sent into the problem area to make an assessment: in this case, they were stock market regulators. Then solutions were outlined, with the temporary assistance of the chairman responsible. When the initial survey was complete and changes agreed, a new head was appointed, with the competent technocrat left in place to supervise detailed solutions. This showed China had not lost its ability to regroup after setbacks. All was completed within five months, from the day when an expert technocrat became the securities regulator's number two in late October 2015 to the February replacement of the China Securities Regulatory Commission (CSRC) chairman. Personnel changes were followed by institutional change and regulations once problems were better understood.

Regulatory supervision of all financial markets was then addressed. A State Council body was given ministry status and enhanced overall powers, effectively ending autonomous silos throughout finance. In late 2017 a powerful entity was created to improve financial supervision. The Financial Stability and Development Commission under the State Council has financial oversight for financial regulation and local government financial development. This is no toothless co-ordinator.

It is headed by the vice premier responsible for the economy, politically outranking all other government entities in these areas. From this would follow changes in practice and policy so as to avoid future disasters, just as happened with air safety, food safety and epidemics. Finance is no different. It will take several years for this all to be proven, but by early 2016 the stock market fix was in. The market stabilized and finished the year little changed. Unlike the 2008 global financial crisis, the stock market boom and bust of the first half of 2015 was much simpler to solve. The process began with selection of a key technocrat, well trusted by Beijing reformers.

Fang Xinghai has a résumé and reputation that states his credentials. He is no *apparatchik* or simply a safe pair of hands. After his Stanford economics PhD, Fang worked at the World Bank before returning to China in the long tradition of serving the country. Whilst deputy secretary of Shanghai's financial affairs committee, Fang came to know Xi Jinping during his brief tenure as Shanghai party secretary. In 2013, Fang was brought up to Beijing from Shanghai by Liu He, secretary general of the key party economic institution, the Leading Small Group on the Economy and Financial Affairs. Harvard-educated Liu is the man that Xi Jinping told foreign reporters was his economics adviser: number one on the economy in all China. In 2017 he joined the Politburo.

Fang's appointment as Deputy Chairman of the CSRC indicated Beijing placed the highest priority on stock market reform to prevent it threatening China's economy or credibility ever again. He was a natural for the World Economic Forum at Davos, conveying calmly a grasp of economics in the way that previously earned China's technocrats accolades for competence but which some questioned in 2015. Not only was Fang a noted reformer within the party's apex economic institution, he had direct experience as deputy CEO of the Shanghai Stock Exchange and in management of one of China's largest brokerages. His articles appeared in the reformers' favourite outlet *Caixin* as well as in foreign media like the *Wall Street Journal* and *Financial Times*. Feng's ideas endeared him to them while his online photo, complete with open-neck casual shirt, said California, not China.

This appointment, though, was not about one person but about a system and its ability to manage change. It demonstrated that China has a process that generally works, for China. If it does not, then alternatives are tried, until solutions are found to change for the better. Healthcare has been one example.

Healthcare

Rapid income growth leads to rising expectations, especially in healthcare after the major shocks of SARS in 2003 and widening income inequality. Philosophically, China is attuned to the long-term nature of medicine and life sciences. Things, though, take time. Like the stock market, healthcare is a work in progress.

Laying the foundation first required the physical infrastructure. Some $124 billion was spent from 2009–2012 on building community health centres and hospitals. China also revamped the State Food and Drug Administration to bring regulation in line with global safety and certification standards. Things had become so bad that consideration was given to closing down China's drug regulator. The head, Zheng Xiaoyu, was sentenced to death in 2007 for taking bribes over 10 years to approve drugs and medical devices.

Much more than just construction and regulation are needed to provide healthcare for 1.4 billion people. A proper national healthcare safety net had to be woven but no appropriate model exists in the West, where there has been no really new healthcare thinking this century. China cannot wait for incremental change. Its population is greying and expectations rising while people are dying younger from the diseases of affluence like cancer and diabetes.

China must figure things out for itself, as in many areas. Unable to afford healthcare costs soaring to 18% of GDP, as in the US, it needs its own models. China has to drive down drug development costs and retail prices, target disease prevention, minimize costs of serious long-term illness, discover breakthrough drugs and develop new treatments: quite an undertaking. At least China has no expensive legacy systems holding it back. Also, it can tap into China's resources, scale and new technology to design its health system. These range from returnee scientists to patient screening, combinatorial chemistry and big data. All are formidable advantages with which to start.

An estimated 80,000 Chinese with Western PhDs worked abroad in life sciences in 2009. In biological sciences, more Chinese graduated in the US with masters and doctorates than did US students. Two-thirds in 2010 indicated they would consider returning to work in China. The government has been hot on their heels. Using academic and scientist talent spotters, it gives incentives, financial and physical, for the best talent to return. Life science parks have sprouted around China, long-term plans made.

Genomics has revolutionized the pace of innovation in drug research. Understanding human biology before was severely limited to about 300–400 "drugable" targets, biological mechanisms that drugs can alter for therapeutic benefit. DNA sequencing raises the potential number to more than 30,000 targets. The Beijing Genomics Institute (BGI) has rapidly created the world's largest gene sequencing capability, after buying the second largest equipment maker and establishing facilities in the US and Europe. At UC Davis, it hired 5,000 maths graduates and game programmers. Nowhere else is approaching it on such scale.

China is good at collecting data, having done so for thousands of years. Big data can link patients' medical records, enabling large-scale research. BGI studied 12,000 people with depression: large numbers in a single area. This may have identified depression's key markers, testament to the progress China has made in creating an investment ecosystem to develop healthcare critical mass, with research, venture capital and government support for drugs and medical devices laying the foundations for a much better health system.

Environment

The number one immediate concern for many urban dwellers is the environment, especially air quality. There is also growing awareness about water and soil pollution, which may be even worse for health. Anything that concerns the public now matters to politicians.

Beijing was not unaware of the problems. Several years before the 2009 Copenhagen climate change talks failed, the China head of Cambridge Energy Research Associates (CERA), Jim Brock, stated bluntly that no capital in the world "got" the seriousness of climate change like Beijing. "Getting" it and getting anything done quickly though can be two very different things.

Traditional thinking is clear. Nature and humanity cannot be separated; there must be harmony, as environmentalist Dr Yang Fuqiang puts it. That is what Laozi taught almost three millennia ago and what people have traditionally believed. However after 1978, economic growth became the government's top priority: China's ecology deteriorated, everywhere. Mention of environmental and economic sustainability was first made in the 2001 five-year plan but this merely put down a green marker. Economic growth was still of paramount importance.

By 2009, this was not so clear. Believing it can correct problems by regrouping, China set about formulating new environmental policy, but conflicting goals limited its ability. The skies became darker, especially over Beijing itself, the air fouler. By then the government had already begun to appreciate the role Non-Governmental Organizations (NGOs) could play in resolving the growing environmental crisis and its consequences not just in knowledge at home but through communication abroad.

At home, the 2008 Wenchuan earthquake highlighted individuals' desire to help. Thousands packed their cars with emergency supplies and headed for quake-hit Sichuan, even though this was technically illegal. The government could use their help; it was too stretched. Acknowledging this was a major reversal of a long-held insistence that the state could care for everyone, meaning there was no need for individual action. Yet the plausibility of this was wearing thin, especially with a better-educated and more prosperous populace wanting greater participation in their nation's life. Finally, when some in the West blamed China for the Copenhagen climate change talks failing, Beijing realized NGOs could help answer its critics abroad. At home they could monitor polluters and policy implementation. The public could be watchdogs: see Ma Jun in Chapter 6. A promising development, but change did not happen overnight.

Change only came in 2014 after public anger, especially on social media, erupted when the Beijing Municipal Government failed to respond adequately to suddenly worse air pollution. This forced central government to intervene, ordering Beijing's local government to change policy. As a result, Beijing's 2015 PM2.5 readings fell a dramatic 27%, though remained well above the WHO's recommended limit: still a work in progress.

New levels of interaction between government and people occur because the national consensus goal is to combat pollution. It affects everyone, leaders as well as led. There is still a long way to go before Beijing gets the blue skies and clean air it craves as the economics, politics and chemistry of pollution are complex. Indeed, the environment may be the last major economic-related problem to be resolved fully, but at least it has turned the corner in terms of social and political will.

Orphans and left-behind children

China has some one million orphans in state institutions that lagged behind world best practices for many years. During the Cultural Revolution, social workers even came under ideological fire, making matters worse. In the 1990s, foreign media exposed neglect in some state-run orphanages, including "dying rooms", where young orphans were left to die.

Realizing it had much to learn, China was open to suggestions in 1998 when a small group of foreign parents of adopted Chinese orphans wanted to extend their nurturing beyond their own families. They contacted the orphans' state institutions to see if they could help train child development staff there. A non-threatening group with no agenda, no religion and no celebrity involvement appealed to China. Understandably sensitive, not just because of any resulting adverse publicity but also after the history of foreign interference in China during the 19th and first half of the 20th centuries, Beijing is wary of giving Western groups access to the grassroots. In the 19th century,

French Catholic missionaries in the interior vied with local officials for influence, acting, as Bonavia put it, "like Imperial magistrates". The "Colour Revolutions" and "Arab Spring" have given a more recent reason to be suspicious of NGOs, while the prospect of Madonna's involvement would alarm many.

Contact between foreign parents and China began informally, developing familiarity and trust. Once trust was established, the Ministry of Civil Affairs authorized two pilot projects in Anhui and Jiangsu, using Western approaches to teach childcarers. From these contacts has grown China's largest foreign NGO, becoming one of the first batch of 14 foreign NGOs registered in China. By 2016, OneSky, originally called Half the Sky, had helped transform the lives of over 138,000 children at risk.

All staff working with institutions or with caregivers and children are Chinese, as are the Beijing office staff and 49 trainer teams. OneSky employs 829 Chinese nationals working in 44 institutions. There are 19,541 trained caregivers: its distance learning programme has 2,900 carers registered to learn online from each other and experts. Although OneSky is inspired by the Italian *Reggio Emilia* system, developed after World War II when children without families to care for them were a common post-war problem in Europe, there is nothing about it at odds with Chinese culture or global best practice.

Between 1998 and 2006, OneSky developed programmes for different ages, from babies to youths. This was done only in government institutions, fitting in with Beijing's goals of systemic reform. Then two disasters happened that changed the way Beijing looked at the likes of OneSky. The disasters provided a pilot scheme in real time, especially when the 2008 Wenchuan earthquake occurred. This showed China was efficient in providing disaster relief and rapid response but lacked the skills to help newly-orphaned children, and children emotionally shattered in the wake of natural disaster. This led to OneSky bringing in US specialists, including some China-born, who had worked in similar circumstances, counseling orphans in groups so as to create communities that would build normality in a sea of trauma and chaos.

Wenchuan was the second natural disaster of 2008. The first was record cold and heavy snow in normally temperate southern China which cut off supplies at some orphanages where OneSky had programmes. OneSky provided much-needed support for this vulnerable community in the midst of winter's disaster. Seeing all this, Beijing asked OneSky to help build model children's centres in each province. OneSky now provides its knowledge to every one of China's child welfare workers in a co-training initiative, The Rainbow Programme, helping create a generation of professional childcarers.

In the course of almost two decades, China has found a way to reform care for orphans, improving both the hardware (facilities) and, critically, the even more needed software (nurturing caregivers). These approaches are now enshrined in China's five-year programme along with the more usual economic reform projects. In essence, the approach differs little from other sectors. Reform is a lengthy process but once started, there is no going back, only plenty of room for discovery and adaptation.

New challenges constantly appear. Previously, orphans were largely abandoned girls, now 90% have disabilities. Some can be corrected, others are serious, requiring intensive treatment and care. The more OneSky contributes, the more it is asked to do. Previously, all fundraising had to be done offshore, as international NGOs could not raise funds from the public in China. In 2012, OneSky helped establish its sister foundation, Chunhui Children, so Chinese citizens, foundations and corporations can support the most vulnerable children. Registered in Beijing, Chunhui is committed to financial transparency. Apart from encouraging local philanthropy, Beijing is also focusing attention on 61 million left-behind children in rural China, whose parents have migrated for work.

OneSky renamed itself from Half the Sky at the end of 2015 because it felt ready to take its knowledge of training orphan carers to an even larger group, children outside orphanage walls, so that all children, vulnerable and secure, can share the same sky. By the end of 2016, some 46 pilot projects had started to provide preschool learning as well as family skills programmes. When working well, after three years it is hoped, they will be replicated for the early education and nurturing of China's 23 million children under the age of seven. These have been left behind with their grandparents and relatives, who struggle to feed them in China's 680 rural "poverty counties".

Family centres are at the heart of the approach. Five days a week, centres are staffed by a trained mentor/leader from the village. Children play while adults, often grandparents, learn effective parenting. These lessons change the way adults think about children, making them appreciate how capable they are, and to value them. Some come every day with their children, becoming involved in village initiatives sparked by the family centres.

Often this changes how adults think about themselves, making them realize how important they are and how they make a difference, especially in the critical first 1,000 days of a child's life. Family centres post video clips on social media to connect migrant parents with their children, showing them dancing, learning and playing. China has found a way not just to learn from foreigners but to involve them more directly in helping its most vulnerable children, without losing any of its culture or importing unwanted influences. Like much of China's reform, there is largely local execution but with some foreign experience and thinking.

Chapter 6

The Overseas Connection

The ocean takes from all rivers.

Zhuangzi (late 4th century BC)

The people who sometimes promote change the most are those with overseas connections. They are the quiet revolutionaries of reform and opening up, often born or partly-educated overseas. Much of China's initial overseas *yanjiu* learning for reform came from related Confucian cultures in East and Southeast Asia. However, in some fields, Confucianism offers little.

In economics, business and finance, knowledge often comes from those who have studied in the West, especially in US universities or business schools. Understanding can also come from multilateral institutions like the World Bank and the International Monetary Fund (IMF) or Chinese who worked there. Similarly, Chinese companies have hired Chinese from Hong Kong, Taiwan and Southeast Asia who worked for world-leading companies. Knowledge about the environment and social welfare has been acquired more informally by building on foreign individuals' initiatives. NGOs like the National Resources Defense Council and OneSky have been among the most successful in helping shape and communicate policy, with approaches that understand China from a Chinese perspective. Even where Chinese knowledge is lacking, the approach to finding it, to devise and implement policy, is Chinese.

Overseas and returning Chinese have played important roles in China's economic and social transformation. Each has their own story that illustrates how China manages change. Also how extensive that change has been.

It was no ordinary action in 1975. A young 25-year old American, Charles Liu, born in Taiwan, son of a KMT officer and grandson of a Hunanese general, returned his two passports: the first to Taiwan, the second to the US where he migrated in 1961 at the age of 11. Liu took up Chinese citizenship instead: not an everyday occurrence anywhere, let alone in New York during the Cold War, when the US did not even recognize the People's Republic of China as a legitimate state.

Chinese culture, especially its literature and history, was a strong pull for Liu as he contemplated taking Chinese citizenship. His reading of Chinese classics, which began in Taiwan, drew Liu to his roots. His liberal arts courses at Princeton exposed him to the literature and history of the West but he often found their Chinese equivalents more profound. This is not uncommon among Chinese well versed in both. The only place where they often find greater profundity in Western arts is classical music, a feeling Liu shares.

China's large population means human relationships, social or economic, have always been much more complex than elsewhere, making them inherently more interesting to Charles. Chinese behaviour naturally reflects this complexity: so did the palace intrigues, novels and drama of China's past. Strategy was much deeper, whether in *kung fu* novels or *The Art of War*. After doing community work in New York's Chinatown, Liu was looking for a way to use his law degree and Princeton education to "do something for the Third World". A chance came to satisfy his youthful "idealism to defend the underdog" when China's delegation to the United Nations asked if he would like to be a UN officer as part of China's quota. That involved a life-changing UN requirement that any employee must be a citizen of the quota country. This hastened Liu's decision to take Chinese citizenship. After working as a UN simultaneous translator for two years, he became part of the UN secretariat, working on economic topics from commodities to trade, before becoming secretary of the G77 economic group of Third World countries.

Liu's first trip ever to China came when he took his UN "home leave". This was in 1977. China was now his home, not just of his mind but in all respects, including his passport. How did he feel? "Thrilled to have come," he recalls. What struck him most? "The country and people were so poor."

China's reform and opening up in 1978 started to see a trickle and then a growing flow of overseas Chinese visit China for business, mostly from Hong Kong and Southeast Asia. China had been effectively closed, both at the China end but also in their adopted homelands like Singapore, Malaysia, Indonesia and Thailand that banned or restricted their citizens from visiting China after 1949, especially while Southeast Asian communist insurgencies continued during the 1950s and 1960s. Few settled, let alone changed their citizenship, something so personal to their identity and fundamental to their security. Many came as traders, boosting and broadening China's exports. Often the products were made in Guangdong, neighbouring Hong Kong, where overseas Chinese introduced operational skills, professional management and global standards to run factories — even if initially only at the very low end. They also gave access to global information, networks and, most important of all, capital.

Liu had none of these skills. He was not a businessman nor interested in profit: he styled himself an altruist with a legal training who worked for the United Nations. Charles continued working for the UN until 1990 when he decided to live full-time in China so as to learn about commerce in order to promote investment and trade. There was much change already, compared with his first visit in 1977. Life was "frantic, vibrant and full of opportunities". In China he was seen as a window on the outside world, while to outsiders he was a way into China. Charles headed the investment bank Lazard Asia in China from 1990 to 1998 before moving into private equity investment. In 2004 he founded Hao Capital, financing a wide range of early stage companies. During China's initial rapid growth, much of the investment was opportunistic. Now he is more concerned with long-term ideas like alternative energy where China is rapidly becoming a world leader.

How does Charles see China now? "Overwhelmingly complex: it is a society composed of people with mindsets from different centuries," he observes. 21st-century Beijing and Qing era Gansu have to get along, fitting in together. "China's transformation is to a totally different normality." Quality of growth and quality of life are becoming people's main objectives. Compared with 1977? "My thoughts have changed, sometimes annually, but often monthly or even weekly. It is impossible to describe," he concludes.

Many more go in the opposite direction, born in China seeking education abroad. From a village in the Hulun Beir grassland near the Russian border on the steppes of northern China, where the temperature falls to minus 35 degrees Celsius in winter, to tropical Singapore near the equator is the journey that Zhao Ya'nan made to further her education. Paying her own way, after saving up for over a decade in business and consulting, she studied international business management before returning to China. Ya'nan is just one of the estimated 550,000 Chinese who go overseas to study each year. Her story is one of a new generation of Chinese increasingly comfortable abroad and very interested in it.

In this age of the internet and social media, it seems appropriate I had never met Zhao Ya'nan before her return; we had only met virtually. I felt as if I had known her for years, as her story is far from unusual. She is the real friend of my former colleague, Anna Kieryk, who would relate Ya'nan's latest adventures and what they illustrated about a changing China. Through related emails and conversations I could visit her world. Anna stressed two points: Ya'nan does not consider herself to be particularly interested in technology nor at 35 is she especially young and hence obviously adaptable to new technology or systems. Furthermore Anna does not think of her as being exceptionally adventurous, though even that is changing. Nor did she come from the wealthier and more "open" coastal China but from Inner Mongolia. In fact, apart from her university education, nothing makes her in any way unusual.

Yet, over the last five years, Ya'nan has backpacked all over Southeast Asia and Australia in her holidays, even taking her mother for several weeks to India. What motivated her to travel abroad originally was her love of learning new things, to encounter new experiences and enjoy the processes that went with them. She wanted to participate. Gradually she noticed how travel and foreign knowledge were changing her. Then she saw how similar experiences changed people around her and China as well.

Almost 40 years ago, I was at Sun Moon Lake in Taiwan. As the sun went down and the moon appeared, my wife commented that mainland Chinese would love to visit such a beautiful and serene place. Of course the chances of that happening seemed very remote. With so many scenic spots in China I asked why mainlanders would want so much to visit this particular one. Everyone in China, she replied, had heard of Sun Moon Lake from literature and history, and like other famous places around the world of which they had read, heard or seen on television, they would want to visit, if only they could. They would be driven by a combination of reconnecting with their history, breaking out of a world that had been closed and feeding an insatiable curiosity.

Apart from much easier visa and passport regulations, what enables Ya'nan and millions of other Chinese to travel independently are advances in technology and Chinese social media. These spread information in much greater detail and a lot faster than traditional guide books ever could. On top of that, there are new business models to support travellers, from the shared economy to online enablers. Very popular mobile apps help Chinese swap information and tips in Chinese, including about which establishments are exceptionally friendly to Chinese as well as those that are not and to be avoided. There are now many online city and country guides with features or comments like, "I am a 40-year-old female office worker, who likes skiing and watching old movies. Here is one perfect day I have spent in Prague: try it." Try it, share the experience, just do it.

A survey showed that Chinese tourists post 42% of comments on luxury travel websites. This disproportionate response reflects that commenting is all part of the journey, the experience, adding to the interest and excitement. It is also what tourists think they should do to help others and raise standards, just as they do in China. That is how this generation deals with the lack of trust in companies and institutions: people do their bit.

Ya'nan's response to change differs from that of most Westerners of her age, enabling her to embrace change through technology, not merely the changes in technology itself. Anna invited Ya'nan to spend Christmas 2015 in her native Poland and was struck by how comfortable she was in planning her first trip to Europe, all 30 days of it. With her first week in Poland confirmed, she booked her flight one month ahead. However she waited until the eve of leaving Poland before arranging her trip to Berlin, by simply going onto Airbnb's website to look for a place to stay. There were five or six cities she wanted to visit in Europe and, since she valued flexibility, she booked each stay only 12 to 24 hours ahead of arrival, all done from her phone. Ya'nan might not have had the same confidence booking hotels this way but with Airbnb she believes that quality control is high (it automatically bans any host that does not reply to a request within 24 hours). Again this shows how lack of trust drives decisions. Those who address it benefit those who do not lose custom and may go under.

Such trust in technology and new systems was in marked contrast with Anna's 40-year-old Polish guests visiting her shortly afterwards in California. They asked her to buy a paper map (in her email to me an exclamation mark was added after the word paper) and requested she confirm with a leading car rental company some information on its website. This had to be confirmed by "an actual human being". Only then would they make their booking. Anna explained Ya'nan's more trusting and speedy approach as being rooted in her generally very positive experience of technology, which had opened so many new worlds. All the positive change of the last four decades has made most Chinese optimistic about the future, Ya'nan included.

Her optimism, Anna figures, comes from many Chinese having moved quickly from relative poverty to relative affluence, making them more optimistic about what lies ahead, even if it is still unknown. Therefore they more willingly risk new technologies and experiences. Anna feels, "There may even be a 'bit of change addiction syndrome' among younger Chinese: how about this, how about that, should we try this, this may be a good idea, this promises to save some money, let's try it", just do it. "If it turns out to be a scam, they just move on quickly to the next opportunity," she concluded, no longer surprised by such pragmatism.

The quiet revolutionaries of modern China include some of its top technocrats. Chief economic adviser Liu He and central banker Yi Gang have used their partially foreign-acquired knowledge to help reshape the economy. In other fields, especially in science, the specialists have been less evident but have nonetheless contributed much to China's change.

The environment is one example. Many concerned with the environment tend to be outside government but work with it to advocate further change. I have known three for over a decade and seen how much can be achieved, even when working with the existing system. The system has changed, in part due to their thinking. Without their work, and that of many others like them, China's environmental future would be worse, quite possibly a lot worse. Dr Yang Fuqiang graduated in physics in 1977 before joining the central economic planning agency where he worked on renewable and rural energy policy. Then in 1984 he went to Cornell as a World Bank visiting scholar in city planning before doing his energy and industrial engineering PhD at West Virginia. These seven years of US education and scientific background enabled him to work eight years at Lawrence Berkeley National Laboratory in California on energy and the environment.

On his return to Beijing in 2000, with Chinese government experience plus US education and research background, Yang joined what was then a rarity in China, an environmental NGO. For another eight years, he headed the China office of the US-based Energy Foundation that promoted alternative energy and conservation, funded by various families, including the Hewletts and the Packards. He subsequently became senior adviser at the Chinese World Wildlife Fund and the Natural Resources Defense Council, two other prominent global NGOs whose work extends to climate change and sustainable energy.

Yang's expertise is in great demand at home and abroad as the world becomes more concerned with climate change, alternative energy, sustainable development and reducing pollution. As a NGO participant, he understands Chinese thinking on all these issues: he has influenced it. He has regularly attended global climate change conferences from Durban to Copenhagen, Cancun to Paris. At home, he mixes freely with former colleagues, providing informal input to policymaking.

Yang's warm, smiling eyes are familiar to many in China's green community, together with his breadth of knowledge and connections. Following Chinese tradition, he has mentored younger policy scholars. One of them, Wang Tao, studied Environmental Economics at England's York University and is now an assistant dean at the Chinese Thinktank, as well as visiting scholar at Beijing's Tsinghua–Carnegie Center.

Tao ascribes his interest to when, aged 17, he realized he "could no longer take for granted the lush green landscape of my native Sichuan and the crystal blue of its waters". This led him to study environmental science at Shanghai's Fudan University where he discovered solutions lay more in policy than in technology. On graduating in 2002, he found that, for all the talk about this being a sunrise industry, there was no private sector demand for his skills and very little from the public sector. That would take time, possibly a very long time. The environment was not a cause with a dedicated following. Government environmental bureaus were primarily meal tickets for officials, not a vocation. With the main focus on economic growth, everyone wanted a better material life for the country, not to mention for themselves: greening China then was not a national priority.

There were very few NGOs at the time: even those such as the World Wildlife Fund, which in 1980 had set up in China, operated only in areas of interest to the government. Pandas, forests and water were of interest, pollution, the direct byproduct of excessive unsustainable economic growth, was not. Fortunately for Tao, the Energy Foundation was starting to look at policy that would address that and explore the applicability of alternative energy. If foreign NGOs were not set up to do the most compelling work, could private Chinese individuals? That would seem to have been even more unlikely, yet that is what began to happen on a limited scale.

The first time I met Ma Jun, around 2005, I expected to be impressed by his knowledge of China's water problems. He had written the definitive book on the subject, and I was not disappointed. However what struck me most was his command and analysis of the Chinese politics that bore on his area, the environment. Also at the dinner was the head of a leading foreign consultancy advising major multinational companies on how to navigate the shoals and deep waters of Chinese politics and policy. He talked about the environment but after 10 minutes of discussion stopped giving his own opinions. Instead he just listened as Ma Jun laid it all out, from his analysis of the environmental institutions to the individuals in charge and the forces that influenced them. I was not surprised that Ma was about to spend a year at Yale as a visiting scholar. He had a breadth of knowledge that foreigners could not match.

I reflected that Ma's grasp of politics was not unique. Everyone, just to survive in China, let alone prosper, has to develop a personal computer in their head to log all relevant information on Chinese politics and to review it constantly: *weixin*, renewal. Not restricted to just those involved with politics at the highest levels, it goes all the way down to the village: not just an interest of the urban, chattering classes but a national phenomenon. I learned this from Eldest Uncle in 1990. We were standing on the top of his house, another red brick and granite mansion, where I was taking in the beauty and tranquility of Fujian with its green rolling, bamboo-clad small hills and rice fields, when suddenly Eldest Uncle announced what he wanted to know. His question came out of the blue. It was eight days after Margaret Thatcher resigned as British prime minister.

"What impact will Margaret Thatcher's *overthrow* have on the development of British politics?" Eldest Uncle asked. I was taken aback, not having thought of it in this way. The word "overthrow" had such violence, yet of course it was correct. Such an event would impact Britain's future. It just seemed too early to think in such terms. I was stunned to hear the question asked thousands of miles away in rural China. I could not recall discussions in rural Herefordshire in 1976 about the impact of Mao's death.

As I took in Eldest Uncle's question, I went weak at the knees. The profundity and unexpectedness of the question was compounded by standing beside a low roof-top balustrade, three stories up. Once I steadied myself, mentally and even physically, I began to think about what lay behind his question and what it implied. Here he was in rural China, had never left the province as far as I knew, and was asking with a great command of the essence about an event that occurred half a world away barely one week before in my own country, provoking thoughts that I had not considered in such terms. Nonetheless Eldest Uncle thought in such clear-cut analytical terms, while I, who had studied politics at university in England, had not. How "closed" was China?

More to the point, with such clarity, what did he think of the village head, the party secretary of the nearest town, the province's governor and what of paramount leader Deng Xiaoping? I could not even guess but I knew that he had thoughts on all of them, as well as the systems they operated. He followed and processed the news, official and unofficial. It was the only way to survive and pursue life. He had his own personal computer, just like Ma Jun and many millions more.

When Ma Jun established the Institute of Public and the Environmental Affairs (IPE) in 2006 to look into air, water and soil pollution, China lacked not just the regulations to control them but, most importantly, the will. Economic GDP growth was the goal, if not the god: the very top national priority. Even where environmental regulations existed, there was little-to-no enforcement. The judiciary was not doing its job, the public was largely silent and government had not changed its priorities of growth, incomes and jobs. IPE was the first Chinese organization devoted to addressing these environmental issues through transparent and public participation. Its first major initiative was Green Choice in 2007, designed to help green the supply chain, to ensure that firms purchased in China from companies that produced with at least some thought for the environment. Multinational corporations (MNCs) became the primary focus as Western consumers were demanding higher environmental standards in the production of goods they bought. This made MNCs vulnerable to domestic pressure, which gave them leverage over suppliers in China.

The timing was good. In 2008, as part of a wide-ranging initiative on more open government, China's State Environmental Protection Agency outlined its information and disclosure requirements. This provided the all-important raw data that any monitoring NGO would need: not overnight but over time. From it could be created an environmental quality database and indices. By 2015, all the top 338 municipalities, across the whole of China, were regularly reporting data. China was also making its first amendments in 25 years to the Environmental Protection Law. By 2016 it was publishing the third 10-point action plan, with soil following on from air and water. Previously, soil information was a state secret: quite a change in under a decade.

Ma Jun has a quiet but determined manner. He does not raise his voice, possessing the calm so characteristic of government officials, like any traditional scholar. He merely applies logical solutions to very evident problems, fully aware of China's scale, speed, philosophy and strategy. The IPE now has over 30 staff; and government listens to its views. Most important are the luridly coloured online maps pinpointing polluters in real time: no one can fail to grasp their meaning. Some are literally stunning. Used to enforce regulations, *Weibo* links viewers directly to local government. Based on IPE's real-time government-sourced data, they can report violators immediately, among them paper factories discharging chemical waste into rivers, power stations belching pollutants into the air and petrochemical plants emitting dangerous gases. In the two years after mid-2014, over 500 cases were addressed and corrected because the maps pinpoint the problems while social media relay the information, and central government can then enforce change through its authority and discipline. Without the maps, Beijing would not have the capacity to act. They could of course create the maps themselves but realism tells Beijing that the follow-through would fail, only public participation can make it work: see Chapter 5.

Listed by the *Guardian* as one the world's top 50 environmentalists, Ma won the Goldman environmental prize in 2012. IPE's databases and maps are revolutionizing public knowledge and participation in public affairs, with three million people downloading the Blue Map app to check their city's air quality. Like other technicians in China, such as fellow environmentalists Yang Fuqiang and Wang Tao, Ma Jun uses foreign and local science and methods to change China not overnight but over decades.

In some cases foreigners have directly helped China change. Jeronia Muntaner left her native Majorca in Spain to backpack around India for three months in 1984. Over three decades later, she says she is still on that trip. India led to Nepal, Thailand, Hong Kong and finally China. She liked China the most, falling in love with the language, Beijing's austerity and the fact that the foreign community was very small, enabling her to fit in all the more easily.

After having two biological children, Jeronia and her husband Clinton Dines, decided to adopt baby Maria. Having done research on orphans in China, Jeronia noticed that Maria was less withdrawn than she expected, recognizing love and responding to it fairly quickly. She wanted to know why this was, so looked into Maria's background and found she had been in a OneSky project in Hefei, Anhui. Soon Jeronia was in touch with its founder, Jenny Bowen, to learn more.

When Jeronia and Clinton moved to Shanghai, she volunteered to do some work for OneSky. Initially she evaluated the seven or eight centres it had, making suggestions and giving guidance based on her Montessori work with infants under three. She worked as a field trainer for a few years before taking over as a director of the infant programme. Then, as a director, she designed the training manuals for the 1,500 nannies in the 51 centres. When I caught up with Jeronia, in Clinton's native Brisbane, after their next move, she was still involved, even from thousands of miles away, busy designing with two others new training materials for OneSky's latest and most far-reaching project.

There are 61 million children in rural China left behind by parents working in towns, often far away: see Chapter 5. This is one of the greatest prices that China has to pay for its rapid, migrant-fuelled growth. They are not orphans but have major needs, separated from their migrant parents and left alone in the village with grandparents, other relatives or even unrelated minders. Their emotional well-being and long-term development suffer.

A 2013 Swedish-funded report concluded that this "separation results in a common sense of failure and anxiety for the parents and often in broken relationships with their children". 80% of parents felt inadequate, while 70% had strong feelings of guilt and anxiety. Left-behind children tend to be less optimistic, suffer from anxiety, isolation, low esteem and self-awareness, depression, behavioural problems and reduced learning ability: left-behind often means falling behind. This comes along with much pain and problems for the whole family.

There are some similarities with orphans but also major differences. A sense of rejection is common. The settings, though, are very different. The orphanage provides no privacy, no personal space and no private time as orphans are constantly surrounded by other orphans: undivided attention is hard to come by. No adult can spend sufficient time with each child, so there is no-one to whom orphans can get emotionally attached. They feel very insecure. OneSky provides that adult with whom an orphan can build an emotional attachment.

Left-behind children may seem more fortunate than orphans but their very different settings create other problems. In the increasingly depopulated villages, they are surrounded by much older people, usually grandparents, who don't know how to help children develop. They have "old ways" and toil in the fields all day, largely in silence. When they return home their silence stays with them. They do not communicate well. Consequently a child's emotional growth is stunted. At least those trained to be nannies in orphanages are selected on the basis of being good learners. They understand a child's development needs and the importance of communication. Grandparents and other guardians of left-behind children may not recognize the need to learn until OneSky gives them the opportunity to "learn Chinese essence from foreign means". So too did one of China's leading industrialists.

The founder of Geely Auto, Li Shufu, decided in 2004 he needed advice on what was expected of a publicly listed company, so he looked in Hong Kong. Whereas Chinese companies are generally ruled by a "king", usually the founder or a founding family member, Li realized that his ambition to create a leading global company could not be achieved in such a purely Chinese way. Western ideas of governance had to be learned and digested if Geely were to raise the funds required to achieve its long-term global objective. For this, Li found Lawrence Ang with over two decades of working for three global giants under his belt.

Lawrence began work in the 1980s at IBM, which was then in its original incarnation as Big Blue, the world's leading computer maker, very much a cutting-edge firm in both technology and management. Everything was laid out precisely. Responsibilities were well defined, so was the work to be done and how to do it. After that, Lawrence moved into financial research, first with what became UBS, the world's second largest bank, and then with Germany's leader Deutsche Bank. All had one thing in common.

These very successful global firms were all run by rules and systems, not by a king. At Merrill Lynch in the 1980s, I found that those who organized the money-making were called battalion commanders, each competing aggressively against each other for ever more resources with which to do business and battle. This was what successful publicly listed companies in the West can do, mobilize enormous resources. The battalion commanders competed by promoting the brightest ideas. Those whose business plans proved the most successful received even more resources. That is what Li Shufu realized he needed, a system that could convert his small kingdom into a much larger land of opportunity and heroes. Lawrence's role was to make Li a hero, maybe *the* hero, but certainly to take him beyond being a very minor monarch.

In 2010, Li became a national hero. He acquired Sweden's Volvo, one of the world's most distinctive auto brands, known for its quality and safety, but living on past glory and losing money. After the financial crisis, Ford needed to cut its debt and so put Volvo's car assets on the block. For $1.8 billion, Geely acquired access to world-class technology, research and brand. With this bold move, Chairman Li became a minority shareholder. He had to respect others' wishes for the first time in his life. Li was no longer the king. He had to listen to a diverse range of independent directors representing everything from local government and labour unions to manufacturing knowledge learned in leading global firms and academe. His plans were scrutinized as never before. This was a big change but, to make more affordable quality cars, he had to win the trust of customers through innovation: no longer could he do it alone.

Li knew both he and the majority could benefit from this but he needed his main board executive director, Lawrence Ang, to ensure that proper corporate governance and laws are followed, teaching Geely's management about the principles involved. This is an integral part of wanting to be a leading automaker, something all Chinese firms with global ambitions have to learn.

The third non-Chinese national to become a senior financial adviser to China was Andrew Sheng. In a *curriculum vitae* that ranged far, wide and deep in finance, he had the very experience that China knew it lacked. Born in Shanghai, he was brought to British North Borneo in 1951. From Sandakan, a small timber town perched on Borneo's northern shore, he went to study economics at Bristol University in England, qualified as a chartered accountant in London, then returned to Malaysia as a central bank economist. His businessman father was a French- and Belgian-educated engineer from Sichuan who travelled to France on the same ship as Deng Xiaoping and other members of the founding generation of Chinese communist leaders who went as student/workers to fill the gap in the French labour force after World War I. When the 1949 revolution came, rather than stay in Taiwan or Hong Kong, he migrated to *Nanyang*, the South Seas, as Chinese had done for centuries.

Andrew joined the China Banking and Regulatory Commission (CBRC) as an adviser in an initiative of Premier Zhu Rongji's. This was widened in 2008 to become the One Thousand Persons Plan to tap top overseas expertise from the Chinese diaspora, mainly in Asia and North America. These experts went to various institutions, from Chinese academies and universities to the bureaucracy and even state-owned enterprises (SOEs). Andrew became the CBRC's chief adviser in 2006. Very well qualified, he had headed Hong Kong's Securities and Futures Commission, been deputy head of the Hong Kong Monetary Authority and worked as a World Bank economist on financial restructuring in Latin America, Eastern Europe, Africa, Pakistan and China. More importantly he was different. In Malaysia, where I first knew him in 1980, Andrew was interested in the real economy, not in abstract theories based on dubious, incomplete data or flawed by ignoring reality. Property was central to the economy's volatility, so were commodities and foreign direct investment, but data on these was generally unavailable to the extent decision makers required, be they businessmen, families or government officials.

To make good the data deficit, everyone had their solution through *guanxi*, connections. We would swap new information gathered through the highly effective Malaysian means of talking, eating and drinking, be it in coffee shops or hotels, with everyone from leading businessmen and small town entrepreneurs to politicians, officials and bankers who all needed to know the same thing. Where was the economy going? What was driving it? What about the politics? This was Malaysia's favourite conversation topic, like sports in other countries, following all the ups and downs, intrigues, achievements, victories and defeats. Everyone was trying to manage uncertainty, see around the next corner and have a longer-term sense of everything. Some sought to profit, some to control and some for the sheer fun of trying to figure out the future, especially in a highly political multi-ethnic country. Malay statecraft is very sophisticated, complex and not without its hardball moments. Chinese businessmen came with the Confucian tradition and a natural understanding of change from the *Yi Jing*, reinforced by hard experience, while Indians brought their forensic skills in argument and story-telling.

Andrew had his "Sandakan Index", which, one day on a visit home, flagged an economic recovery. He had complete confidence in the signal as it reflected reality, even if only one part of reality. At the very least, he had told me, it should be monitored, kept on the radar screen. Much to his delight, several months later, the official data confirmed the new trend. The swing indicator was the karaoke component: for the first time in five years, karaoke bars were opening in Sandakan rather than closing. This was a clear inflexion point, reflecting the financial health of the timber tycoons, whose lavish entertaining was legendary, not just in bars and hotels but in restaurants and jewellery shops too. Cash flows were increasing, leading to consumption rebounding, a very early recovery indicator. This experience was a good warm-up for a much more complex task, trying to fathom China.

Andrew brought with him knowledge and, more importantly, real world experience that China lacked. This included a deep understanding of markets, the rule of law, transitional economies and developing countries, especially Malaysia and Southeast Asia where he experienced bank runs, sorted out Malaysia's deposit-taking co-operatives, which today would be called shadow banking, and resolved problems in an emerging insurance industry. In Hong Kong, he had handled a full-blown currency crisis, with global roots.

How little he really knew about China quickly dawned on Andrew in his CBRC role, so he started to read its history and classics in the original. Wu Jinglian, the leading economic reformer among academics and government advisers, suggested he write a column in the widely read *Caijin* magazine. This projected his experience to a broad audience well outside government as well as within. He found it difficult to translate Western ideas into Chinese concepts, better to do so in stages: classic gradualism. Direct criticism does not normally work in China: far better to use analogies and recount what he had seen. This enabled him to say things in a Chinese way, with messages wrapped in his international experience.

Andrew has written two insightful books, one about the Asian crisis and the global financial crisis, the other about shadow banking. Under way are two more books on financial regulation and Chinese philosophy, specifically how it differs from Western thinking when considering how to cope with uncertainty, a central idea of economics and finance. He is a leading Asian voice on *Project Syndicate*. Much more than the average central banker, Andrew is the sort of wide-ranging thinker that Asia increasingly produces.

The high calibre of China's top technocrats is often mentioned by global counterparts. China's elite technocrats are at ease and familiar with their opposite numbers at the likes of the IMF, World Bank, foreign treasuries and trade departments. Equally important to this understanding, their counterparts are familiar with the technocrats in Beijing. It is a two-way case of soft power in practice. The technocrats are led by people who have been in these roles, or are at least preparing for them, for almost a quarter of a century, ever since Deng Xiaoping, then Jiang Zemin, tapped Zhu Rongji to head economic reform, especially of finance, banking and investment. The process developed a group of very capable people, including Zhou Xiaochuan and Liu Mingkang, with whom Andrew worked closely over the years. He considers both to be Renaissance Men, capable of rising to the top in any field, in any system, anywhere. They epitomize the essence of the traditional mandarin elite.

Liu Mingkang, who was the first head of China's banking regulator the CBRC, missed out on his formal education during the Cultural Revolution, but through sheer determination and hard work (grit) got a job at the Bank of China, learned English on his own and was posted to the bank's London office. While there, he studied at the City University of London, getting his Masters in Business Studies at the age of 41. An open and charismatic leader who speaks fluent English, he is not only highly respected in the international banking and regulatory community but also as a talented photographer and painter.

Zhou Xiaochuan, Governor of the People's Bank of China, is another financial leader who demonstrated his abilities early. After completing his engineering PhD at Tsinghua University, he became part of the young reformers' group around Zhu Rongji, working on international trade, domestic finance and structural reform. A person of considerable personal charm and diplomatic skill, Zhou communicates easily in central banking halls from Basel to Washington. Accomplished in Chinese and Western classical music, with an interest in Broadway musicals and their impact on China, he is also an avid tennis and badminton player.

Such technocrats are comfortable with the world as well as with subjects from art to literature. I once invited a senior official in Beijing to watch the Royal Ballet from Covent Garden. As I handed her a chocolate, she smiled and reminisced that the first time she ever tasted chocolate was when, as a child, her parents took her to see Markova dance in 1957. Both were special treats. Parts of the world are a lot more connected than many realize, even if in this case it is at an elite level. China's technocratic elite, with formal or informal foreign education, is a major part of making reform and opening up successful.

Chapter 7

Wen's *Xun* and Wenzhou Theatre

The fix is in. Beijing will fix it first in Wenzhou and then in the rest of China.

Michael Taylor, *Coldwater Economics,* October 2011

Complexity is the hallmark of Chinese problems. To see how reform is handled administratively, politically and publicly, Wenzhou provides an extensive case study, illustrating how China actually works.

A few days in October 2011 brought together the key people to solve China's then most pressing problem. Three things were at risk: China's banking system, private sector and economy. By isolating the individual elements, government could weave a solution, combining long-term reform with pragmatic dealmaking and without any immediate bailout. The poster child for bad borrowing and lending, Wang Xiaodong, a local entrepreneur, was back in town. So too was the premier of China. While the rest of the country took time off for the National Day holidays, Wang and Premier Wen Jiabao, along with his entourage of some 30 senior officials, including the central bank governor and finance minister, were hard at work in the Zhejiang coastal city of Wenzhou.

This was a classic high officials' inspection tour, a *xun*, of which Mencius had written over 2,000 years before and Deng Xiaoping had copied in 1992. Their presence was part policy, part drama, signifying the fix was in. Beijing had worked out solutions to the problems caused largely by the excesses of the 2009–2010 stimulus and unfinished reform of China's command economy. Now was time for action. That was the message. What followed was Chinese government theatre at its finest.

Underground Finance

The problems were very real. Banks had lent unknown quantities of stimulus money to, among others, government officials and other favoured borrowers, who then lent it on to the informal or underground capital market at interest rates of 20% or more. Increasingly the privileged borrowers did not get their money back from their loans, and therefore, nor did the banks. Often, new loans were made to cover up initial losses. A pyramid of debt was built, which eventually collapsed.

Much of the money had gone to develop property. When property became oversupplied, homes were left unsold and cash-starved developers had to borrow at even higher rates to survive, often merely delaying the day of reckoning. Slick informal financiers looked for funds at ever higher rates to keep businesses afloat, usually a vain hope, but for some a lucrative game of pass the parcel until the music stopped, as it did in Wenzhou. I knew Malaysia's informal capital market and had looked into it in China, so was familiar with its workings.

One day in 2010, someone I had met while researching attractive private equity investments in rural Jiangsu, called my office in Shanghai, said he was in town and asked to meet. No longer was he introducing interesting rural projects, he had moved on. Like a man on a mission, he launched into the benefits of informal capital market lending, blind to the absurdity of what he was offering. He assured me that any lender could get annual returns of 30%, even 40% in some cases. That was for sure. I recognized the familiar patter of the hot-idea salesman whose cousins I knew from Malaysia to Taiwan, Philippines to Indonesia. As a way to decline politely, I enquired about the sustainability of the scheme, as no legitimate business could survive paying such high interest for long. He quickly assured me that there was no problem, everything was taken care of.

His scheme worked "perfectly". To ensure all permissions came automatically for any projects funded by the loans, officials in each level of the local government were allotted some of the funds, he explained, as smoothly as an insurance salesman describing how a policy worked. The largest share was given to the person at the top. This was the clincher. The local government, or at least its officials, would take care of everything, having been cut in. They would clear any problems with a bit of influence, threats or money. He believed this was a flawless scheme: watertight. That was how it worked in theory and in practice, until it didn't. He had overlooked the market, as do many neophytes in business.

In Wenzhou the sums involved were truly eye-popping. They were not the invention of China sceptics, they were very real. Local entrepreneur Wang Xiaodong himself was estimated to owe banks Rmb 1.2 billion ($190 million). A further 200 delinquent borrowers supposedly had skipped town to avoid creditors. Wenzhou, famed throughout China for its post-1978 private entrepreneurs, many of whom received their start in business with funding from the unregulated informal capital market, was awash with debt, and this was highly priced debt at that, averaging 20% a year. Some was even at 30% or 40% on an annualized basis when distressed borrowers became really desperate. To understand how this all came about, it is necessary to go back to October 2008 when the global financial crisis hit.

Uncovering Reality

Faced with a global financial collapse that threatened to bring down the economy, China outlined in early October 2008 plans to keep at bay the contagion then engulfing the world. While a clear success, the government's stimulus doubled financial credit in 2009, an enormous expansion. Beijing had averted an immediate crisis but had not achieved the desired economic soft landing. How could it avoid a hard landing?

First, the central government had to understand the problem's full extent and nature. Everyone knew the root causes. Local governments only received 50% of the nation's taxes and revenues but were responsible for 70% of spending. The fiscal gap could not be made good by borrowing from banks, which was formally prohibited, or by issuing municipal bonds. The creative solution was to set up local government financing vehicles to which banks could lend, especially local banks that are often partially local government-owned. These then funded projects, usually in infrastructure and housing, which involved the sale of government-owned land. Land sales were ramped up to average about 25% of all local government income, sometimes up to 40%–50% or more: unsustainable levels given the size of residential property demand, which was large but not that large.

Officials in Beijing knew all this. The leaders invariably had made their careers in the provinces: President Hu Jintao in Gansu, Guizhou and Tibet, Premier Wen Jiabao in Gansu for almost two decades. They knew the dodges as well as vices that distorted local economies and hid reality. Beijing's financial regulators and policymakers in 2008 had been the engineers of bank reform in the early 1990s and the foot soldiers in the financial cleanup that followed. Therefore Beijing knew the nature of local government finances, methods and practices as well as the central role residential property played in the economy: what was needed were the details. How large was informal lending, how big a threat was it for the banks and how to resolve it?

Since late 2008, Beijing's senior financial officials and bankers had been trying to figure out the impact of the global crisis. Even before the stimulus money reached the provinces, they travelled to where they knew senior officials whom they trusted, often because their relationships went back several decades: see Chapter 10. Such assessments became more formal and widespread by mid–2009. These continued for another two years, studying problems on the ground, often only getting the picture after dragging details out of reluctant local officials and guessing at the true state of affairs.

Problems were the result of many complex, intertwined factors: some universal, others unique to China. These made clear-cut analysis and instant policy solutions very difficult, if not impossible, due to China's economic history, unfinished reform and stage of development, especially its financial development. Sometimes there was a lack of it or at best only partial reform since the days of the command economy when banks were cashiers for the government and managing risk was not the job of bankers. Although banking system reforms had been introduced in the 2000s, they could only be tested by experience, and Wenzhou made clear that China still had much to learn.

Property

Central to rapid economic growth and any problems linked with it has been China's acute housing shortage. This made residential property China's single largest industry: see Chapter 13. In 1990, China's average urban living space was barely one quarter of that in Northeast Asia, a mere six square metres per person. It still lagged behind by a good one third in 2016 at about 24 square metres: in Western Europe it was about 45, in the US close to 60. Therefore the 2009–2011 boom began logically enough in response to China's housing shortage.

Space was a political issue within the Chinese context: unspoken but very real. A scorching thirst for more living space fed frantic demand for everything from steel to cement, timber to white goods. Much infrastructure was needed to support associated urbanization, while rising incomes meant more demand for cars and public transport. Water, sanitation, waste treatment, drainage, roads, rail and power all had to catch up with the new living space. Construction, not surprisingly, became about 25% of China's GDP, the major economic driver.

Like any bonanza, property attracted fortune hunters and rent-seekers. The new industry grew largely after late-1990s reform ended state responsibility for housing. For the first time since 1949, families could buy their own homes. Whereas residential construction was not a high state priority before housing reform, afterwards, more and better living space became households' top priority. Suddenly there was a gold rush to build for potentially half a billion urban dwellers. The industry's infancy meant that developers were very inexperienced. Few had lived through a full property cycle. None had two decades in property development. Many mistakes were made but strong pent-up demand often bailed out developers. The trend was their friend in the new El Dorado, until it wasn't.

All finally came unstuck in late 2007. For that is when the longest and largest boom gave way to bust: nothing to do with the 2008 global financial crisis, it should be said. Tantalizingly high profits dazzled developers until finally the market collapsed as unaffordable property prices cut demand just when excess supply came onto the market. Under the weight of oversupply, the stock of unsold homes soared: prices plummeted 20%–30% to clear the surplus. Developers new to real markets were bound to come unstuck, especially those in the least developed new markets in smaller towns. Before and after the global financial crisis the downturn lasted only about 15–18 months, shorter than many feared.

Like manna from heaven, the unexpected stimulus funds, together with still large pent-up demand, sparked a new housing cycle in mid-2009. Demand was strong. Buyers for the first time across all China routinely used mortgages, adding demand that previously lay untapped, particularly inland. Everyone was in new territory. Neither developers nor buyers had been here before; the scale and apparent opportunities were unprecedented. It looked like a sure bet: time to return to the property races with even more borrowed funds. Of course, there is no such thing as a sure bet. Imagined profits eventually turned to painful losses: a mirage evaporated.

Wenzhou's entrepreneurs were among the first to appreciate the property sector's potential in the 1990s. As Mark O'Neill recorded in the *South China Morning Post*, bus tours took adventurous Wenzhou property investors to other cities looking for the next new market, first along the coast where Shanghai became *passé* by the early 2000s, then inland before finding the final frontier in western China, ending up in Ordos, Inner Mongolia, the most ghostly city of all. The post-2001 WTO-entry export boom generated large cash flows for many to invest, until the 2008 crisis.

Then most struggled frantically and some Wenzhou manufacturers were lured onto property's rocks by the siren call of apparently easy annual financial returns of 30% plus. Property development made crisis-hit manufacturing look pitiful and frequently pointless. Often two decades of painfully accumulated wealth in manufacturing was pledged to lenders, banks and the informal market alike, only to see property hit the skids as demand failed to keep up with recently over-leveraged supply in 2011, when the apartments and houses funded by the easy money of 2009 and 2010 flooded the market. Most developers tried to hang on by postponing sales; the weakest, usually the least experienced, went to the wall, making life difficult for even well-managed survivors.

The Fix and the Theatre

Beijing therefore knew that a fiscal gap and another property roller coaster were the root causes of the problems from the stimulus, both in China in general, and in Wenzhou in particular. However, officials also knew the economy still had many strengths: see Chapter 12. With these, China could get through the crisis, if given enough time. So they acted.

The Wenzhou visit signaled the end of stimulus. Handling its consequences now began. To announce this, obliquely, but in language that everyone understood, Beijing chose Wenzhou as its stage, the city at the epicentre of the lending boom-and-bust shock in the informal capital market. In the next wave of economic reform, it showed what China had to fix to haul itself out of dependence on state-led growth. Well-funded private sector companies were needed. They in turn required banks disciplined by market forces rather than administrative fiat, and a lending culture without the distortions that had bedeviled China, Wenzhou included.

By the time Premier Wen departed Wenzhou, the problems' details were confirmed and action under way. As Michael Taylor put it in early October 2011, "the fix is in". Having witnessed first-hand China's fiscal and financial crises of the early 1990s as Morgan Stanley's Asian economist, he could see what was happening. Indeed the fix was in, both locally and nationally, understood by those who could follow Chinese political theatre. Wang Xiaodong had provided the central government with a full list of lenders and borrowers that named names: dramatic and informative. At the top were those local officials who for a time had grown fat on borrowing heavily from banks in order to lend to the informal capital market, where 5% stimulus bank money could be lent out at 20% or more.

Wang's list, along with other investigations, gave Wen and his officials a sense of the magnitude and precise nature of Wenzhou's problems so that policy initiatives could be readied: policies that reformers were only too keen to unveil anyway. Wang Xiaodong, with savvy that Wall Street could only admire, was reported to have negotiated a 30% haircut from the banks, who reduced the debt so as to get something back, making good on all his debts.

The central message after the visit was that Beijing was on the case, action would be forthcoming. Stability, that much long-cherished virtue and goal, would be restored with the help of state-controlled media and even non-state media. Propaganda is an ancient craft in China. This was all very precisely choreographed for maximum effect. Nothing was left to chance. First the unannounced headline-capturing grand official visit, the imperial *xun*, then the daily explanation through the drip, drip of detail, all made for October holiday viewing, when families get together and are likely to discuss such events. Something was going on, but exactly what was not immediately clear. It was a case of stay tuned: classic Chinese communication strategy in any campaign.

After the official announcement of Wen's visit, the respected *Caixin*, a regular non-party outlet for financial reformers' ideas, broke the details about Wang to put some flesh on the bones. Then the *Global Times*, normally a hard-line nationalist tabloid and, in a diplomat's words, Beijing's attack dog or rottweiler, weighed in with its analysis of Wenzhou's problems. The solutions it prescribed were music to reformers' ears. It advocated the need for greater interest rate liberalization and more lending to the private sector, especially to smaller companies.

The point was to make the problem appear manageable, easier to grasp and less alarming. This was all about Wenzhou, which was not as large as Beijing, Shanghai or even the provincial capital of Hangzhou. However it represented something much larger than all three combined: China's private sector and its future: see Chapter 12. For it was announced that banking licenses would be given to some private groups. In Wenzhou, the capital of China's private sector, this was very welcome as it finally gave private enterprise legitimacy, helping remove the stigma that had attached to it since 1949.

National Application and Underlying Principles

By working out how to fix Wenzhou for the long-term as well as in the short-term, Beijing demonstrated it knew how to handle the rest of China. Show the fix and intent first in Wenzhou, then fix the rest of the country. Reform was to be given a shot in the arm, even if much of it was done after Wen retired. The fourth generation of leaders together with the fifth built the bridge that led directly to the 18th Congress and reform's landmark Third and Fourth Plenums in 2013 and 2014 respectively. These enshrined in the party's canon the "decisiveness of markets" and the rule of law, two of the key finishing touches to economic reform.

Beijing also showed its flexibility in finding solutions, another traditional virtue. Forging consensus to carry agreement among numerous competing constituencies is no small achievement. Contrast this with the EU over the euro or refugees, and the US with the Middle East or trade, particularly as China's population is almost treble that of the EU's and quadruple that of the US. Solutions to thorny problems were hammered out. Beijing allocated losses and punishments among the various parties, be they individuals, companies (state or private) and government (local, provincial or national), showing that China is not constrained by ideology or dogma: very pragmatic.

All this, though, did not mean that everything was plain sailing after October 2011, either for the economy or financial markets. Sentiment was constantly buffeted. In many ways, the hard part had only just begun. The economy's stimulus teat had to be withdrawn just as new property supply surged, fuelled by stimulus-engorged banks and the stock market, causing home prices to plummet. Some developers went bust, but these were the aftershocks that could be managed.

Three messages emerged from the Wenzhou *xun*: the stimulus problems were being addressed, the private sector would have a greater role and the government could cope. The end game was on, supported by China's misunderstood strengths and realities. Yet China sceptics still maintained in late 2011 that reform was dead and that the "fragile" system would collapse, notwithstanding the evidence from Wenzhou that action was forthcoming. Their doubts would not go away.

Realities, Perceptions and Timing

The realities of China's economy often are not what they seem. In the good times, they lead the consensus to be overconfident. In bad times, they can appear to spell disaster. As far as Western perceptions of the world outlook were concerned, there were no worse times since 1945 than immediately after the 2008 financial crisis for everything, everywhere. This highly negative view was the prism through which the West saw China's adjustment to the crisis, missing a great deal of positive progress China was making.

Foreign expectations of overnight reform in China were and remain unrealistic. Central planning and administrative measures cannot be replaced immediately, far from it. Reform in one area often has negative implications for others: the Rubik's Cube effect. Change is a very complex and lengthy process; mistakes are made. The danger from mistakes is that they could undermine support for further reform. Therefore sequencing correctly the many stages of reform must be considered very carefully. Every Chinese politician and bureaucrat knows the dangers, both to China and to their own careers. None want to get ahead of what is possible. None want to be another Wang Anshi, the Song prime minister who took on the system some 900 years ago and tried to change it. Even though this was done with the emperor's blessing, Wang was brought down by conservative vested interests: see Chapter 1.

However, it is equally dangerous to be too slow, as the Empress Dowager Cixi found when she belatedly opted for reform but failed to prevent the Qing Dynasty collapsing in 1911. She had resisted reform for decades, including by her nephew whom she removed from the throne in 1898, after his 100 Days of Reform met similar conservative opposition at court. Chief policy advisor Kang Youwei fled China while most of the other reformist advisors, the Six Gentlemen, were executed. No one today wants to be a latter-day Gentleman. Every official knows the importance of timing and judging what is practical and, most crucially, when to implement policy. That is the reality of dealing with change. In policy implementation, timing is all.

As in many countries, China can get mired in a system that can be its own worst enemy. To bring about real change, leaders then have to go outside or reshape the existing system to ensure change continues. Deng Xiaoping in 1992 and Xi Jinping since 2012 illustrate this.

Reform and Change

Deng China's reform and opening up began in 1978, symbolized by rural Shenzhen becoming within four decades almost double the size of Hong Kong and a world innovation centre, notably in telecommunications and transport. Deng Xiaoping, the leading pioneer of reform and champion of Shenzhen, still features on city billboards.

Xi Jinping Reform's second major date was the 2017 19th Congress when Xi Jinping revitalized and expanded it, setting new domestic development goals out to 2050 to make China an "advanced society". Xi, backed by what could be the world's largest economy by 2025, has taken China to centre stage in world affairs, playing leading roles in the Paris climate change accord, above, and defending freer multilateral trade at Davos. Xi has termed this a New Era, as indeed it is, not just in China but in an increasingly disrupted world.

Chapter 8

Battling Within the Party for Change

Xi Jinping doesn't hold his cards close to his chest. He has them tattooed to the inside of his palms.

Western diplomat, 2013.

Standing apart from the teeming crowd of often ragged travellers at central China's main railway junction, a group of largely older men in their tailored Mao suits gathered alone. In this quieter part of Wuchang Station, they must have looked like a welcoming party for some passing senior official. In fact, they were. However the visit was far from routine. Unknowingly, this small group in southern central China was about to become a part of history on that winter's day in January 1992.

The provincial leaders waited patiently for the special train from Beijing to draw in to Wuhan, the capital of Hubei, which was the first stop on a journey that was to help change modern China. Time was short. After the brief pleasantries, the senior "official" from Beijing launched quickly into his thoughts: ideas he would repeat continuously for the next couple of weeks as he sought to change history's course by attempting to secure for China the "Wealth and Power", dignity and recognition it had sought unsuccessfully since 1840. This would transform China's economy.

There is no published official account of those snatched minutes with Hubei's party secretary and governor, but it seems likely that as words flowed, the 20 or so people crowded closer round the visitor. This was a cold winter's morning, but more important was the fact that the message clearly did not have the approval of Premier Li Peng, let alone the revolutionary elders above him who still had ultimate power in China. Instinctively, the greeting party could tell this was no ordinary visit, nor exactly where it might be heading. As they heard the official speak, some could have been forgiven for thinking they were part of a plot, a budding insurrection against China's conservative economic leaders.

The octogenarian's words were incendiary, scornful and direct in equal measure. Whoever is against reform must leave office, he declared bluntly, taking deliberate aim at those stifling China's economy and risking its future; "markets are not capitalist or socialist", he avowed, sounding like a stern economics professor chiding a dim party ideologue; and there are "more documents than hairs on a cow", he thundered, attacking bureaucracy and its endless, useless meetings, as told in Ezra Vogel's definitive account. There was more in a similar vein from the man who had famously said, "If you don't have anything to say, keep your mouth shut … the purpose of meetings is to solve problems." Productive meetings, not mass meetings, were to decide policy henceforth. They were to be practical problem-solving occasions, not propaganda or political opportunities.

There was a sense of urgency rather than one of intrigue at Wuchang station. Time was running out for both China and the party, not to mention for the senior official himself. In 20 minutes he was gone, off to the next stop on his whistle-stop tour, more like a barnstorming American politician than a largely retired revolutionary going on a family holiday. He had the energy of a man half his age. People's gaze rarely left the animated figure of the 87-year-old, drawn in by the intensity of his words, all the more powerful because they came from such a small frame. He was acting more like the covert underground operative that he had been when dodging Chiang Kai-shek's killer squads supplied by Shanghai's deadly triad, Green Gang, in the late 1920s and 1930s than the Paramount Leader he was called.

His real plans were known to only a very few: not even to the security forces that protect China's leaders. The occupant of a special train that slipped out of Beijing on January 17, 1992, with his true purpose unannounced and undetected, was supposedly China's most powerful man — Deng Xiaoping.

Deng Xiaoping's Last Guerrilla Campaign: By Stealth

Contrary to the image of a strong man at the helm, we see how very limited the position of China's most powerful man really is. It was the limitation that forced Deng to wage the last guerrilla campaign of his life, and this was different from Xi Jinping's approach in the details but shared the same strategy of stealth as a primary weapon to manage change.

Deng staked all his prestige on shifting economic policy in one final attempt to revive the post-Cultural Revolution 1978 reform and opening up which had run out of steam. Conservatives, strengthened by the events of June 1989, were dead set, for the time being at least, against further radical economic reform. This is what led Deng to board the train, heading south in great secrecy, with the connivance of the People's Liberation Army (PLA) police, as Harvard's Vogel recorded in *Deng Xiaoping and the Transformation of China.*

The immediate trigger for Deng's journey was the 8th Plenum in November 1991. This had left the economic conservatives firmly in control of the party and government. Deng Liqun, the party's former propaganda head and arch-opponent of reform, had warned in the *People's Daily* against "peaceful evolution", which was code for an end to communism as the conservatives knew it. He reflected the winning side at the Plenum. Deng Xiaoping's one-man two-year campaign against economic conservatism had failed. Unable even to get his thoughts into China's leading paper, the *People's Daily*, Deng had left the capital for a time in early 1990 for Shanghai that was more open to reform ideas. There, under an alias, he had at least managed to get published in the *Liberation Daily*, but Beijing's *People's Daily* counter-attacked directly. Deng was shut out of power and policymaking, so he had to adopt another strategy.

With meticulous attention to detail, Deng organized the greatest guerrilla campaign of his life. This time it was on the economic battlefield, where everything from finance to foreign trade and investment needed fundamental reform. Under the cover of a family holiday in southern China, Deng took 17 of his family, children and grandchildren included, to the relative warmth of the south, away from the northern winter's biting cold. Many leaders did this: it was not unusual, so aroused no suspicion. Neither Premier Li Peng nor General Secretary Jiang Zemin had any idea of what was happening. They were left in the dark.

To preserve the element of surprise, arrangements were left until the last minute, down to providing Deng a spittoon. A hastily arranged itinerary drew up a series of meetings and visits for an 11-day Inspection Tour of Guangdong. The southern province had been the first testing ground of economic reform, endorsed by Deng himself in the late 1970s and reaffirmed by his last visit there in 1984. Deng not only wanted to gather information in his own *yanjiu* but, more importantly, to broadcast his views to a responsive audience that was already seeing the benefits of economic reform.

Provincial politicians were generally more fertile ground for new ideas. Often, with scant resources, they had to deal directly with problems arising from policy: Beijing merely had to defend or change it. Those who had benefited from the first wave of reform were natural allies. Deng hoped he could use them to pressure Beijing into accelerating reform, in effect to do a major U-turn. There was no guarantee the strategy would work. Similar utterances had been made for two years, to no avail. So, after the seemingly conclusive 8th Plenum in November 1991, Deng felt he had no alternative but to make one last attempt.

What came to be called the *Nanxun*, the Southern Tour, named after the old imperial practice of rulers visiting the provinces to discover what was happening on the ground, was part political strategy and part symbolism. The symbols were clear: places spoke louder than words. The "holiday" took Deng and his family to places steeped in history for communist veterans and younger party members alike, even if they were not the normal destinations for warmth-seeking northern holidaymakers in the depth of winter.

Wuhan was the cradle of the 1911 revolution that overthrew the last imperial dynasty, the Qing. Changsha, the next stop, was the capital of Mao Zedong's home province of Hunan. Mao and Deng were different personalities in many ways but each managed to tolerate and even appreciate the other's differences for most of their lives. Mao saw Deng's administrative and political capabilities while Deng appreciated Mao's overall leadership qualities that had secured the party's military victory in 1949. Only in the Cultural Revolution, the "Eleven Years" from 1966 to 1976, did they fall out badly. However they were reconciled before Mao's death in 1976 when Mao placed Deng as vice chairman of the Central Military Commission and chief of staff, putting Deng at the head of both the second generation of leaders and the government. However, he could not put Deng in charge of the party: Deng's arch-enemies the radicals, led by the Gang of Four, would not have worn that.

The principal destination on the 1992 Southern Tour was Guangdong, where Deng had previously blessed the two leading Special Economic Zones of Shenzhen and Zhuhai that pioneered the first wave of reform. More symbols were all around, providing powerful reminders from history or opportunities to reflect on important ideas. As Deng crossed the Pearl River Delta he passed the old Qing customs house, a remnant of China's period of weakness and "humiliation". "Those who are backward are beaten.... We've been poor for thousands of years but we won't be poor again. If we don't emphasize science, technology and education we will be beaten again," Deng declared to the officials in the boat.

Yingtian in neighbouring Jiangxi province, the next stop on the *Nanxun*, was a reminder of 1931 after Deng fled Shanghai to fight in its remote mountains, helping secure the Jiangxi Soviet. This was the party's last remaining major base after its rout by Chiang Kai-shek's Kuomintang (KMT) forces. Holding Jiangxi enabled it to regroup, before beginning 1934's Long March that launched its eventual victory 15 years later over the KMT. It also prompted more recent memories: after being ousted during the Cultural Revolution, Deng worked there from 1969–1973 in a tractor factory.

The final stop was Shanghai, China's economic heart until 1949. Variously dubbed the Manhattan of Asia and the Wall Street of Asia, it had been famous worldwide for the foreign facade of the Bund, along which stretched the offices of banks, insurance companies, shipping lines, telegraph agencies, trading houses and manufacturers, local and foreign alike. Japanese shipping lines, French banks and the headquarters and original home of the Hong Kong and Shanghai Banking Corporation (HSBC) were prominent, flanked by countless other enterprises that packed its riverfront. After 1949, Shanghai was seen as a pariah, the former home of capitalists and foreigners. Yet local officials still harboured hopes it could recapture its former glory of the 1920s and 1930s. Development of the largely empty swamps and farmland of Pudong, which Deng championed, was seen as the symbol of Shanghai's renaissance in the early 1990s, but Beijing blocked its way.

The Bund had what Shanghainese still relate today with pride — *yangqi*, foreign air. The style was unrelentingly modern and cosmopolitan, reflecting global, though mainly Western, architectural tastes. These ranged from parts bearing more than a passing resemblance to England's great northwestern port of Liverpool, which dominated trans-Atlantic shipping for two centuries, to Art Deco architecture from New York, then the very symbol of modernity. The Bund's grand sweep along the western banks of the Huangpu River, close to the Yangzi's mouth, was the equal of any waterfront in the world during the 1930s. Shanghai had become one of the great cosmopolitan cities, with everything from textiles to finance and shipping linking it to the rest of the world. Deng wanted to restore those connections while reviving the technical skills and systems that had made them possible. If China were to become successful globally it would again have to build an international financial and trade centre. That centre would be Shanghai.

Drawing on all his knowledge of how China, the party and society worked, as well as calling in old favours and appealing to shared hopes or fears, Deng launched his last campaign. Like good politicians anywhere, Deng kept his messages simple and repeated them frequently. Everywhere he went on his Southern Tour he urged people to continue reform and opening up as mandated in 1978. He was not breaking new ground, merely reminding people of the party's previously agreed mandate which had not been fulfilled.

Deng tackled head-on the charge that markets were capitalist by reiterating that planning is not the same as socialism and markets are not the same as capitalism. There could be planning under capitalism and markets under socialism, he argued. The important thing for Deng was that socialism "liberated productive forces" as "its ultimate goal is to achieve common prosperity": socialism is not poverty was the message. "Development is the only hard truth. It does not matter if policies are labeled socialist or capitalist as long as they foster development," Deng said, very pragmatically.

Deng demanded China catch up with the small dragons of Singapore, Hong Kong, South Korea and Taiwan within 20 years. Singapore was a model, doing "things strictly": with approved echoes of China's Legalism from over 2,000 years before. He took great heart from Singapore and Hong Kong being Chinese-dominant societies, concluding that "we should manage things even better", which in terms of GDP growth China has done. Deng also urged people to experiment: "Do not fear making mistakes. Just make sure that when they are made they are corrected." Mencius would have approved: again very pragmatic. These few simple messages he repeated throughout his visit. Words, though, were not enough if Deng was excluded from the national media.

Guangdong provided a major strategic media opportunity for Deng. It was next door to Hong Kong. Inevitably the local media there would pick up news of Deng's Guangdong tour and its strong reform message. This would then find its way back into China. Deng was not the first or the last Chinese politician to use this media route. Despite initial reticence by the mainland press in Hong Kong, the non-mainland owned *Mingbao* ran its first story on Deng's visit to Shenzhen and his calls for accelerated reform only four days after Deng left Wuchang Station.

Next day, Hong Kong television stations picked up the news: just as Deng wanted. Chinese on the other side of the border watched these broadcasts whose message spread like Mao's proverbial prairie fire. By the time Deng reached Shenzhen, his lone accompanying photographer was joined by another 50 or 60 others, all snapping and recording Deng. That did not mean that China's official media picked up the news immediately: far from it. China Central Television reported Deng Xiaoping and President Yang Shangkun arriving in Shanghai without mentioning the Southern Tour or calls for greater reform. If Deng's guerrilla campaign had relied only on publicity it would have failed: Beijing conservatives had the media sewn up.

However they had no response when Deng played hard-ball politics in Zhuhai. This was bare-knuckle combat, no more factory visits exhorting people with happy faces to accelerate reform. Instead, Deng attended a specially arranged "military planning" meeting in Zhuhai. Vogel, who was the first to detail this, records that Qiao Shi took the chair, one of the six members of the Politburo's Standing Committee (PBSC) and the person directly responsible for China's domestic security. Also present were two vice-chairmen of the Central Military Commission (CMC) and head of the PLA's Political Work Department. All were involved at the highest levels with China's security. All agreed with Deng about accelerating reform. This formidable quintet gave opponents a strong idea of others who could be mobilized, if necessary.

This was a direct shot across the bows of Jiang Zemin. Deng had already made plain that if Jiang did not back reform fully, he would support others for top party positions. Qiao Shi would have been a very plausible candidate for either the CMC chairmanship or China's presidency, two posts Jiang hoped to obtain in 1993 so as to secure his primacy at the head of the third generation, consolidating his grip on power. Jiang may have owed his position to Deng in the first place, but for the two previous years Deng had expressed disquiet about reform's slow pace.

Jiang could not take Deng's support for granted. Deng's assertion in Wuchang Station that whoever is against reform must leave office was designed to make Jiang feel more than a little uncomfortable. Before long, word reached Jiang, who quickly changed his tune, saying that

China should accelerate reform, revive opening up and cut out interminable and unproductive meetings. Outside normal protocol, Jiang phoned Deng in Shanghai to give his Spring Festival greetings. However Jiang knew that words alone would count for nothing unless action followed to prove intent: that is the Chinese belief and expectation, actions count much more than words.

Matters then moved on apace. On March 10, the Politburo under Jiang endorsed a summary of Deng's main Southern Tour ideas, especially on the need for more reform and opening up, even though as recently as February 23 the *Nanxun* itself was not even mentioned when the *People's Daily* ran an editorial entitled *Be Bolder in Reform.* More important, this full Politburo meeting chose reform as the main theme for the upcoming 14th Congress. Xinhua, the New China News Agency, announced this on March 11, and finally, the *People's Daily* ended its silent opposition to Deng's ideas by reporting the same on March 13. In less than two months, Deng's final guerrilla campaign had won a swift victory. Two years in the political wilderness, fighting his one-man battle, had ended.

Results

Results started to flow almost immediately. At the March National People's Congress (NPC), China's legislature, both military and academic delegates attacked leftism (economic conservatism). Military commanders of China's seven military regions visited Shenzhen and Zhuhai that spring, so did 57 generals. In May, five cities along the Yangzi opened up to foreign trade, receiving the same privileges as existing special economic zones. So did nine border cities and 30 prefecture cities. Shanghai was pronounced the economic dragon head of the Yangzi. This was all happening at dizzying speed.

To underline the total shift in official thinking, Jiang Zemin addressed the graduate class of the Central Party School, which educates the party's and hence China's future leaders. His subject was "Deeply Understand and Implement Comrade Deng Xiaoping's Important Spirit, Make Economic Construction, Reform and Opening

Go Faster and Better". This was the equivalent of a US president addressing West Point on a major change in military policy, though without a snappy title like "Pivot to Asia".

Jiang said GDP growth should be raised to 9%–10%, well above the 6% five-year plan target conservative Li Peng had announced in March. China should look overseas for ideas and not bother discussing whether they were capitalist or socialist. Jiang boldly referred to this as a "socialist market economy", in contrast to leading economic conservative Chen Yun who talked of a "planned socialist market economy". When Jiang asked Deng if he liked his Party School speech, Deng replied, "Actually, Shenzhen has a socialist market economy." There was no need to talk any more about central planning.

The 1980s had increasingly revealed the limitations of earlier reform and its slowing pace, as Edward Steinfeld described in his 1998 book *Forging Reform in China* and subsequently *Playing Our Game*. Bolting on 1978's Four Modernizations to the old system did not work. Fundamentally new structures and principles were needed. With a new "reform and opening up" script, Jiang laid out four ideas at October's 14th Congress. There was no need to question any more if something was capitalist or socialist; while retaining state ownership as the main form, State-owned Enterprises (SOEs) could become more independent, with experiments done in shareholding structures; markets should be expanded beyond agriculture to all main sectors, including capital, technology, information and housing; and science and technology were now a "primary" productive force. Economic reform was to accelerate.

Like any well-managed political convention, the star arrived at the end, but only after a long build-up to his entrance. Deng was praised by Jiang Zemin for all his contributions and the policies he advocated. The party veteran, and now its indisputably most powerful man, was 88 years old, an auspicious number for Chinese. This would most probably be Deng's last party congress, his grand finale. No more speeches, just some very symbolic moments of continuity as he handed over power to the younger third generation before fading into the background.

The frail Deng entered the 14th Congress in the Great Hall of the People to a hero's welcome. He immediately went over to Jiang Zemin to signify he was the new leader, at the head of the third generation, endorsed by the Paramount Leader of the second. Deng stood by Jiang for 20 minutes as bulbs flashed, film cameras rolled and the message went out to over one billion people. Jiang was the "nucleus" of the third generation. This was Deng's version of Mao signaling he had handed over power to Hua Guofeng by saying that "with you in charge my heart is at ease". Like Mao before him, Deng was ensuring the succession was in place before he died. Only, his more thorough and long-term succession plan turned out to be far more durable than Mao's, enabling lengthy economic reform to continue rather than be jettisoned by factional or ideological rivalries. Very lengthy political peace was needed if the decades-long reform of China's economy was to succeed.

Deng not only blessed Jiang's primacy but also made it easier for the third generation to establish its authority by persuading other party elders to retire. There were no more lifetime appointments. The Central Advisory Council of elders was abolished, removing the elders' constant shadow over affairs. Deng also shaped the future through appointments and positions. First he helped change the Politburo's composition in June 1992, a key turning point. While retaining reform-minded Foreign Minister Qiao Shi and Foreign Trade Minister Li Lanqing, the party reversed inland provincial domination of the Standing Committee by selecting five new members, all from the reform-minded coast. Deng's ideas and men replaced conservative economic rule.

The most important appointment for economic policy and financial transformation was ex-Shanghai Mayor Zhu Rongji, who came to Beijing in 1991. Zhu was mayor when Shanghai gave Deng a base from which to spread reform ideas, providing a platform through its *Liberation Daily*. In Beijing, Zhu steadily moved up the ladder, first overseeing the economy then becoming vice premier with specific responsibility for the economy. After taming rabid inflation and resolving near-crippling triangular debt, Zhu achieved an economic soft landing, avoiding a repeat of the 1988–1989 hard landing that many feared. At 1997's 15th Congress, Deng's point man on the economy became premier, a crucial appointment for reform.

Earlier, looking ahead to the political transition in a decade's time, the 14th Congress under Deng's influence addressed selecting the fourth generation leadership. Although not directly a Deng appointee, its youngest Politburo member, Hu Jintao, emerged ahead of his peers to take over when Jiang Zemin retired in 2002. Other appointments enshrined the principle of favouring experts over ideologues with only red credentials, as had been practised after the mid-1960s. This enabled technocrats to rise up the ranks to handle the system's problems.

All this extended Deng's influence for another 20 years. Crucially, Deng broke the cycle of political instability that had gripped China. The next two leaders were identified, setting the precedent for subsequent power transitions. The turbulent and often violent times of the 1950s, 1960s, 1970s and 1980s became a thing of the past. From this political basis, an era of economic pragmatism replaced the already waning ideological battles that had held China back since 1958.

The dramatic nine months in 1992, which ended three-and-a-half decades of turbulent argument, violence, politics and ideological division, show how China works in practice: rarely smoothly and with many challenges along the way, very unpredictable and complex. Not only did 1992 launch a new economic era, but Deng's battle for reform illustrates how decisions can be made or blocked, and how difficult this can be, even for supposedly China's most powerful man. Everyone has to develop a supportive consensus: dictation from above does not work.

Xi Jinping: In Full Sight

Whereas Deng had to launch a secret, swift guerrilla strike from Wuchang Station to ensure change continued, 20 years later, Xi Jinping had to pull off an inside job from within the heart of the party in full sight of everyone without setting off alarms, and over five years, not a few months. The same meticulous planning, strategy and stealth were required.

Unlike Deng who had nearly half a century in the party's top leadership, Xi had just half a decade. Deng's seniority and achievements gave him the right to speak out, even to dissent from Mao. Xi had no such record. He had kept his ideas largely to himself in the years spent climbing to the top. No one before had ever clambered from the lowest level of the party to its pinnacle: stealth was an unnoticed virtue. Once there, Xi showed he should not be underestimated, consolidating power far faster than most expected. Rapidly, he came to be described as the most powerful leader since Deng and then, erroneously, since Mao.

Xi created four new Leading Small Groups, covering just about everything that mattered: all reported directly to him. His next key focus was to get the party to mandate the concept of the rule of law as the bedrock of civic and commercial life. This was a critical achievement, not just for individuals' rights but for the economy. It is the Cultural Revolution generation's response to ensure that such arbitrary lawlessness never occurs again.

Approach

The party has its own procedures, timelines and rhythms to which it adheres closely. Gradualism and strict observance of process were a reaction to the chaos, violence and lawlessness of the late 1950s, 1960s and early 1970s. Acknowledging these guiding norms, Xi crafted a long-term strategy with everything carefully sequenced, recognizing that it would be two years before anything substantial could be done in detail and that some of the ideas would only be implemented fully during his second term after 2017. All this followed traditional precepts of governance.

Like Deng, Xi displayed a palpable sense of urgency in dealing with new challenges. Standing still was not an option. Xi and his inner circle approached reform very methodically. Patiently building a solid foundation brick by brick, they garnered broad support without alienating too many people at once. Vested interests, the equivalent of economic conservatives for Deng, may have seemed entrenched, but when subject to party discipline, reinforced by the 2013 Mass Line disciplinary campaign, they were impotent. A war of attrition was their only option, though that was risky as officials' future appointments and promotions were on the line.

Like any good political campaign, this one was prepared thoroughly and executed one step at a time. Xi did not rush: Confucius would have approved. After the initial announcement of the key points, he allowed each one to sink in to gain acceptance before moving on to the next. There was a clear sense of sequencing. Starting with the bare outlines of reform and corruption in late 2012, party members were slowly but steadily introduced to the details of what it would all mean. The whole picture only emerged one frame at a time, until the full unveiling of his long-term ideas at the 19th Congress in October 2017.

Xi's choice of Shenzhen to make his first public statements after becoming party general secretary in late 2012 was very deliberate. Shenzhen resonated with symbolism as China's most changed and innovative city which Deng had done so much to build. Xi wanted to evoke the memory of Deng and become China's paramount leader like him. For party members there was also the implicit reminder that it was Xi's father, Xi Zhongxun, who persuaded Deng to make Shenzhen a special economic zone. Deng suggested the term "zone" in reference to the military zone Xi's father helped establish in the northwest, where the party was able in 1935 to end safely its Long March: a subtle reminder of Xi Jinping's party lineage.

One year later, the 3rd Plenum gave an uncontested broad mandate for further change. In a system that places great importance on mandates, this was very significant. The party was then ready for the most important change of all, the introduction of the rule of law at the 4th Plenum in 2014. Without this, all the other changes could well fail. Xi avoided stirring up unnecessary resistance to reform by leaving the rule of law proposal until the end of a two-year campaign. First, Xi cleared his plans with the party elders: no longer a formal requirement but still a practical necessity. Then he gained the military's public admission it was under "civilian supervision", while the other major power centre, the Politburo Standing Committee (PBSC), similarly had to proclaim all its members should play an "exemplary role". Both subjected all members to party discipline.

This enabled Xi to pursue the mighty "tigers", putting the vested interests on the back foot whilst demonstrating the power he could wield. The party then spelled out what was expected in its 89 million members' behaviour and work practices: code words for corruption, efficiency and abuse of power. Two years of asserting his authority made Xi much stronger in the party than the consensus ever expected.

Xi took a different tack from Deng. Deng had no choice but to confront the economic conservatives head on. Xi's task, arguably, was even harder than Deng's. Deng had the element of surprise. Xi had to pull off his change in full daylight. Only he and his chief lieutenants know how radical his conception of change is, but it could be very radical in the long run from the viewpoint of conservatives and vested interests. If he intends to alter the power of state enterprises and even institutions while allowing the private sector's expansion and individuals to have better lives, which would be considered a rightward turn, Xi has to be seen turning to the left first, even if that is not his ultimate destination.

Therefore, Xi adopted a strategy of divide and rule. This he did by appealing to each on areas of common ground, such as anti-corruption for the left or by taking a firm stance on national security for the military. This is the carrot. The stick is the threat of party discipline for those such as foot-dragging bureaucrats who contemplate resistance, let alone rebellion. This way, Xi created a seemingly broad church ahead of the crucial 19th Congress in October 2017.

China under Mao was riddled with factionalism, which led to turbulence, violence and destruction. Politics without factions, at least nominally, is how Xi approaches ruling. He prefers a broad-based approach for as long as possible, hoping success breeds success, thereby ensuring support or at least stemming outright opposition. Reuters China political specialist Benjamin Lim captured the idea in a piece wittily entitled *Four Funerals and a Wedding*. He noted that in 2015, Xi went to four party members' funerals across the whole spectrum of opinion even though protocol did not require it. These ranged from Marxist ideologue Deng Liqun, who bitterly opposed reform and had been a fierce opponent of Xi's father since the 1950s, to Zheng Yanxin who was the first to be purged during the Anti-Rightist Movement in 1957. He also attended the funerals of Qiao Shi, the NPC chairman and former anti-corruption head, and Zhang Zhen, the former vice-chairman of the CMC: both represented important institutions.

The wedding of the title was his own. Xi had kept his personal life so private that when the first guest to a low-key dinner expressed surprise to find Peng Liyuan there, Xi had to explain that Peng was his wife, and his superior, the mayor of Fuzhou, was hosting dinner to celebrate their wedding. Nothing had been said in advance. One ambassador who met Xi several times before he became president said Xi was "very comfortable in his own skin": very self-confident. He seems to have the touch for 21st-century politics even while hiding it behind a veil of Confucian restraint.

Xi does not have so much a poker face as a completely smooth surface that occasionally ripples into a smile: most of the time, Xi gives no hint of what he is thinking. One foreign diplomat who met him several times noted that Xi does not play his cards close to his chest as commonly said; he "has them tattooed to the inside of his palms". He keeps his enemies guessing, catching them off-guard.

In political terms, Xi seems prepared to take risks, as Russell Moses observed. Although Xi gives little away, he has displayed a willingness to "think outside the box", as he urged one leading economist to do. This sometimes unorthodox approach, along with popular support to cut corruption and abuse of power, enabled Xi to gain and keep the upper hand. Taking on the tigers in the anti-corruption campaign by bringing down a former Politburo Standing Committee (PBSC) member and the leading military officer, were far from risk-free.

Xi struck very quickly to reorganize the all-powerful PBSC. In fact he moved so quickly that many, unused to such rapid and far-reaching change during the Hu–Wen decade, did not recognize it for what it was: a fundamental redrawing of power lines at the very top of the party. This streamlined how the party and hence government works, providing a 360-degree view to improve policy and implementation.

The party created four new Leading Small Groups: reform, security, internet security and informatization, and the party. They are not small in terms of power. Little of importance is not under the purview of at least one of the four groups — be it SOE reform, economic liberalization, domestic security, foreign policy, military affairs, cyber security, the internet or the party itself. With the general secretary heading each group, this gives Xi formal power that is unprecedented in China's last two decades, indeed, since Mao. The key difference is it is institutional and therefore more sustainable: titanic personality or revolutionary credentials are no longer the criteria.

Previously each major area of party work was under a particular member of the PBSC. This had been Deng's device to prevent the monopoly of power by one person, as Mao had seized. Over time though, this reform created its own problems. Silos or fiefdoms arose, allowing abuses and factions to flourish. That led to the greatest internal challenge to party stability since 1989, when, in the run-up to the 2012 18th Congress, PBSC security and legal affairs head Zhou Yongkang and Politburo member Bo Xilai tried to disrupt the party's earlier selection of Xi and Li as the two leaders of the fifth generation. If Zhou had succeeded, it would have derailed any smooth transfer of power from the fourth to the fifth generations, with incalculable consequences and turbulence. The silos were closed by Xi quickly making an end-run around all of them by creating the four new leading small groups under the general secretary's direct control.

While ideas in increasingly consensual Chinese politics can often best be considered in terms of a particular generation and its experience, the strategy to maintain reform did come down largely to one individual, Xi Jinping, and his inner circle who shared the same seminal influence in their lives, the Cultural Revolution. Political scientist Li Cheng at Brookings calls this the Shaanxi group, people who came from or, like Xi, lived in Shaanxi during the Cultural Revolution. In Li's words, this is Xi's "brains trust, eyes, ears, voices, chief lieutenants and enforcers". Foremost among them, Wang Qishan and Yu Zhengsheng, retired at the 2017 19th Congress but the younger two key members of the Shaanxi group remain. Li Zhanshu first worked with Xi three decades before in Hebei and, under Xi, headed the party's General Office that prepares all papers and work for the PBSC: the party's chief of staff. Zhao Leji headed the Central Organization Department in Xi's first term, responsible for thousands of top appointments in the party, government, military, state-owned enterprises and other institutions. At the 19th Congress, he took over from Wang Qishan to head party discipline and root out corruption: Li ranked third in the Politburo, after Premier Li Keqiang, while Zhao became sixth.

Displaying Power and Intent

Xi had plenty of opportunities in his first two years to outline his ideas, assert authority and demonstrate power. The anti-corruption campaign under Wang Qishan shackled opponents to change; the once seemingly all-powerful military was brought to heel; and the Diaoyu/Senkaku Islands dispute generated support among the nationalist majority. Through these, Xi won three clear victories in what could have been problem areas — corruption, military and nationalism — enabling him to develop soft power and create acceptance for the rule of law.

Corruption: Xi is serious about corruption. It is more than just a one-off against his rivals, exceeding any previous campaign in intensity, duration and results. Again, Xi can look back to Deng, who observed that what was so striking about Singapore and Hong Kong was not just that they built successful modern commercial centres but these predominantly Chinese societies had brought corruption under control.

Singapore and Hong Kong are now ranked by Transparency International among the world's least corrupt places. Before introducing anti-corruption systems, both were notably corrupt. Indeed, the early-1970s quip was that colonial Hong Kong with its British-led police possessed the finest police force money could buy. Although, to many people, such a transformation in China may seem impossible, it is doubtless part of Xi Jinping's China Dream as it was of Deng's. China had been studying corruption in other countries for well over a decade. Back in 2003, a mainland friend in Hong Kong with strong ties to Beijing asked me to recommend books about corruption in Southeast Asia: tackling corruption was already on the radar screen.

Xi does not have to reinvent the wheel for how a Chinese society can overcome corruption. Lee Kuan Yew wrote the manual in Singapore and the Independent Commission Against Corruption did the same more than 40 years ago in Hong Kong. Both introduced strict laws (something Deng liked) and decided to pay civil servants well, in fact, very well — unlike systemically corrupt countries like Indonesia and the Philippines where officials were paid very poorly but compensated for it by extracting "squeeze" and wealth through the abuse of power, unhindered by the legal system. Indeed President Ferdinand Marcos was the top law student of his year in the Philippines just as President Chen Shui-bian was a leading lawyer in Taiwan. Both ended their political careers in disgrace after betraying the very law they had sworn to uphold and protect.

Military: Xi has been involved with China's military longer than any active senior career officer, an advantage neither of his two predecessors had. His military connections began over 35 years ago when, straight out of Tsinghua University in 1980, he became assistant to the vice premier responsible for defence. After that, he strengthened his understanding of the military, building ties during his career along the coast in Fujian, Zhejiang and Shanghai: all major strategic areas on the front line opposite Taiwan. This doubtless gave Xi great insight into the military and geopolitical strategic issues, as well as ideas for senior appointments.

Xi has used institutional power to bring the military under firm civilian control, something not always clear under Jiang or Hu. Xi's Mass Line spells out lines of authority within the party. This forced the military to declare its subordination to civilian leaders at a high-profile 2014 meeting, where it reaffirmed that the party retains "absolute leadership" of the military. This was written into the Party's constitution in 2017. Clipping the military's wings further did not end there. Auditing of the PLA was taken away from the General Logistics Department and placed directly under the CMC, headed by Xi. The ultimate expression of Xi's power over the military was to have the former top-ranking military officer Xu Caihou investigated and dismissed for corruption. Xu was the other major "tiger", along with former PBSC member Zhou Yongkang, caught in the anti-corruption campaign: two formidable beasts.

Nationalism: Japan's government purchase of the Diaoyu/Senkaku Islands was a foreign policy gift for Xi. It enabled Xi to play the strong protector of the nation card in defiance of perceived resurgent Japanese militarism. In a country where an estimated 90% of people view Japan unfavorably, that is quite a gift.

In the dispute with Japan, Xi seems to have been able to control events from the moment he took over, never letting them get out of hand at home nor permitting others to force the agenda abroad. He brought the icy stand-off to an end at a timing of his choosing: ahead of the 2013 APEC meeting where Xi met Shinzo Abe for the first time since either came to office. This defused tension sufficiently through diplomacy, though as Japan became more assertive, no major improvement in relations followed. Xi also demonstrated to his military who is in charge of relations with Japan: the civilian-led party. By standing up to Japan and not blinking first, Xi burnished his credentials domestically, strengthening his popularity. Subsequent challenges over the South China Sea reinforced this.

Soft Power: In response to the US Pivot to Asia, Xi focuses on soft power to project China's influence beyond that of its military, which clearly cannot compete with the US. Soft power is part of the China Dream. Suspicion surrounding China's economic re-emergence is taken as inevitable: being able to manage it without conflict is the goal. Xi, using China's financial and trading power, along with international institutions and events, has played his cards well, so far.

Xi has splashed the cash, as the cliché goes. Instead of building ever-threateningly large foreign exchange reserves, China decided to diversify its holdings into overseas investments, some in US dollars, some not. Creating the Asian Infrastructure Investment Bank (AIIB), New Development Bank (BRICS Bank) and other funds along with the Belt and Road Initiative, China has put financial flesh on the bones of its soft power. This began to shift the world's geopolitical centre of gravity from its post-1945 moorings, even before the election of President Donald Trump. The UK's own breakaway pivot to Asia, by joining the AIIB in late 2015, drew a public rebuke from the US, its closest ally: China's influence, especially its hard dollars and, for its neighbours, its Asian identity, are more powerful than many acknowledge.

Rule of Law: Xi left the most important of his changes till last. Potentially the most controversial, Xi only made the rule of law the central theme at the 4th Plenum, two years after coming to power. Now, party leaders see it as being in the interest of the state, especially one that holds harmony and stability as its highest priorities. They realize their very legitimacy and efficacy are undermined by the lack of the rule of law. The more the economy develops, the more it needs a firmer foundation in law, particularly for the markets that the 3rd Plenum deemed "decisive". Without it, the economy cannot rise to the heights of sophistication, stability and prosperity for which China aims, and could spell the party's doom.

The anti-corruption campaign, with which the party hopes to win back and maintain its standing with the public, requires the development and enforcement of the rule of law. So does environmental protection. Without defined laws and systems, polluters will not be brought to book if they bribe officials. With one billion people linked together on *WeChat*, the main social media platform, and 900 million on the Internet, this could spark discontent among people now acutely aware of safety and environmental standards, from food to water.

Increasing prosperity has led to a growing sense of people's rights and desire for protection from harm. Property ownership as well as commerce requires clearly defined and enforced law, interpreted by a trusted judiciary and government. Happiness, the object of Xi's people-oriented approach, depends on a belief in an effective and clean government, driven by a sense of justice. Xi's initial description of China's government is that it is effective but not clean. Abuse of power can only be checked by the procedures outlined at the 4th Plenum, rooted in the rule of law.

The party's credibility is on the line. If it does not deliver, party support would drop even more than it did after the 2011 Wenzhou high-speed rail crash killed 40 people. Corrosive cynicism would undermine the broad support the anti-corruption campaign has won. This could be fatal for the party and Xi. At the very least, loss of confidence would certainly hit sentiment, reducing economic growth further.

The Cultural Revolution Generation

This is the Cultural Revolution generation in power now. In its most formative and impressionable years, it saw at first hand the damage done by abuse of power and absence of rule of law. Since then this generation has had over four decades to reflect and decide what to do when its turn came to take up the reins of power.

This fifth generation of leaders has very different formative influences from the fourth. The latter were described by one fifth-generation official as grey, cautious people who grew up in the early years of New China, as "True Believers" in Communism. The Great Leap Forward and Cultural Revolution came as a great shock, making them even more cautious when they saw what happened to society and senior leaders.

To rebel is glorious, the fifth generation learned in its youth: to question official doctrine, a virtue. Each individual rebels in their own way, but a fear of change is not inherently characteristic of this generation, only a fear of the wrong sort of change. After the Cultural Revolution, Premier Li Keqiang undertook an interesting assignment while at Peking University. He helped translate into Chinese *The Due Process of Law* by Britain's leading jurist, Lord Denning, who as the Master of the Rolls was the UK's third most senior judge for 20 years. Denning was most famous for his judgments involving abuse of power against the individual, either by the state or powerful corporate interests: very relevant after the Cultural Revolution.

Li's wife, Cheng Hong, was, until Li rose to prominence, a professor of English language and literature at Beijing's Capital University. Her book *Tranquility is Beyond Price*, written after being a visiting scholar in 1995 at Brown University in New England, focused on her interest in nature and ecology. She wrote about Henry David Thoreau, the 19th-century American writer-philosopher, best known for *Walden*, a reflection on two years in a rural Massachusetts log cabin. Cheng has translated several books from English into Chinese, popularizing nature writing in China. What might her husband draw from her work as he tackles China's environmental problems?

On more directly political topics, Li Keqiang is reported to have recommended in 2012 that party members read Alexis de Tocqueville on the fall of the French monarchy. This was seen as detailing the dangers of rulers' detachment from ordinary people, and corruption. Cheng Hong presumably knows of the French historian and political theorist from his writings about New England, most notably his *Democracy in America* written in 1841: more food for thought.

The Response to Arbitrary Rule

No group lost more in the Cultural Revolution than either the "educated youth", who largely lost their education, or officials, who were the target of much humiliation, lawlessness and violence. Premier Liu Shaoqi lost his life as a result of the abuse of power. Former Red Guards, like Xi and Li, are now China's top officials, potentially vulnerable to the same uncertainties and arbitrary processes that plagued their predecessors half a century ago — unless they do something about it. The rule of law is their solution.

The 2014 4th Plenum did for the rule of law what the 3rd Plenum did in 2013 for overall reform. It gave a broad mandate. Wide-ranging changes to the judicial system were promised. Xi warned that there are serious problems in a judicial system that is "neither effective nor complete". He pledged "to end judicial injustice in a system dogged by unfair trials and corrupt judges". These are strong words, with which the party has raised expectations and dashes them at its peril. Social media and rising incomes have changed China fundamentally: Xi and the party know that.

Xi was quoted as saying that the law would set up a list of government powers and would ban officials from extralegal activity. It would spell out the functions, authority, procedures and responsibilities of officials, "squeezing out room for rent-seeking". Officials would be specifically banned from interfering with cases before the courts.

To ensure fair trials, Beijing would consider whether judges and procurators from outside the local jurisdiction could handle such cases to prevent local interference from vested interests. It may also allow prosecutors to pursue public interest litigation. Courts are to be encouraged to take on cases against government departments, which will be required to appear before the court.

All this seems very radical in the Chinese context, but Xi and other fifth-generation leaders see that there is no alternative, just as Deng and even Mao before him saw there was no alternative to economic reform. Doing nothing is not an option. Even if legal reform happens only gradually, it will bring significant change over time. In fact, the Central Committee has said that the anti-corruption law should be expedited so that officials "dare not, cannot and do not want to be corrupt": again, words that could come back to haunt it unless acted upon.

Transparency and efficiency were enhanced in 2014 with all court judgments required to appear online within seven days of being made. Pilot schemes began in Shanghai and Shenzhen to make judges more professional and independent. The first intellectual property court was established in Beijing. These are the things that a modern economy and society need in order to be successful — Beijing's abiding concern. Implicitly, Beijing has accepted the concept of the rule of law.

One weekend, I sat among alumni of a foreign university, held in one of China's most famous halls of learning. Presiding was a member of the Central Committee: one of less than 400 people whose party rules 1.4 billion lives. First, portraits of Hobbes, Locke and Montesquieu appeared on the screen; gone were Marx, Engels and Lenin. Then the lecturer left little doubt that China is serious about legal reform and the rule of law. It is not window dressing: there is no alternative. There may be some Chinese characteristics involved, but its relevance for society, the economy and all that flows from that in terms of stability is fully understood.

Professor Edward Steinfeld's insightful book about reform bears the title *Playing Our Game.* In the early 1990s, China decided to discover the source of the West's "Promethean Energy" and to copy it. Capturing this flame was Deng's objective after visiting the advanced Western economies. It was the rules, regulations, processes and procedures that underpinned the West's rise to power and dominance. China's leaders believe the rule of law is a fundamental part of the West's formula for success.

What materializes in China will doubtless be a hybrid of traditional thinking and Western law. For instance, Chinese may feel, as Professor Lanxin Xiang from Geneva does, that "it is impossible to accept that having more lawyers and litigation would be the right way towards social justice: rather they would be seen as a symptom of social chaos and moral decay". That may be a traditional Confucian view but one with which Xi has sympathy. Hence there will be much more about the China Dream and traditional Chinese values in an attempt to instill in people a moral compass and knowledge. These are deemed to have gone missing after the chaos and violence of the Great Leap Forward and Cultural Revolution, followed by the often crass materialism and rising corruption of the last three decades.

The rule of law is the critical enabler of change, needing support from a "basic law" that the Central Committee says is required. These are the rules required to Play Our [Western] Game. Politics will thrash out the mechanisms: in China they are as complex as anywhere else. No neat diagram can describe how they work as they constantly evolve, responding to changes in priorities and circumstance. Both Deng and Xi, the two greatest agents of change since Mao, tore up the old models. Both used stealth and timing: one through a guerrilla campaign and the other in full sight of his adversaries to consolidate power and push forward reform. Position does not in itself mean power. Strategy alone can acquire that, as Xi showed in his first term before the 19th Congress where he emerged pre-eminent.

Chinese politics can be difficult to grasp for those from different systems: putting them in context or even following them is not easy. Furthermore, there are common misunderstandings about China that hide its reality: the next two chapters explain why.

Chapter 9

Why Many Misunderstand China

There in the mist, enormous, majestic, silent, and terrible, stood the Great Wall Solitarily … Menacingly … Grim … Stark … Ruthlessly … Fearlessly … in utter solitude, mysterious like the great empire it guarded.

Somerset Maugham, *On a Chinese Screen,* 1922

China obscures, you say; and I reply China obscures but there is light to be found. Look for it.

Blaise Pascal (1623–1662), *Pensees 397*

Why do many people misunderstand China? Unsurprisingly, it is because many look at China through Western eyes. Even in the rest of Asia people are influenced by Western perceptions. Misunderstanding is the same everywhere. Its roots lie in fixed ideas of what it true. These are strongly influenced by ideology, beliefs, popular culture, media and direct experience. People do not take sufficiently seriously others' history, philosophy or politics that are based on different experiences and hence thinking. In fact, most lack adequate knowledge of them.

Theirs is too often the view of the observer rather than of the observed, as Oxford's Raymond Dawson wrote half a century ago in *The Chinese Chameleon.* He also noted that "Communism conceals China from us". It still does today, especially in the US. Even without ideological or cultural prejudices, it is often hard for Westerners to get their heads around China. The sheer scale, differences, distance and unfamiliarity are barriers to understanding. There seems to be so much that is new or unknown that most do not know where to start.

Vast and Mystifying

China can seem to be too much to take in all at once. First there is its forbidding size: "very big, China" as Noel Coward drolly noted in his 1930 comedy *Private Lives*, which was partly written while overlooking Shanghai's Bund. James Kynge observed that,

> China defies classification and is especially resistant to all-capturing ideologies that Chinese and outsiders try to impose upon it. This makes it a nightmare for those who believe that China should fit into any set of narrow ideological tramlines that they have constructed for it. The only durable framework for China watching is to accept that the place embraces every energy, vice and virtue known to man.

Then there is the very different language and China's ways of thought, which can be confusing, especially to Cartesian thinkers rigidly adhering to their understanding of logic. The concept of *yin* and *yang* mystifies many Western minds. How can seemingly contradictory negative and positive forces embrace and support each other? Yet Niels Bohr put the *yin* and *yang* symbol on the cover of his ground-breaking paper on quantum physics as the way to explain this major advance in Western science: not all Westerners are incapable of grasping the concept and using it to gain real insight into universal ideas.

Reared on a strong belief in the future, be it from Hegelian thought in Europe or from a sense of manifest destiny in the US, it is difficult for many in the West to know what to make of a country that can think so differently and has so much history. Looking for guidance on the present and the future to their peaks in the Han and Tang dynasties, which occurred respectively over 2,000 and 1,400 years ago, perplexes many Westerners, but to Chinese this is not the distant past but the relevant comparison. Chinese seem steeped in their history in a way few Westerners are.

Imagine being asked by a museum curator, while looking at a magnificent three-foot-tall 3,000-year-old monumental Zhou bronze vessel, who was the King of England during the Western Zhou Dynasty of 1046–771 BC? When stumped by that question in Huangshan, Anhui, my mind frantically delved into obscure and largely unknown British history: some petty chieftains, was all I could answer. More to the point, very few Westerners would even think such knowledge to be relevant today. In China, many do. For most Westerners, 3,000 years is an awfully long time when their countries then did not have organized states in the way China did.

The concept of human progress is deeply ingrained in the West. The broad assumption is that the future will be better than the past. This is especially true in "young" cultures, which can only conceive of history in terms of a few hundred years or, more likely, decades, like the US, rather than in millennia, like China. The former supports belief in straight-line progress. The latter believes in cycles.

Whose Great Wall?

The Great Wall is a wonderful metaphor for a barrier to understanding. It also raises the question of whose great wall is it? The problem, as seen from China, lies much more in the observer than the observed. The great wall belongs to the observer. Ideology and prejudice create barriers, reinforced by fear, popular culture and, especially, the media. Communism and Orientalism do seem to conceal the real China from the West.

In economics, Beijing's data and policy intentions do not always help an understanding of China either. First, there is a long tradition of secrecy. Then there is exaggeration and theatre used as an integral part of Chinese political campaigns, and economic policy is often presented as a campaign. When things have to change, the government often exaggerates the negatives or creates a very ugly straw man, described out of context or missing some key perspective. Chinese grasp this oversimplification and adjust accordingly, but foreigners, lacking local knowledge, cannot. Instead, many take it at face value, finding justification for their negative views from official pronouncements.

Furthermore, as Somerset Maugham, who showed insight, understanding and empathy in writing about China almost a century ago, said, "Nothing hinders friendly relations between different countries so much as the fantastic notions which they cherish about another's characteristics." He was not writing about China but France. However, he could have been talking about much of the world, including how China is misunderstood today.

Reactions to new rising powers are rarely generous. Emotions can be raw. When the US was on the rise in the mid-19th century, Charles Dickens caused a storm of controversy with *Martin Chuzzlewit*. As Simon Callow wrote in an introduction,

> Dickens plunges the knife into America from the very start in page after page of wild satire tinged with personal animosity: the sense of grievances being settled is palpable. His personal loathing of the pomposity, bragging, lying and spitting he found are not counter-balanced by any intimation of merit whatever.

Selfishness was his theme, a charge often made against those on the rise as President Obama showed when criticizing China's "free-riding" on the region's supposedly US-brought peace. Xi Jinping quickly invited everyone to ride on the Belt and Road train China was building, something that the US has chosen not to do, although US companies like GE have leapt aboard with great enthusiasm and expectations.

Roots of misunderstanding often lie in four main factors.

1. People's idea of themselves defined in terms of "significant others": not what others are really like but what they are or represent in contrast or in juxtaposition to themselves. This psychologically gives them a positive view of themselves, often accentuating a sense of superiority and difference, while heightening the element of threat.
2. This then informs news flows that normally reflect the bad rather than the good: bad news sells.
3. Opinion leaders, be they in journalism or markets, tend to hunt in packs. Therefore, often one idea rises to prominence in the main narrative, shutting out alternatives.
4. Finally there is ambiguity. Some cultures are more comfortable with it than others. At one end of the spectrum are Asians, including Chinese, who see its merits and generally feel comfortable with it.

At the other end are many Westerners whose Cartesian minds cannot accept the lack of precision, the many shades of grey. Not all, though, as Niels Bohr demonstrated. Studies show that creative people are more comfortable with ambiguity.

These root causes of misunderstanding are then accentuated by a lack of familiarity with the country. This often leads to asking the wrong questions, which in turn sets enquirers looking for the wrong information whilst missing what is more relevant in the context of a country's norms, history and economic development.

China is seen as being in a "mist", presumably lacking clarity. To summarize Maugham, China is clearly enormous, with the world's largest population, far more than any country in Europe or the Americas, and the fourth-largest land area. China's long history, with its finest silk and peerless porcelain illustrating its quality, has created an aura of majesty, but to a foreign mind there may be more to it than that. It is silent: Malaysia's fiery former Prime Minister Mahathir Mohamad once observed that Westerners in general and Americans in particular are uncomfortable with silence, whereas Asians are not. To Westerners, it may hide intentions, express antipathy. Silence is sinister, unnerving and threatening.

Very much not like us: China is solitary, isolated and distant. Therefore it is menacing and ruthless. Moreover it is fearless.

> Solitarily, with the indifference of nature herself, [the Great Wall] crept up the mountainside and slipped down to the depth of the valley. Menacingly, the grim watch towers, stark and four square, at due intervals stood at their posts. Ruthlessly, for it was built at the cost of a million lives and each one of those great grey stones has been stained with the bloody tears of the captive and the outcast, it forged its dark way through a sea of rugged mountains. Fearlessly, it went on its endless journey, league upon league to the furthermost regions of Asia, in utter solitude, mysterious like the great empire it guarded.

Maugham wrote the above in *Arabesque,* a very short fragment in his 1922 book *On a Chinese Screen*. Repression and difference: both very current themes. This was the common foreign view Maugham saw, overall a very negative and threatening image.

The Negative Narrative

The Coming Conflict With China (1997), *The Coming Collapse of China* (2001) and *The River Runs Black* (2004) chart the recent evolution in book titles of the China threat or disaster-waiting-to-happen genre. They may include elements of truth, of which Beijing is usually only too well aware, but their alarmist titles do not help grasp the more likely long-term outcome. Namely, that most problems will be overcome as they have been in the recent past: for many reasons, not least of which is China's ability to understand and adapt to change in the pursuit of its clear interests.

Without sufficient long-term perspective, the titles seem to be a continuation of the thinking in Fu Manchu movies almost a century ago: an ominous threat of no-good people, who will come to a sticky end. *Death by China* in 2011 by Donald Trump's China adviser, Peter Navarro, is just the latest manifestation. This reveals much more about Western fears, ignorance and prejudice than about China. Myths abound: "Don't let the facts get in the way of a good opinion", as *Far Eastern Economic Review* journalists used to quip about others.

China has proved sceptics wrong with its continued high growth, in stark contrast to the OECD economies, trapped in slow or no growth since 2008, still adjusting to their financial boom and bust. Given this is where most global commentators sit, it is not surprising their judgment is clouded on all likely economic outcomes, China's included. A faltering China fits with the talk of stagnation or worse.

How seriously the West really takes China is still unclear, and that is part of the problem. Asia, with China at its heart, may have overtaken the EU and US in 2011 to become the world's largest economic and trading area, but learning anything of significance about China still seems of little importance to most people outside Asia, preoccupied with their own issues after the 2008 financial crisis. At best, it remains exotic, at worst, a threat. Excerpts from three European academics half a century ago help grasp why many misunderstand China.

"There is no better or finer fiction than the reality of others," Francois Geoffroy-Dechaume, who grew up in Beijing in the 1930s, commented in 1967's *China Looks at the World.* This is an example of the self-defined in contrast to "significant others". The French writer continued, "Our failure to understand the Chinese starts … with a failure to understand ourselves, to recognize … what they reject in us and about us." The latter is rarely given so much as a passing thought by many Westerners, yet is central to misunderstanding, both of Chinese and about how Chinese see Westerners. Being often studiously misunderstood, Chinese are bound to feel some rejection, harbouring reservations and even resentment.

"Western civilization appears to be the most advanced expression of the evolution of human societies *but things are by no means as simple as that,*" leading anthropologist Claude Levi-Strauss wrote in 1963. Certainly they are not as simple as that today, as world powers become dysfunctional domestically while mired abroad in conflicts they do not understand. Their use of military and financial might, with unintended consequences, causes new and deeper problems which seem to be unending: not the signs of being the most "advanced" societies that should be emulated, let alone being capable of understanding something as complex as China.

Raymond Dawson wrote in 1967:

> We have a long way to go before our general understanding of Chinese civilization corresponds adequately with the Middle Kingdom's past achievements and future importance. For the great majority of people China will continue to be slightly unreal: a country of fans and lanterns, of pig-tails and slant eyes, of chopsticks and bird's nest soup, of pavilions and pagodas, of pidgin English and bound feet.

How much has this perspective changed since to create sufficient understanding? Apart from a few notions about Mao and high-speed trains, certainly not enough now that China has 1.4 billion people, is the world's largest trading nation and the second-largest economy. Again to quote Dawson, it is difficult for many to be objective about "a remote country with an alien civilization". This was especially true during and after the Cold War, when views were set about Communism in general and China in particular. As post-2008 global economic adjustment grinds along, tensions rise.

Alterations in perceptions largely reflect changes in Western intellectual trends rather than changes in China. Many foreigners are self-absorbed, relating China to what is familiar and of interest to them. The earlier sympathetic views of the 1930s, in the US of Pearl Buck and Edgar Snow, or in the Europe of Malraux and Marx, gave way to those of the Cold War and then to the era of Reagan and Thatcher in the 1980s. Since the 2008 financial crisis reinforced by Brexit and Trump's election, Western intellectual fashions respond to stress and anxiety about the future, catching China in the crosshairs.

Human beings are reluctant to change or adapt to it, according to psychologists. Many people just want the future to be like the present or recent past. Inertia is powerful. Behavioural finance talks of recency bias: in plain language, rear-view mirror driving. Rather than believe the recent trend is one's friend, it is better to look ahead, assume discontinuity, figure out what that could be and when it might occur, so as to be prepared. To many this is counter-intuitive; they think change is slow and fairly predictable, a very mundane, grey word.

In 2002, I was doing some research into the Chinese car market, which seemed attractive to me, but a noted China sceptic dismissed my notion with the withering comment that yes, China's car market was now as large as Australia's, a country of only 26 million people: not interesting. His frame of reference was the early 1990s when many consultants forecast double-digit annual growth for China's car demand. The experts were very wrong. It only averaged 6%. This single-digit growth was the recent past, which presumably would continue: recency bias. My reference was different, having lived for two decades in richer Southeast Asia. There car demand grew at double digits for many years, driven by a steep and long S-curve as incomes rose on industrialization and urbanization. S-curves show demand growth for products at different income levels. As incomes rise, self-evidently more people can afford to buy cars so demand accelerates. China entered this point when annual incomes reached Rmb 80,000. Only 10 years later, China became the world's largest new car market: no longer does anyone compare China with Australia.

China is seen differently by different types of people. Those with a positive mindset look for progress. Dawson gives the example of a visitor interested in basketball who decides China is progressing because the number of basketball courts is growing. Those with a negative mentality are absorbed in their own politics, standards and issues. He specifically mentioned press freedom and civil liberties, ignoring the questions by which to judge and assess China in its own terms or priorities.

Preconceived misconceptions abound. Everyone has an opinion on China, just as on the US. This is expressed in easily digestible sound bites, usually based on their own experience, normally gained outside China. Each has their own world view, largely formed several decades earlier during the Cold War for the older generation and with matters closer to the present and to home for younger people. The root of much ignorance is the sheer lack of knowledge of current reality, history or geography. In the US, Henry Kissinger blames the education system.

Fear is the problem for some: fear of the unknown, fear of the other and fear of the Western world losing privileges derived from its pre-eminence and economic dominance. These fears haunt those who assume and crave an unchanging world. Demography is starting to determine economic weight, which in turn translates into power and influence. First it is China, then India, to be followed by the likes of Indonesia, Pakistan, Bangladesh, Brazil and Nigeria, eventually vying in numbers with North America and Europe, and collectively far outnumbering them. This is the unsettling prospect for those who feel threatened. The West is in danger of becoming like the Tea Party, representative of the old local elites, unable to come to terms with the new world. Regardless of the economic arguments for the all-round benefits from growing global prosperity, fears persist.

Popular culture has not helped. Demonization of Asians in general and Chinese in particular has created stereotypes from Fu Manchu in American cinema to the Yellow Peril, the term first coined by German Kaiser Wilhelm. The world has moved on, though supposedly serious Hollywood productions like *Apocalypse Now* and the *Killing Fields* did nothing to calm Asian nerves or correct the biases against them.

Confucius became not a respected philosopher but a figure of fun to be mocked with squinted eyes, high-pitched nasal intonation and the words "Confucius, he say" before some banal and concocted saying. Clearly a large difference exists between the crude racism of *Punch's* doggerel about John Chinaman in 1858 and today's media, but xenophobia and myopia are not dead. It is hard to read this piece from *Punch* without wincing, not least because some of the racist elements, conscious or unconscious, are alive over 150 years later.

> John Chinaman a rogue is born,
> The laws of truth, he holds in scorn:
> About as great a brute as can
> Encumber the earth is John Chinaman.
> Sing Yeh, my cruel John Chinaman,
> Sing Yeo, my stubborn John Chinaman,
>
> With their little-pig eyes and their large pig-tails,
> And their diet of rats, dogs, slugs and snails,
> Of that nasty feeder John Chinaman,
> Sing lie-tea, my sly John Chinaman,
> No fightee, my coward John Chinaman,
> John Bull has a chance — let him if he can
> Somewhat open the eyes of John Chinaman.

Racial superiority has been increasingly replaced in Western attitudes towards China by a different but still negative presumption: Chinese should be like us. They should follow our rules, our institutions and our thinking. Anything different is deemed to be inferior, and a challenge, quite possibly a threat. Edward Said's critique of Orientalism drew principally on the Middle East, but there are many features in common with China. The exaggeration of difference, presumption of Western superiority, exoticism, the Inscrutable Orient, irrationalism and inherent weakness are still part of some Western perceptions, even if only held subconsciously.

Communications

The age of instant communications and ready opinion have not necessarily improved matters. The media cannot escape blame for why some misunderstand China. Editors and subeditors back at head office, thousands of miles away, have storylines, some would say agendas, that correspondents in the field know they should satisfy if they are to get ahead. For many, the lure of peer or editorial approval, let alone a Pulitzer Prize, is too great.

Many journalists in Beijing live in the same bubble, recycling the same oxygen of what is and is not "the China story". They generally hunt in packs, with some honourable exceptions. Increasingly it has become an impending disaster movie, played out in slow motion, day by day. With 24-hour news cycles and non-stop deadlines, it is no surprise. All too often, journalists talk to the same people and share similar knowledge. Don't, though, only blame the correspondents labouring long hours in the field.

Start with the editors, for as the saying goes, "The fish rots from the head." They set the direction for others to follow, and fast, emotive news is what grabs viewers or readers. There is no room for slow news, developing over years or even decades, though that is often the main long-term news. Wars, famine and death come and go but fill the bulletins, while longer-term social and political change is harder to make interesting and hence less covered. Global editors, who view the world from their US- or Euro-centric perches, are unlikely to abandon a lifetime's worth of knowledge in favour of a different world view, of which they know very little. They have invested heavily their whole careers in this 20th-century perspective. These are also the areas they know best. Stick with fixed, comfortable, existing ideas; life is easier and safer.

Admittedly, it is hard to gain a balanced perspective on a country the size of China. "Ah yes, balance", a veteran journalist sighed nostalgically when reminded of the guiding principle 40 years ago in his early days of reporting Asia. Globally, viewspapers are replacing newspapers, and social media is replacing reporting. The internet and social media have replaced network television. So much has changed and with it journalism. Balance seems rather quaint, like memories of afternoon tea with a respectable and very proper maiden aunt: no longer with us, regrettably, in this disrupted and changed "post-truth" world.

As *New Yorker* writer Evan Osnos recalls in *Age of Ambition,* a journalist's day in China could start in the morning interviewing a new tycoon and finish in the evening meeting with a dissident under house arrest. Not exactly a balanced reflection of about 1.4 billion people's lives: hardly typical. As in the US and Europe, news in China is mixed: some good, some bad, some boring. Trying to convey this to a global audience, which to begin with is very poorly informed about China, is a great challenge, even with the best will in the world. This is especially true when time and space is much more limited for "foreign" news than for news nearer home. Bad news sells is more than a cliché, it reflects demand and grabs headlines. This is nothing new. Anthony Trollope in 1857 wrote about the press in *Barchester Towers*, "It is so easy to condemn; and so pleasant too: for eulogy charms no listeners as detraction does." Detraction sells.

China does not always help either. The *Dao De Jing* said over 2,000 years ago that "those who know don't talk, those who talk don't know". Following the dictum more than most, senior officials provide very little regular access to journalists. This will doubtless change as China understands soft power more. Government knows it needs to work on its communications, just as companies learned the need to make their case to investors. Indeed at Davos in 2016, Fang Xinghai, the Stanford Economics PhD and deputy chairman of China's securities regulator, did respond to IMF Managing Director Christine Lagarde's comments about China's poor communications affecting the currency markets. He admitted that China's communications are not set up to guide markets. Fang said, "We have to be patient because our system is not structured in a way that is able to communicate seamlessly with the market": patience and gradualism, two traditional Chinese virtues. This was no brush-off: he knew the fix was in. One month later, Xi Jinping and Li Keqiang separately talked about the importance of communications, which has risen up Beijing's list of priorities as part of soft power. In 2017, China launched the China Global Television Network, hoping to provide its own Al Jazeera.

Whether greater accessibility will change the problem of unbalanced foreign perspective is debatable. Two incidents involving James Kynge, once of *Reuters* and now the *Financial Times* emerging markets editor, arguably the most balanced Beijing economics reporter over the last two decades, illustrate the problem of bias. In the autumn of 1989, Kynge reported that China had had a good grain harvest, which was true. In the post-June 4 world though, he was told this was propaganda, diverting attention away from the deaths in and around Tiananmen, and should not have been covered.

In 2006, while promoting his book *When China Shakes the World* at the Shanghai Foreign Correspondents' Club, Kynge ran into heavy foreign *negatavista* flak from the floor. Initially, he answered the points with geniality. When this failed to stem the hostile questions about China, he confronted the questioners with one hard fact. The World Bank said China since 1980 had lifted 400 million people out of poverty (around 700 million by 2016), wasn't that enough achievement, Kynge asked, to balance the other criticisms and to put them in perspective? For some it was not. However, it is a good reminder that in the China argument, the wood often gets lost for the trees: less conspicuous broad-based slow advance is ignored in favour of very visible problems, even if they are no longer as representative as they were.

As part of opening up, will China take a more accommodative attitude to foreign journalists? After all, they, not the state media, are on the front line reporting China to the rest of the world. Time will tell. As mentioned, the nature of Western journalism often involves an unbalanced diet, which brings journalists into conflict with official China. In addition, journalists face the constant stress of Chinese life, beginning in Beijing with its air pollution, where the great majority congregates. It is not surprising that many are ground down by it: China burnout. The pace and intensity of living in China's high-speed transition is more than many can take. China burnout affects more than just journalists. Some in business, diplomacy and academia suffer too, taking their grievances back home with them.

Soft power should lead China to find remedies for this, though other greater priorities and sequencing, just as in economic policy, may prevent that happening immediately. As ever, nothing will be rushed: gradualism is the guide. It is not that Beijing is unaware. Pulitzer Prize reporter Ian Johnson acknowledged in *Wild Grass: Three Portraits of Change in Modern China* that without the help of their official minders, foreign journalists could not even do the reporting they manage to do. There is some sympathy, but then there are rules.

Different Approaches are Not Wrong, Just Different

It is not just about getting information, though. That is only half the problem. Interpreting it is the other part. Foreigners should not assume that the interpretation of information will be the same in the Asian teahouse or coffee shop as in a London bar or on the New York trading desk.

They should reflect on a lesson Joseph Needham learned in 1943 on his first day in China. Winston Churchill sent Needham, a Cambridge academic, to China's then capital, Chongqing, to see what assistance Britain could give the numerous universities that had retreated there to escape the Japanese invasion. After a stressful three-hour-long flight in a battered DC-47, over the Hump of the Himalayas from Calcutta, Needham was recuperating at the British Ambassador's house when he noticed the gardener grafting fruit trees, Simon Winchester records in *Bomb, Book and Compass*. Needham knew about grafting and this was being done all wrong. Yet it was clear that this was the head gardener. Puzzled, Needham kept his eye on him. As the afternoon wore on, it dawned on Needham that the gardener could not be doing it wrongly, for China had been growing fruit trees a lot longer than Britain and the man had risen to be head gardener: he was just doing it differently. Needham's first lesson in China was to learn that things could be different without being wrong: a hard lesson for many to learn.

Plenty of tripwires lie in wait for those trying to fathom China, but that does not mean China is unfathomable, far from it. There are many resources to aid understanding for those prepared to put in the effort. This should not be underestimated, but given China's current importance, let alone the future position it may well attain, it is well worth it. Often overlooked is that only with knowledge of China's background, especially its history and philosophy, can come a true understanding of

China. Not that there is a single China. There are many Chinas and many interpretations of them, ranging across the whole spectrum from optimism to pessimism.

Without knowing the history and philosophy, China will remain unfathomable, even to those who speak the language, as they will only be able to comprehend China in their own terms rather than in China's terms. It has to be the China of the observed, not the observer, not the fiction of others' reality. Difference need not be wrong, just different.

Sometimes there seems to be no other explanation for misunderstanding China than the psychological. Cognitive dissonance is the term, occurring when new information is presented that contradicts existing beliefs, causing great discomfort, especially to those heavily invested in particular ideas. As Frantz Fanon summarized it:

> Sometimes people hold a core belief that is very strong. When they are presented with evidence that works against that belief, the new evidence cannot be accepted.... And because it is so important to protect the core belief, they will rationalize, ignore and even deny anything that doesn't fit in with the core belief.

Core beliefs seem to come no stronger than in economics.

Chapter 10

Why China's Economy is Misunderstood

In theory, there should be no difference between theory and practice. In practice there is.

Attributed to Yogi Berra, New York Yankees (1925–2015)

Fixed ideas about how economies best operate have bedeviled much Western thinking about China's economy. Familiar with only mature economies, many assume China should be just like those in the successful West. No allowance is made for differences in stage of development or background. This has to be a Chinese economy imagined by the observer rather than known by the observed.

After 1978, China chose a pragmatic path that mixed the concept of development economics with other approaches, including an increasingly important role for markets and competition. However, as Western intellectual fashions changed, with Chicago replacing Keynes, a new orthodoxy spread to emerging economies, the Washington Consensus. This was propagated globally by a new type of evangelist, the "hamburger economist," who has stymied understanding ever since.

Turning Points in Thinking

As post-Cultural Revolution China changed from a Marxist approach to economics towards something that worked, Western economic theory separately underwent a major shift of its own. The rise of the Chicago School sidelined development economics and Keynes, leaving no clear orthodox path for developing economies to follow other than copy what Chicago preached.

Increasingly there was only one approved model in most academic institutions, governments and multilateral agencies, particularly the International Monetary Fund (IMF) and the World Bank. This neo-classical view of economics was dubbed the Washington Consensus, though its thinking was done largely in Chicago, centred in the US heartland rather than on either coast at Harvard or Berkeley, let alone overseas at Oxford or Cambridge. No allowances were made for structural differences. In its pure form it presumed that one size fits all, which it didn't. Not that Chicago was all wrong. Its emphasis on market forces was a much needed correction to the state being a major allocator of resources. However, development economics and Keynes provide ideas of equal value. They possess a long-term perspective based on structure, insights to overcome market failure and solutions to some emerging economy's problems. These Chicago lacked.

Enter the hamburger economist, a missionary for the faith: see this chapter's "The Hamburgers". Younger cousins, the hamburger analysts and hamburger fund managers, followed in his wake, fanning out into emerging markets in the 1990s and 2000s. They ignored anything outside the Chicago economic model and associated theories of finance, including context, perspective and background.

To the Hamburger family, data is all. It drives markets perfectly. The wheels of markets and commerce whirr effortlessly, unimpeded, powered by a constantly changing rich fuel of data. They overwhelmingly focus on the same data as used in mature markets and economies, overlooking large amounts of very relevant data such as trade data, education levels and R&D spending, let alone its structure. Incredibly, they miss China's single most important trend this century, the private sector's rise to dominance, which is ironic as Hamburgers are great believers in the superiority of private enterprise, which China has proven.

Development Economics and Chinese Thinking

One of development economics' great strengths is its in-built assumption of change, conceptualizing development over the long term as a series of steps to be taken in an appropriate order. As sensible as this may seem, Western institutions largely ignored this. Instead there was the rise of Chicago, rational man (never woman apparently) and mathematical economics for three decades, informing the Hamburger family along the way. In China this was not the case.

China never abandoned its interest in development economics, best described as a broad range of ideas rather than a particular school, all rooted in the observed experience of developing economies. This was not an exclusive diet. Beijing also readily embraced more recent macro theories to manage the economy and create a more sustainable system. These included some of Chicago's ideas, especially its strong emphasis on markets.

China's current long-term economic thinking borrows much from development economics' analysis of basic building blocks, a process that develops in stages. This was mainstream Western thinking for a decade or more, outlined in 1960 by US President Johnson's security adviser Walt Rostow in *The Stages of Economic Growth: A Non-Communist Manifesto*. There was nothing Marxist about it all. Rostow, an economist and Henry Kissinger's predecessor as national security adviser, was anti-communist, believing in the efficacy of capitalism and free enterprise. Appreciating an economy's stage of structural development before tailoring policies Rostow considered critical. For economies are constantly evolving, making an understanding of change central to policy prescriptions.

Such thinking helps frame and inform the path China is taking. An insight into this comes from the introduction Liu He, China's chief economic adviser, wrote for a book about leading development economists of the 1950s and 1960s. They contributed to a common global language until the 1970s, which went largely quiet in the West for three decades. Like Keynes, it is now making a comeback.

Particularly interesting among the book's profiles are Hirschman and Schultz who endorse two concepts that fit squarely with traditional Chinese thought — the importance of education and the idea of learning by doing. Schultz helped coin the term human capital. He held that development requires an educated workforce to solve problems as opposed to just financial capital and investment. As Shaun Hargreaves

Heap of Kings College, London noted, "Hirschman saw development at the ground level and located it crucially in individuals grappling with problems" or as the Chinese would say, "crossing the river by feeling the stones" to discover reality in order to manage uncertainty. People have to learn for themselves. Failure is an integral part of learning, for this is when people are at their most creative, stressed by failure or the prospect of it, and hence discover solutions. Creativity really is "the fuel of growth and transformation". The notion of individuals grappling with problems on the ground resonates in China with officials and entrepreneurs. They call it innovation. This is much more important to growth than relying on foreign economists with top-down models and very little experience of China: divorced from reality.

Among other economists, Liu included Lewis who showed that growth's initial driver is the transfer of surplus labour in subsistence agriculture to manufacturing. Once the surplus is exhausted, then wages rise: the Lewisian turning point, explaining China's current situation, driving consumption. Myrdal is interesting as he saw the importance of economic history determining the path it would take, an idea sitting well with Chinese philosophy. Bauer opposed agricultural support schemes, deeming them to be inefficient subsidies that wasted resources, while Mynt was a liberalizer who ascribed development largely to free markets. Along with Nurkse, Rosenstein-Rodan, Prebisch, Singer, Vinet and Haberler, this is a broad church of economic thinkers chosen for their relevance to China.

The important point about this group is that it does not exclude any major school nor supports one over another: neither Keynes over Chicago or vice versa, as often happens in the West. China is looking for practical, non-ideological ideas. The Hamburger family, in contrast, took Western free market prescriptions lock, stock and barrel to China. Not surprisingly, they found China deficient and highly inefficient. It was simply bound to collapse; after all, the Soviet Union had.

The Hamburgers

"Hamburger economist" was the ultimate putdown at Oxford graduate seminars in the early 1970s. The term describes a foreign economist who advises developing economy governments using knowledge largely gained from mature economies which only change slowly.

Why "hamburger economist"? This is where the withering disdain enters into the term. It is because the economist's principal acquaintance in the country he advises is with foreign luxury hotel coffee shops, eating homogenised American hamburgers and eschewing local delicacies, customs or experience. Local knowledge is in short supply, and visits usually short too. When Robert Wade, author of *Governing The Market* and an on-the-ground-observing social anthropologist by training, asked fellow economist Mynt why his research visits to Taiwan were so short, Mynt explained, only half-jokingly to Wade's mind, that if he stayed any longer it might confuse his thinking. In contrast, Wade spent six months in Taiwan researching his definitive account of the state's role in supporting enterprises, looking for more than hamburgers.

Most research trips entail visits to the central bank, ministry of finance and, possibly, department of statistics: a limited menu, reinforced by discussions with local academics, many of whom were students of the economist or her university before garnering impressive credentials from the likes of the IMF and World Bank. What more need the Hamburgers know that cannot be acquired from such authoritative sources, schooled abroad, who think like us?

That is where Angus, replete in loud floral shirt acquired in a local market somewhere between Bagamoyo and Bali, launched into his denunciation. The country is much more than just the capital city with its beautifully manicured lawns and reassuringly familiar coffee shops. It is very diverse, usually much poorer and much more complex. How wrong could anyone be, he thundered? The hamburger economist is just Graham Greene's well meaning but naïve and meddling Quiet American in another guise, out of his depth in a foreign land.

Unlike the hamburger economist, Angus derives his information literally in the real market from his loud shirt seller. She does not have a bank loan (unsound credit risk, unlike the President's children and other scions of the elite or kleptocracy) but knows everything about the informal capital market where she borrows at 3% if she is lucky, but usually up to 6% when times are tight — *per month*. She manages her finances and survives, even with these punishingly high interest rates.

Her country's recent economic and political history she has lived, and knows more vividly than most academics, let alone foreign advisers. Knowledge of previous times is passed down by parents and elders. She knows how to interpret government plans and pronouncements, discounting much along the way. The market is the centre for information, which flows in from every corner of the country and overseas, as it has done for hundreds of years. Name checks can be done by tapping into its extensive networks: no advanced degree is needed, just common sense and local knowledge. Her finger is firmly on the economy's pulse, unlike any hamburger economist's.

Fast forward two or three decades: enter the hamburger cousins, the hamburger analyst and hamburger fund manager, criss-crossing the globe with their instant opinions, ways of viewing markets and sound bites made for financial television or social media. Usually building on theories developed elsewhere, they are often backed by numbers that the local market would largely dismiss as mumbo jumbo, incomplete and clearly failing the straight-face test: laughable. For the last decade, the cousins' prime destination, even if only on virtual visits, has not been Bagamoyo or Bali but Beijing.

The Next Big Thing

The Next Big Thing draws people like bees to honey. Few have the right experience to fathom it completely but that does not always matter. Indeed, it can be an advantage in short-term-oriented markets. Knowledge might get in the way of clear-cut conclusions. What matters is to know one's audience. What will it find credible?

China became the Next Big Thing, a vast canvas on which anyone could paint bold ideas to grab attention. This began in Hong Kong in the mid-1990s when bulls greatly exaggerated short-term claims for China's economy and markets. The more eye-catching the hues the better: the simpler the idea, the easier a talking-head or salesman could spin it to an audience of largely momentum traders who invest based on price movements rather than because of fundamental valuations.

However, economies and markets are more complex than this. As H.L. Mencken wrote, "There is always a well-known solution to every … problem — neat, plausible and wrong." Bulls and bears are equally guilty as they do battle in the financial media and markets. There is no room for complexity, nuance or even, as it often turns out, reality. Partial and partisan analysis is appreciated: it generates clicks. The dynamics are that investors, especially hedge funds, frequently hunt in packs. They are not trying to gain an edge through superior information as Nathan Rothschild did after the Battle of Waterloo, when he made a killing in British government stock on his exclusive knowledge of Napoleon's unexpected defeat. More than having an exclusive scoop, many investors today are most concerned with how other fund managers might respond to news. If they will follow, and packs are full of followers, they will create sufficient momentum to move prices from which to profit: fundamentals are irrelevant.

Stock market bear Jim Chanos apparently never visited China before pronouncing that its property collapse, which he believed was a given, would be 1,000 times bigger or worse than the 2008 Dubai crash. Chanos had great credibility as his forensic accounting was the first to rumble the gigantic US corporate fraud Enron. He presumed he could do the same with China's property market and economy. However, he ignored the fact that accounting and developing economies can be very different, and that China is a very long way from Texas, both in distance and in history. Did this matter in financial markets? Presumably not, as "1,000 times bigger than Dubai or worse" served its purpose. Impressionable investors took it to heart, comforted by the familiar, and so the China bear market gathered steam in the West, to the great benefit of all who held short positions in the expectation that prices would fall. (Short sellers sell stock they do not own. To cover this shortage, stock can be borrowed from owners for a fee.)

The important point to know about financial markets is that opinion-makers do not have to be right in the long run to succeed and profit. They can be completely wrong. All they need do is convince other investors that their predictions could be right and their lead should be followed. Then in the short-term, markets may well move in the desired direction before a real world-based verdict on their claims is clear: game over, success. Since markets are supposed to discount the future, this is often the case: move first, prove later. Therefore it does not matter that China's property market did not collapse like Dubai's, let alone 1,000 times worse, or that average Chinese property prices have since doubled. As long as share prices fall for whatever reason, even if an erroneous one, a short investment is the "correct" call.

This is where financial markets, like banks, differ fundamentally from markets in manufactured goods. If a new car model were so badly designed that it crashed repeatedly, killing thousands of people, it would have failed to meet its top goal, to transport people safely. It would be deemed "unfit for purpose", in management speak. The car market would probably inflict the ultimate sanction — collapsed sales followed by bankruptcy. That is why manufacturers test, test, test and test again before unveiling new models or products. Not just carmakers, ask car airbag maker Takata about the price to pay for inadequate testing.

Financial markets function differently. They do not exact the ultimate price on those whose predictions prove to be wrong. Market-movers can reappear time and again if they have been right initially in terms of price direction, even if wrong about causality. Many follower investors forgive easily. Constantly on the lookout for new ideas couched in familiar, plausible terms, they often can believe even those previously badly wrong.

Three Myths and a Loss of Common Sense

Many market participants, who usually are not trained in economics, have biases not so much about economic theory but derived from ideology and belief. These distort important assumptions about China's economy, as three myths illustrate. The conclusion of all three is negative, reinforcing conviction about the likelihood of China's impending trouble.

First, competition, the life-blood of sound economies, is presumed to be lacking since China is ruled by a communist party: the state is all-powerful, private enterprise is discouraged and handicapped, if not outlawed. Yet, as Michael Enright once exclaimed over a decade ago at a Research-Works workshop, "Harvard Business School has no words to describe the *intensity* of competition among firms in the Pearl River Delta." In only six out of 40 industrial categories in China do leading state firms possess over half the market, and two of these are natural monopolies, which are often monopolies in market economies: see Chapter 12. So, no dead hand of the state smothering the economy here. Large parts of it are very competitive and market-driven.

A second assumption is that entrepreneurship must be lacking in a communist economy, and that pre-1949 China had no entrepreneurial culture. Rather, China was weighed down by a near-feudal system and traditional economy under the dead weight of conservative Confucianism. Yet Jiangnan, the lower Yangzi delta region around Zhejiang and Shanghai, was on par with the Netherlands in the early 19th century as Li Bozhong observed in *The Economy of the Lower Yangzi Delta in Late Imperial China*. Billy K.L. So, the book's editor, described the Yangzi delta as a highly developed market economy. Clearly there are animal spirits and entrepreneurship in China's social, cultural and mental DNA as 18th- and 19th-century Europe knew all too well from their imports of tea, silk and porcelain, as well as ideas in government and the arts.

Thirdly, China is assumed to be mercantilist, as supposedly Japan is, always protecting its own firms. This ignores the fact that foreign companies dominate China's auto market, one of the largest manufacturing sectors in any economy. China has been General Motors' largest market since 2012, larger than the US. Foreign firms also have significant shares in many of the more technologically advanced sectors and segments. An open WTO-compliant economy always needs advanced technology. Chinese pragmatism accepts this: narrow nationalism does not fit the larger purpose.

Like any country, China helps its companies, but when global trade rules are binding and supposedly "markets are decisive", the amount of assistance is more limited than many imagine. Rather than assisting its state-owned enterprises, Beijing is more often on the side of its consumers, as Andy Rothman, then of CLSA, observed in 2003, for they can withdraw the mandate of heaven by revolting or leaving. Hence China has no problem with foreign companies owning over half its car market, albeit often in joint venture with local companies, if that gets the better cars that consumers want.

When the Hamburgers turn their attention to China, it is remarkable how often basic common sense deserts them. Eager to stay on what they think is safe ground they speak from the familiar narrative about China's overbuilt infrastructure with roads to nowhere and ghost cities. Knowing so little about China's reality, they ignore the obvious: that the Chinese talk endlessly about traffic jams and congestion. In the crowded streets around their five-star hotels people push, jostle and shove, elbow-to-elbow, often with barely anywhere to breathe let alone relax. The subway systems are jam-packed, they are told, and hence to be avoided. The reality on the ground about infrastructure is very different from the narrative of overbuilding and misallocated capital.

As market penetration is still relatively low, China knows its car population may well rise to nearly 200 million by 2020, having more than doubled from 2010 to 2015. As incomes rise, cars become increasingly affordable for more and more people, requiring new roads to avoid gridlock. All this is the talk in China, for those who care to listen. They also know that urbanization is unfinished: some 10–20 million more people become urban every year. That means another 50–100 million to be housed over five years, not to mention many more that need to be re-housed from the existing crowded and poorly built housing of the 1980s and 1990s. "Ghost cities" will therefore fill up: see Chapter 13. The Hamburgers should reflect on what they have seen from their windows and heard in casual conversation, instead of latching on to one piece among myriads of monthly data or a wild generalization so as to make a seemingly powerful point that completely misses the real picture. Traffic jams are a lot easier to find in China than "roads to nowhere".

Perspective, Sense of Proportion and Context

The problem with the Hamburgers' data-driven approach is not that it is necessarily wrong but that data on its own is insufficient. Statistics can prove almost anything. Their user needs a sensible historical perspective, as well as keen sense of proportion: in sum, the context.

Many of the criticisms of China's deficiencies and problems may be valid in a narrow sense. A broader and longer-term perspective, though, is required. First, a sense of proportion is needed to grasp reality. Having grown faster than any other economy in the world over the last 50 years, China still has momentum. This is usually missing, a major omission from any objective analysis. China's GDP grew at 6.7% in 2016, when the advanced economies combined grew less than one-third of that.

Worrying about Chinese exports when the whole world is suffering on the trade front and most countries are doing worse than China also gets things out of proportion, especially when in 2016 China racked up multi-billion dollar trade surpluses every month. Yet markets expect a major devaluation, something not normally associated with the world's largest trade surplus. Hard data on capital flight is difficult to come by. What exists is incomplete. At first sight, China's numbers can seem enormous. However, when the scale of a problem is put in the context of a $12 trillion economy, the second largest in the world, it does not seem quite so alarming.

Again, a sense of proportion is needed. Even when the number is genuinely disturbing, history has shown that China can grow out of its problems: principally by changing policy and structure. China has done so in each of the previous decades. In the 1980s, it turned around the economy after the Cultural Revolution; in the 1990s, Deng rebooted reform with his Southern Tour after the 1980s' reforms proved insufficient and created new problems of their own; and in the 2000s, when reform had to continue, especially in the financial sector, to provide a stronger, sustainable foundation for an increasingly sophisticated economy. What China has always needed is time, something markets are usually too impatient to provide, but something China has created through understanding change.

The hunger for change among individuals has not lessened. Only China's needs have changed from the very basics of calories, security and living space to middle-income desires like better healthcare, education, environment and leisure. This stark change in priorities is all too often forgotten. The images that most come to mind in the West today about China are of air pollution, ghost cities, chubby children and luxury goods-buying tourists: all things that many could only dream of having after the Cultural Revolution. Even air pollution would probably have been accepted as it would have meant economic development and accompanying material prosperity.

The scale is simple. This is the largest economic transformation the world has ever seen. In land area, China is the fourth-largest country on earth. Its provinces should be treated as countries, each with its own history and economic geography. Only with that level of detailed understanding can the overall picture be seen. There are no neat, let alone speedy, solutions to its problems or ways by which to judge China and its prospects easily, but that is the reality.

Data, Surveys and Networks

So what are serious investors to do, especially those with no deep knowledge of any land but their own? A handful of visits to China do not constitute sufficient knowledge. A few interns and junior staff from China cannot make up for this gap: they are too young to know the whole country well. Often they have remarkably narrow knowledge or experience of China, let alone of investment. To some investors, the problem is not just lack of language or knowledge, it is the lack of reliable data. They believe transparency will make everything comprehensible: good luck.

Is the official data propaganda or the truth? This is where many foreigners give up or discount very sharply the veracity of China data. One even went so far as to call it "state-sanctioned propaganda". Another young fund manager dismissed those who broadly accept China's data and version of economics as being captive to a Chinese form of Stockholm Syndrome: hostages falling under their captors' spell. This would come as a bit of a surprise to professional economists at the likes of the IMF and World Bank who scour data continually. They know its ins and outs having worked closely with Beijing to improve it, especially after the 1997 Asian Crisis exposed the poor quality of the whole region's data. Ever since, there has been a steady improvement in data quality though there is still a way to go, especially unfortunately in the all-important property data.

Reared on a data diet from football, baseball and basketball statistics in the US or soccer and cricket elsewhere, then schooled in the accuracy of numbers, company accounts and government economic series, the Hamburgers believe data to be sacred and infallible. Data moving markets instantly because they are credible is fundamental to their religion. Otherwise they are at a loss to explain reality. The world has to be black and white; there is no room for grey. Precision is required. Algorithms have to be created: this is the only way to make sense of any economy or market.

Yet in China, and Asia generally, there is plenty of room for ambiguity. People are comfortable with it: ambiguity disturbs no one. It is assumed to be the case because of great complexity. Not everything can be easily reduced to a formula or fit into neat, precise boxes. That would be a great mistake. This is life; it is messy. In fact, ambiguity can be a lubricant, smoothing the way forward and keeping things on track.

Reality

China has gathered data for over 2,000 years: hardly new to the business, with longer continuous experience of it and data's inherent weaknesses, distortions and manipulations than any other country. From their years working in the provinces, those at the top know how local governments provide data to make officials look good or avoid making them look bad. It enhances their careers. It is a game, an art and definitely not a perfect science.

No one is more conscious of China's data shortcomings than the National Bureau of Statistics (NBS) itself. I recall a long visit in the 1990s to the NBS in Beijing with a colleague, Geoff Lewis, who previously worked for the UK Treasury. After being grilled on their data for nearly a couple of hours, the junior of the two officials asked if we believed their data. Diplomatically, we asked if they did. They burst into quiet, nervous laughter. There was a long silence. After all, they were obviously compiling the statistics on well over one billion people and dealing with career-minded officials on a continental scale. The silence continued: the sound of silence. The question needed no answer; it answered itself. It was self-evident; there was no need to discuss uncomfortable truths. Like everything else in China's reform, it is a work in progress and better than it was. That was the truth that mattered.

In China, the data is often the message: more than just a way of keeping score. No one worried that when Premier Wen Jiabao set the 12th plan real GDP target at 7% Chongqing, which is funded directly by Beijing, projected handsome 14% GDP growth, while other local governments forecasted numbers well in excess of 7%. No one expected the target to be hit; all assumed then it would be exceeded. What mattered was that everyone received clearly the central message: long-term growth should slow compared with the last plan and the plan before that when growth targets were 7.5% and 8% respectively. The fact it came out around 10% was ignored. The precise number was less important than the message: growth would slow and quality now mattered more than quantity.

Solutions

So what should investors do in this apparent data nightmare? Best look at what Chinese premiers do. Premier Li Keqiang said he follows just a few key variables. Zhu Rongji constantly ordered bespoke surveys. Given their track records over the last 30 years it is well worth considering how they cope.

As US President Ronald Reagan said, trust, but verify. It is the same with China's top officials. Start with some healthy scepticism about the data's precision, though despair should be avoided. If it is any consolation, the trend, increasingly, is usually correct. What may be in doubt is its magnitude. Each decade, the quality of data gets better but it is never going to improve completely, let alone overnight.

To avoid flying blind, those at the pinnacle of government have to operate with some undistorted data. Former premier Zhu Rongji was once asked if he believed Chinese government data. He put his hand in his pocket, pulled out some coins, added them up and pronounced these were the data he believed: the only numbers he could verify himself. Zhu, who had headed economics and business at Tsinghua, China's top university, brought some hard-headed realism to national government in the 1990s, when he was vice premier in charge of first the economy and central bank, then the country as premier. He tried to make up for the potential unreliability of the data by commissioning regular surveys on all sorts of issues to find out what the official data missed.

Various monthly surveys are done in leading industries like property, autos and steel as well as private sector ones like *CLSA's China Reality Research* and the *Financial Times' China Confidential*. Between them they provide a realistic overview of economic trends in what is a complex, continental economy. Car dealers and jewellers are another indicator, though the gold data has to be navigated carefully, with gold's new-found status as a momentum trade understood. It is not just a store of wealth.

In China, it is all about definitions. Residential space in China is often 30% greater than the Western definition would calculate. China includes common areas like hallways, lobbies and lifts. Disputes and misunderstandings often arise simply because two sides are talking about different things without realising it. Before getting embroiled in an argument in China, check the definitions. They may differ from what is understood elsewhere. The devil indeed is in the details, and particularly the definitions.

Apart from surveys and healthy scepticism, government officials draw on their networks: their legendary *guanxi*. Be they with former colleagues, current officials, corporate executives, academics, classmates or family and friends, people in Asia know the fine art of building information networks to solve problems and capitalise on opportunities: not unlike elites everywhere. The difference in China is that almost everyone builds *guanxi* from migrant workers to businessmen and officials.

The best *guanxi* provides trust, truth and predictability in an uncertain world, as was proven in 2008 after the global financial crisis when senior officials fanned out across China to get an initial idea of the problem's scale. Old acquaintances, including powerful party secretaries and provincial governors, had great local knowledge as well as solutions to avert a collapse. Officials returned to Beijing not only with a much clearer understanding of reality on the ground but also with much less fear of an economic collapse. The Chinese term *guanxi*, literally connections, often has a negative connotation because it is used regarding influence with officials, often corrupt influence. Yet someone's *guanxi* is much more than that: a major source of economic, commercial, market, political and financial intelligence, it is an important part of operating where the media and markets, more formal sources of information, are less developed.

The doyen of Philippines business, Washington SyCip, was once asked by a young fund manager for his most important piece of advice. Without hesitation SyCip, then in the 1990s the most connected person in Manila, replied that it was "to eat out every night, except on Christmas Day and mother's birthday". Much knowledge and timely information was accumulated by eating with as many people as possible. Over time, this collected more valuable information and insight than existed in entire newsrooms, libraries, boardrooms or brokers' offices. Little escaped SyCip's network in Manila or throughout the Philippines. Many of its members rose to prominence in business and government, national and local, even regionally. The accretion of knowledge and ability to check a fact or rumour with a quick phone call to a knowledgeable and trusted source is reminiscent of Siggy Warburg's comment that he never read newspapers because he made it his business to know things before they appeared in the press. Warburg was his own newsroom.

Less illustrious figures than Zhu Rongji or Washington SyCip have their own networks. The club or coffee shop in Southeast Asia or teahouse in traditional China was where all businessmen met. Hence the credit rating was the judgement of one's peers or, as the saying goes, "the value of one's face" in the teahouse or coffee shop — how someone was regarded. Were they greeted, and by whom, or ignored, and why? In modern times, restaurants and karaoke lounges have supplanted the traditional venues but the purpose is still the same: unearthing information, maintaining relationships and doing reputation or credit checks.

Despite foreign distrust, China must be getting something right. As a poster on the *Financial Times* website in 2014 put it, "So if I accept the FT's general [negative] narrative of China today: $6.8 trillion of squandered investment, lethal pollution, inability to innovate, terrible demographics, widespread culture [of] graft and corruption which includes day-to-day cheating by the general population, aggressive military expansion (not just islands but also space and cyberspace), out-of-control credit expansion, lack of democracy, wealthy elite (all of whom are corrupt, of course) who have fled the country for a better life elsewhere ... etc. Just to name but a few of the negatives highlighted. And still, it's the second largest economy growing over 7% (1st if you go by PPP, not GDP). So what is China getting right?" In the three years after that 2014 post, China grew another 20%.

So what is China getting right, for China at least? That is the question to ask and answer. Where, as Pascal urged, should one look? The book's final section considers misconceptions and big ideas about China's economy, including how its change will impact the world's future.

Chapter 11

Economic Change — The Difference is Night and Day

In today's China, it is hard to understand the changes taking place without understanding the economy and materialism.

Yu Hua, *The Australian Financial Review,* 2016

Just as China's economy can only be understood by knowing non-economic factors like history, philosophy and politics, so China's overall change only makes sense with strong knowledge of the economy. As novelist Yu Hua noted, the economy and materialism underpin change.

Tracing China's economic evolution shines light on change's path since 1949, a year which of course itself marked very major change. Adjusting to what that brought has been China's story ever since. Temporary stability until the mid-1950s gave way to instability and great uncertainty as ideology took hold for the next two decades before pragmatism clawed its way back to stability, while state planning bowed to a greater use of markets. First, though, a corrective is essential to appreciate the long-term context of the post-1949 path.

A World of Surprising Resemblances Before the Great Divergence

Projecting backwards to the past from today, when Asia's billions are seen suffering disasters from pollution to overcrowding and disease, is a mistake. This error springs from the idea that China, more than any other country, has been the "other" in Western versions of itself: the presumed opposite. Whereas Europe is depicted as uniquely rich, long before its late 18th-century industrial revolution, China is considered to have been poor.

Too easily forgotten is that in 1800 Beijing was the world's largest city, while China's Yangzi Delta was one of the world's five leading economies, along with Japan's Kanto plain, the UK, Netherlands and India's Gujarat, as Kenneth Pomerantz identified them in *The Great Divergence*. All had similarities in agricultural, commercial and early industrial development. Differences were only of degree, not of kind, and no one economy was clearly ahead of the others.

In 1800, China fed, clothed and supported its rapidly growing population whilst creating specialized skills on par with Europe. Pomerantz's view is that Europe and China shared "a world of surprising resemblances", not differences. Economic specialization from food and clothing to housing and transport generally needs large populations for economies of scale to spur output and, with over 300 million people, China had scale even then. The Yangzi delta had some 1,000 people per square mile and 31–37 million inhabitants in 1750, depending on definition, while China's second-most developed region, Lingnan, around Guangdong, had 17.5 million people. Western Europe's largest state, France, had 26 million in 1789, smaller than the Yangzi delta alone.

Rather than Europe being well ahead of China, a better description is that global development in 1800 combined Western European and East Asian approaches. Even though they increasingly used Western technology, it was not simply the spread of Western ideas and achievements. In some ways, Asia was ahead of a Europe that used Chinese and Indian textile weaving and dyeing processes. A damp Manchester reaped the benefit of the 17th-century Shandong discovery that humidity aids cotton spinning. The lower Yangzi region probably produced more cloth in 1750 than Britain did in 1800.

In farming, the Welsh agricultural improvement society dedicated itself in 1753 to Wales becoming "as flourishing as China": note, not as

England. China's irrigation not only watered and extended production but developed well defined water rights. Disputes were handled efficiently in Asia, from Java to Cambodia and northeast Asia: China was no exception. Land management was also well developed. Multicropping was common, more fertilizer was used than in Britain, both animal dung and bean cake, while Britain learned practices from China to combat deforestation and soil degradation.

China's consumption of grain, sugar and energy reflected a thriving economy. Grain consumption in the 18th century, when adjusted for 1930s age structure, was 2,386 calories per capita: for males it was 2,651. China consumed twice as much sugar as Europe, having used it in Buddhist rituals since the Tang Dynasty (618–907). Visitors in the 16th and 17th centuries found wealthy Chinese used much more sugar than did their European peers. Even poor Chinese ate sugared biscuits at festivals, while candied fruits delighted wedding guests. Energy use per capita in 1700 was about the same, though China, with its generally warmer climate and faster cooking methods, needed significantly less fuel than Europe. Chinese stoves were much more efficient for cooking and heating compared with European open hearths.

Many anecdotes, records and travellers' accounts testify to all this. British envoys to China in 1793, George Staunton and Lord Macartney, both commented on how much Chinese smoked. European visitors observed the lack of severe poverty whereas in India they mentioned extremes of wealth and poverty. Staunton noted that rural China, while poor, had the basic necessities. China's extensive transport systems of water (river, canals and coastal) and roads enabled long-distance trade to flourish. China sold much more of its harvest in markets than Europe: its grain trade fed an estimated 14 million people, five times more than Europe did before 1800.

China was more successful expanding its markets abroad as exports of silk, cotton, porcelain and tea testified. Only with the use of force (armed trading and colonization) could European firms beat merchants from China, Japan and India in Asia or the Middle East. Chinese cotton textiles and porcelain became prized items of European fashion, even by those with modest incomes. No Western product held similar importance in China, until opium. China's superiority in long-distance seaborne trade was due to a different approach. China never gave military backing to private overseas forays: it protected Chinese merchants militarily but never overseas settlers. Qing military expansion was inland in Central Asia. Southeast Asia never became as important to China as the New World of the Americas did to Europe. China's top security concern was holding China together: overseas entanglements were to be avoided.

Consumers and traders alike had to pay for overseas goods at market prices, without subsidies or military assistance. They had to wait until after 1850 to exploit the great rice bowls of Southeast Asia — the Irrawaddy, Mekong and Chao Phraya deltas, as well as Luzon. Only then could sufficient capital and labour be attracted to develop them. Not that China lagged Britain in long-distance trade. Manila's Chinese population in 1603 was reportedly over 20,000, in Batavia (Jakarta) it was some 10,000 in 1739, whereas Boston had a population of 10,000 in 1722 and New York City only 6,000 in 1690.

England's life expectancy in 1750 was 40 years, Germany's 35–40 and France's about 30 in 1790. Those Chinese who avoided infanticide to reach one year of age averaged 40 years or more before 1800. Despite popular images of disease and poverty, China's public health, for the times, was developed, with smallpox prevention, maternal and infant healthcare along with the more basic uses of soap and boiling water. Attitudes towards medicine did not lag either. People widely sought treatment from China's millennia-long medical knowledge.

If it had been a question of Adam Smith's markets triumphing, China would have been the more likely winner. Pomerantz records that, "Markets worked well within China's eight or nine macro regions [each larger than most European states] encouraging people in much of the interior to devote more time to making cloth and the like ...18th century China actually came closer to resembling the neoclassical ideal of a market economy than did western Europe." Most land throughout China was more or less freely alienable whereas much western European farmland was considerably harder to buy or sell. Labour markets were similarly constrained.

Migration was much easier in China. Over 10 million in the late 17th and 18th centuries migrated within China compared with just 1.5 million Europeans crossing the Atlantic to the New World before 1800. The Chinese government assisted surplus labour to move into underdeveloped or war-hit areas where labour was scarce, which allowed glutted regional labour markets to clear. Government help extended to travel, loans, seed and land, giving farmers a better chance of making a go of things independently.

Chinese farmers were much less likely to face monopsony, a single buyer. Qing rulers, at least until the 1850s, were very concerned that markets should have many competing buyers and sellers. This competition definitely worked well for China's two main crops, grain and cotton, whose harvests kept up with the rapidly increasing population's demand. Farmers were free to make and sell handicrafts like textiles. There was no urban monopoly on textile making, whereas in western Europe powerful protectionist guilds disappeared only very slowly.

However, after 1800, the Qing Dynasty started to weaken and ossify for economic and cultural reasons. Its infrastructure deteriorated: first, water transport in North China and the Yangzi Valley, then the granary storage system designed to reduce price fluctuations after bad harvests. This created price instability and deterred investment. Farmland expansion was hampered by growing Confucian conservatism among elites and wealthier farmers who scorned women working in fields: much more proper to be indoors, spinning and weaving. Bound feet again became fashionable.

All this was in great contrast to Europe that had technological change, institutional development and New World resources to exploit. China stagnated, though did not de-industrialize. Market mechanisms saved China but could not prevent it entering a long relative decline during the Great Divergence that lasted from 1800 until after the 1978 reforms.

Night and Day

Harvard Professor Dwight Perkins forecast one of the key turning points of the late 20th century, recognizing its importance long before it happened, in *China, Asia's Next Economic Giant.* Capturing the full magnitude of reform, Perkins predicted in 1986 that "Few if any events in the last half of the 20th century are of comparable significance … one quarter of the world's population … [will move] from a closed, poor, rural, peasant society … to an economy … increasingly urban and industrial … fully integrated into the international economic system"; and so it did.

Perkins also identified the key qualifier: "if the political environment remains supportive". Effective government has been critical to economic success throughout Asia. Not so much because of state intervention or planning but because stability brought long-term investment, from physical infrastructure and education to heavy industry and housing. Even with political disruption in June 1989 and the 2012 transition, China continued its transformation. Change has its own strength and dynamics that can survive rough patches, enabling the difference between 1978 and today to be described as "night and day".

Milton Friedman's explanation for colonial Hong Kong's success missed an important part of the equation. Parts were *laissez-faire*, with lots of very healthy competition, especially in manufacturing and trade. However, privately-owned banks, real estate and utilities were cartels. Stability and government, not a free market, enabled all to flourish. There was more to Hong Kong's growth than the invisible hand of Adam Smith. Singapore certainly never eschewed state involvement. Japan, South Korea and Taiwan all benefitted from the stability that better government and some state intervention brought after war destroyed their economies.

The future was not promising in 1978 when post-Mao reform and opening up began. Given what happened elsewhere in Asia, there was no guarantee China would gain the stability to emulate its neighbours' success, especially after the Great Leap Forward and the Cultural Revolution. China could have followed Cambodia, an ideological kindred spirit in the 1970s, the autarkic Burmese road to military-driven stagnation or the Philippines' half-century-long fall from leader to laggard. After all, China had had over a century of political turmoil, war and relative economic decline.

A few more decades of the same turmoil may have appeared more likely than Perkins' forecast when he had a section entitled *Will Reforms Continue*? His answer was a definitive yes. Some questions never change. Media editorials and writers still raise it three decades later. Newcomers keep asking the same question. In 1979, I tried to run a series of articles in the *Far Eastern Economic Review*, then Asia's leading politics and economics magazine, on whether the four modernizations, as reform was first called, would succeed. While no one disagreed they might, so few details existed in terms of capital, human capacity, systems or thinking it was considered too speculative a topic or just plain difficult. There would doubtless be some experiments, parts of China might progress, but the world could afford to watch patiently.

George Baeder, then head of Business International in Hong Kong, recalls with a smile the advice he gave in 1979 to a visiting US shipping line which was very excited about possibly carrying container loads of Chinese textiles across the Pacific. Looking out from Hong Kong harbour to Lion's Rock, behind which China's mainland hid, Baeder quickly disabused his guests of the notion for two self-evident reasons. First, China did not have enough textiles to clothe its own people. Second, China was not known for quality, quite the opposite. Furthermore, who knew where its politics were heading? China was of little interest, just a turbulent backwater. The Tigers of South Korea, Taiwan and Southeast Asia were where the action was. Forget China; reform and opening up were mere words, issued more in hope than expectation. That was the foreign consensus view.

To those schooled in the Western ideological, political and economic wars of the 1950s and 1960s, or later the 1990s' triumphalism, it seemed strange to call reform just modernization: it must surely be a euphemism, a fig leaf for an end to communism. In China there was no such sense. This was not the end of communism, merely its newest chapter. To China in 1978, they were indeed just four important modernizations of agriculture, industry, defence and science and technology, in the tradition of the search for "Wealth and Power" and national dignity. This was no Chicago School critique of a state economy's failings but the ignored 1963 proposals Premier Zhou Enlai made just before China descended into prolonged political turbulence. Over a decade later, to rescue the economy, Mao in 1975 turned to his ailing premier to sort out the economy with the four modernizations. Zhou Enlai then turned to Deng Xiaoping, his frequent assistant over the years, who was close to Mao on practical matters, to revive and implement them.

Deng's eyes were opened to the modern world in the early 1920s when, like Zhou, he spent several years working in war-ravaged France. These were opened even further when he returned in 1978 to see how much Europe had changed for the richer and how far China had fallen behind. Seeing modern Japan made an even greater impression as it shared similar Confucian roots. Zhou and Mao shortly passed into history but Deng carried on the work they decided was needed — a 20th-century version of the 19th-century "Self Strengthening", the reform that tried to cure China's weaknesses by modernizing as Japan did through the Meiji Restoration.

Changing Role of Government

Government's role was not in doubt when the Communist Party took power in 1949. Globally, free markets were deemed to have led to the Great Depression of the 1930s. Even in the US, government economic involvement increased, while in Britain it led to the welfare state and nationalization of many economic commanding heights. Similar changes occurred in most of Western Europe. Asia's second-largest nation, India, looked to the state to build and direct its economy after Independence in 1947.

In China, after two decades of almost no growth pre-1949, the adoption of a Soviet-style five-year plan seemed logical, given the Soviet Union's continued rapid economic transformation. Free markets had done little for China in the 20th century, though they had in the previous millennia. *China Reconstructs* was a baffling title to British Chinese restaurant takeaway customers for a propaganda magazine circulated worldwide in the early 1970s, but its title captured a very potent idea inside China that helped establish communist rule. After the depredations of two decades of continuous warfare during the civil war and Japan's 14-year invasion, rebuilding China's physical infrastructure and education topped national priorities.

Reconstruction needed government. The private sector was in no shape to build roads, railways, bridges or the like, even if government had wanted that. Then, as the Cold War came to Asia in 1950, bringing China to war with the US-led West in Korea, so Beijing looked to secure its borders. Heavy industry was needed to build defence and China required allies, most notably the Soviet Union. These changes did not fail China in the short-term. The first five-year plan saw GDP annual growth average 7%–8% before nationalization in 1955–56 spread to everything except petty trade. Only 7% of land was left with peasants. Agriculture was collectivized, first into co-operatives and then into communes in 1958. Central planning took over. Administrative allocation of resources replaced the market in heavy industry, supplying capital and inputs.

Signs of serious problems emerged. Economic efficiency fell while waste rose. Perkins noted that China ended up using two-and-a-half times as much oil to produce the same amount of GNP as India. Although per capita GNP still grew, household incomes and consumption did not: most people started to lose out. Income differentials remained; incentives were removed. Performance was rarely rewarded. Economists saw the signs of deterioration but did not matter when politics ruled.

Mao wanted to create Socialist Man and Woman, not so much a socialist economy. His military mind sought sweeping movement, breakthroughs and dramatic progress rather than a technocrat's belief in steady, gradual long-term economic growth *per se*. The same military mentality and experience enabled the party to overcome overwhelming odds by mobilizing masses of people. What worked in war, however, failed in peace. The search for selfless Socialist Man and Woman, driven by the social good rather than material gain, was a mirage. As Xi Jinping in 2012 told China Central Television, in a very Daoist way, the "Cultural Revolution was emotional. It was a mood. And when the ideals could not be realized, it proved an illusion."

The attempt to create a socialist society led to increasing absenteeism, shoddy work and even strikes. There was no alternative but to reintroduce material incentives. For the first time in 15 years, wage increases and promotions were allowed, piece-rate work reintroduced and better performance rewarded. By 1978, urban China was returning to full-time work under a new, but elsewhere, normal system.

Change Again

China's formal reintegration into the world economy began in 1979 with joining the International Monetary Fund and the World Bank: not that this meant its financial institutions bore any resemblance to those of other members. Its banks were not banks in the conventional sense; they merely had the word "bank" engraved above their doors. Indeed it only had one commercial bank, the Bank of China.

China opened up to foreign investors in 1979, mostly from Hong Kong and Taiwan, to invest in four Special Economic Zones in Guangdong and Fujian. Capitalizing on China's one comparative advantage, its low cost of abundant labour, exports suddenly boomed 22% a year between 1979 and 1982 as China set off to become the Workshop of the World. Soon there were anti-dumping protests against Chinese tinned mushrooms in the US, the first of many trade disputes: in hindsight a very good sign. Without any inkling, as China re-emerged, the world entered a new era: globalization.

Agriculture was not left behind; indeed, it saw some of the first fundamental reforms. The communes began to disband, rural markets returned, some prices liberalized and production reverted to largely individual family peasant agriculture. Immediately, farmers responded to the incentive of working for themselves while production quotas were cut, allowing people to sell more on the free market. Thai financier Choedchu Sophonpanich noticed the difference over just two years in the early 1980s. The first time he visited, no one was working in the fields at 4pm. On the next visit, people were there until dusk at 6.30pm, then rising again before dawn. Families were given more freedom to decide what to plant. Not surprisingly, agricultural output grew 9.4% annually between 1979 and 1985 compared with just 2.9% in the two decades up to 1978: incentives worked.

Overseas Learning Through *Yanjiu*

Before introducing this major economic correction, China did years of extensive *yanjiu,* field work and research. As a late developer, China supposedly could leapfrog others by adopting leading technology and thinking, but this proved much easier said than done. In fact it could not be done in finance or in more complex manufacturing. China lacked some of the most basic concepts, knowledge or institutions to support the world's most advanced systems.

So China looked most to economies with systems that had been much closer to its own 20–30 years earlier. Successes and failures were equally important. Warnings were as valuable as solutions. China needed to figure out almost everything for itself after studying others' blueprints and regulations. Traditional Chinese thinking knew this, even if many foreigners assumed China would simply copy world-leading Western systems as best it could. Therefore, in the 1970s and 1980s, East and Southeast Asia, with similar cultural traditions and historic experience, were China's natural focus for ideas. Taiwan, Japan and South Korea had Confucian roots and trade links with China for centuries. The city *entrepots* of Hong Kong and Singapore had similar affinities, while providing a window more directly on the Western world, markets, law and systems.

Not surprisingly, Taiwan was the most relevant. The common cultural, government and social foundations were often those that continued in post-1949 China. After successfully developing a state-led economy in the 1950s, Taiwan evolved into a market-driven one where the government still had influence but 99% of companies were small and medium-sized enterprises (SMEs). However, a strong desire for control remained. After all, the Kuomintang's (KMT) forebears created the world's first major bureaucracy, which lived on in Taiwan after 1949, where it faced very similar challenges as China did 20–30 years later, not just creating fast economic growth but also handling its inevitable slowdown. Taiwan's Asian Tiger pace and volatile growth that averaged 8% for three decades had been managed down successfully from 6.8% real GDP growth in 1990 (China's was 6.7% in 2016) to a mature 3%. Banks' non-performing loans fell from 8% in 1990 to 0.4%. Shadow banking, which really was shadowy, complete with gangsters playing a major role in financing local politicians, came into the mainstream financial system.

Taiwan's approach followed traditional Chinese thinking. This interested post-Mao China. Incremental change and pilot schemes cut paths to financial modernization. Interest rate liberalization drove down the cost of capital, while deposit insurance and a maximum interest rate ceiling helped stability. A credit card crisis was brought under control in 2005–2006. There was much from which China could learn within its own terms and historic experience. In manufacturing it was the same.

Taiwan's economic structure had been similar to China's, only more developed: textiles and machinery were its backbone until the 1980s, before moving up to IT industries. The inevitable problems of an ageing manufacturing base, under pressure from lower-cost Asian economies, had been managed successfully. It was not fully market-driven. In the opinion of CLSA's Taiwan head, Peter Sutton, if the US economy is 90% market-driven, Taiwan's is only 75%, with the rest dictated by state policy and politics. State enterprises, though, changed sufficiently to prevent them being dangerous, unlike in China. In the early days, Taiwan's government had to play a leading development role simply because private firms were often deterred by the amount of capital required for major investments and their distant long-term returns. The government-funded 10 Projects, largely in infrastructure and supplier industries like steel, revived Taiwan in the early 1980s.

Among Taiwan's economic architects of the 1950s, there was a traditional Chinese belief in the responsibilities of the educated elite. Public office was not seen by this group as a way to enrich self, family or friends, as had been the case before 1949 when the KMT ruled the mainland. Unused to Western ideas of politics which "imposed a pseudo parliamentary system on China" as David Bonavia put it, the

KMT had failed with "the dictatorship of the Nationalist period, whose most important features were corruption, hypocrisy, inept military leadership, financial bungling and defeat by the Communist 'bandits'". Reacting to the mainland's loss, a traditional elite tried to restore KMT legitimacy in Taiwan by using best practices, Chinese and Western.

Taiwan was 30 years ahead of China in the 1980s in one very important respect. In commerce, international trade and finance, it had adapted Western institutions, law, regulations and systems to the Chinese context and culture. Taiwan very often had the same terms for concepts as China. These made writing laws and regulations much easier, especially when having to find new words. It could also help provide training in culturally familiar ways. Financial systems had been as chaotic as China's became in the 2000s. The stock market had ballooned 10-fold in the 1980s. In banking, getting the balance right between too much and too little state involvement proved very hard. Too much control choked initiative, too little led to chaos. As China set about transforming its economy, Taiwan provided valuable lessons and warnings.

The same was true of South Korea. When Deng sought a transitional model towards a market-based economy, he looked directly east. In 1989, Kim Kihwan, then South Korea's top economic mandarin, flew to Beijing to meet Deng after quickly preparing a 30-page booklet that his host "gobbled up". President Park Chung-hee, pilot of Korea's economic take-off, had a military past and mindset like Deng. Kim Kihwan listed for Deng how South Korea overcame the many trials it faced in the 1980s, including Park's assassination, a terrible harvest, the OPEC oil shock and industrial overcapacity.

Deng came away from Singapore in 1978 with two major insights. First, Singapore's ruling People's Action Party, socialist in origin, had managed to reform its state-owned enterprises (SOEs), so why couldn't China? Second, a predominantly Chinese society had managed to cure the blight of corruption. Despite the obvious differences in population size, China has looked to many of the things Singapore did, notably in enterprise reform: the Temasek model of state ownership and social security.

Like Singapore, Hong Kong's exposure since the 19th century to foreign markets, law and institutions was very instructive. Hong Kong in the 1970s was becoming a global financial centre. As a marketplace, joined increasingly by mainlanders, it provided a perch from which Beijing could observe the outside world from up close: even more so after its return to Chinese sovereignty in 1997. Not only could its banks gain direct exposure to global finance and its norms but Chinese officials could become familiar with them too.

The Hong Kong Monetary Authority and the Futures and Securities Commission have been two important institutions for increasing Beijing's financial knowledge. Not just about Hong Kong but also the rest of the region and global systems. As one Beijing official remarked, it is much easier in Hong Kong to deal with China stock market manipulation by talking there to officials from Taiwan, home of the notorious Big Hand market manipulators, and Hong Kong than to try to manage it only in China. Similarly they could see how global currencies, capital markets and international trade finance worked.

From outside Asia, multilateral institutions contributed considerably to China's change. Initially, in the 1980s, it was the World Bank. By 2000, as China's needs changed from development *per se* and manufacturing to the financial system, so the IMF became the more relevant of the two Washington-based Bretton Woods institutions. The IMF has a technical mission in Beijing, there to advise on whatever China wants to know, resulting in China spending more on IMF advice than any other state, as Bloomberg's economist Tom Orlik recounted. The IMF is not in Beijing to enforce any lending agreements, merely to monitor the economy and financial system. This makes for a very different relationship from the often fraught relations with other members: think Greece.

The IMF has become one of China's most important global relationships. Having transformed itself after the 1997 Asian Crisis when IMF measures had proved disastrous, it became increasingly a sounding board for Beijing's thinking. Apart from technical information, it also purveys the ideas of Beijing's technocrats and top leaders to their less well-informed party associates through its published periodic reviews and pronouncements about global best practice, reinforcing the main messages of China's economic reformers.

Change in Practice

Despair was widespread after Zhu Rongji in March 1998 cut the jobs of four million bureaucrats and 20 million industrial workers. This bitter medicine was administered because 50% of SOEs made losses, while 60%–80% of PBOC policy loans were to failing SOEs.

Edward Steinfeld of Brown University captured the sense of despair in *Forging Reform in China: The Fate of State-Owned Industry*. Beijing was "utterly panicked by the prospect of failing SOEs and massive urban unemployment. There was an air of complete crisis surrounding discussions of the SOEs". Policymakers faced "grim choices ... simple choices do not exist". China was "beset by colossal economic problems"; its banking system and industry were on the verge of collapse. This was a Kafkaesque nightmare.

Partial reforms often made matters worse but there was no going back: Catch-22. Reforms like decentralization, corporatization and even privatization could not work without clear property rights, impeded by a lack of the most basic institutions including proper capital markets, accounting or regulation. Decentralization unleashed animal spirits but also predators and rent-seekers. Overproduction was encouraged by the easy rolling over of bank loans. This led to excessive investment, with funds diverted to unauthorized and hidden purposes. There was no bankruptcy law, no real accountability, no control and no responsibility: all a real nightmare.

Change could only come from strictly enforcing budgets. Property rights and management freedom were insufficient: both could be undermined or abused. Ironically, the central government had to save the SOEs from the state itself, especially from local government interference, as Steinfeld observed. Before the other catalysts of beneficial change could occur, Beijing had to act. The list of what SOEs needed was long. Contracts had to be enforced but the rule of law did not exist, only the rule of man. Professional managers were required in increasingly complex companies, yet the "agency problem" occurred when decision-makers put their personal and short-term interests ahead of the state's and its shareholders. Corporate governance was inadequate or non-existent, so was monitoring.

Interference was rife, especially from local governments that looked on SOEs as their most precious revenue source. There were too many mothers-in-law (competing authorities) constantly interfering. All claimed authority but none took responsibility. Clear lines of authority between firm and state were absent. Supervisory agencies had conflicting goals. Vested interests looted. Accounting was not standardized: some 70 different methods of accounting existed. Regulation was ineffective: a complete mess. Yet, by 2017, progress was made on all fronts from the rule of law to accounting standards. Only time can teach by hard experience, which takes decades to gain, so patience is required. In the meantime, systems and practices become less imperfect as they improve steadily by following, where appropriate, global best practices.

China spent the first 15 years of reform after 1978 focused on agriculture and manufacturing. Agriculture because that is where the bulk of people worked, manufacturing as it was the new growth engine. Only later was it apparent that China needed a modern financial system to provide the funding and transaction services for an increasingly complex economy. Yet there was only one commercial bank, the Bank of China. Even the world's largest bank today, the Industrial and Commercial Bank of China (ICBC), was just a department of the People's Bank of China (PBOC) until 1993. The Banking Law was only promulgated in 1995. The regulator, the China Banking Regulatory Commission (CBRC) was not established until 2003. Until then it too had been a PBOC department.

The CBRC has built a surprisingly effective foundation for the banking system. Under its tutelage, banks developed basic systems from risk management and internal audit to personnel development and information technology. This is as fundamental as change gets. Listing the major banks abroad taught and enforced the basics of transparency; so did teaching global best practices in accounting and investor communications. All these systems were tested, first by the almost overnight appearance of a market-driven residential property market in the early 2000s, and then by the 2008 financial crisis. China came through both successfully, even if with many frayed nerves and a nagging sense that it still wasn't all over.

Perceptions and Reality

That, though, is not how many saw it after 2008. Following Lehman's closure in September, global attention switched to China as the most likely victim of financial contagion from the US and Europe. After all, it was the world's largest exporter whose main markets' economies were crumbling. Furthermore, beneath China's surface lurked all the legacy issues from the command economy, unable to take the stress of a global depression. China sceptics were everywhere. They have not let up since, still alive and well in 2017.

The negative narrative on China is very much stuck in the only partially reformed and still state-led China of the 1990s, often even before that. Nothing is deemed really to have changed. Therefore the coming collapse of the Chinese economy is only a matter of time. Sometimes it is imminent. Yet almost a decade later, despite a stock market boom and bust, China's economy has grown far faster than any other major economy. Unlike the Western economies after 2008, real incomes did not fall, unemployment did not soar for long, there was no sub-prime crisis in which people unable to meet mortgage payments lost their homes, debt was sustainable and prices were sufficiently stable. The consensus picture has not fitted China's reality since 2008.

China's prolonged high growth must be due to more than just hard work and long hours. This has puzzled the development economist, investment strategist and economic historian in me for many years. The answer lies largely in China using history and philosophy to navigate change. The past is no guarantee of future success, though that does not mean it will not continue, even if more slowly now China's labour surplus has ended.

China has changed "night and day" since 1978. The fact this is incomplete does not mean it is untrue. Observers just have to be patient, as Confucius would have advised, and undertake more *yanjiu* of their own, starting with the biggest common misconception of China's economy, private enterprise, and the other three overlooked strong pillars of growth.

Misconceptions

Ghost Cities One of the greatest misconceptions is that China is littered with ghost cities. Temporarily empty areas exist but not whole cities: people rapidly fill the space as an overall housing shortage still prevails.

Urbanization China is not running out of demand for new property, even though the rural labour surplus has ended. Most property demand comes from urban upgraders and new families. On this Guangzhou building site, poor quality older buildings below give way to more modern often high-rise homes above.

Congested Roads Traffic jams are much easier to find in China than Roads to Nowhere but this does not stop the negative narrative repeating the charge. With China's new auto sales seen equaling those of the US and EU combined by 2022, there is no major misallocation of resources on roads: most are still overcoming congestion.

Private Sector Another myth is that the state advances while the private sector retreats. Private firms now dominate the economy, as Jack Ma Yun of Alibaba illustrates on the world stage.

Chapter 12

Four Strong Overlooked Pillars

Through its continual cycle of ruin and rebirth the private sector demonstrated its enormous capacity for survival ... forcing ossified, conservative state enterprises to adapt to the cutthroat competition of the market place.

Yu Hua, *China in Ten Words,* 2011

China ... is the world's largest technocracy ... ruled by scientists and engineers who believe in the power of new technologies to deliver social and economic progress ... in the most ambitious programme of research investment since John F. Kennedy embarked on the moon race.

James Wilson and James Keeley,
China: The Next Scientific Superpower, 2007

China has four frequently overlooked strong pillars supporting economic growth. The now dominant private sector, education, research and development (R&D) and new growth areas are the foundations for 6%–7% GDP growth in 2016–2020 and around 5% in the third decade. This should be plenty enough to address the main economic issues of incomes, employment and price stability.

The Asian Development Bank (ADB) has made similar long-term forecasts, viewing Asia's 2011–2030 GDP prospects through two lenses: one with reform and one without. For China, it saw average real GDP growth in 2011–2020 of 7.0% with reform and 6.1% without. Over halfway through the decade, with China's growth to date having averaged about 8%, the reform number seems pretty secure. For 2021–2030, the ADB saw a slowdown to 6.2% real GDP growth with reform and 5.0% without. The IMF and World Bank expect similar trends as long as reform continues.

Private Sector

The biggest mistake made about China's economy is that it is state-dominated. It is not. Furthermore, China's private companies are now among the most vibrant anywhere. One of the most pervasive and erroneous ideas of the negative narrative for almost a decade has been that the "state advances and the private sector retreats". This is plain wrong: completely missing the major boost private firms have provided to sustain China's economy after 2008. Greater efficiency and vigour have lifted it well above the state sector: not everywhere, but in the economy overall. The data speaks for itself.

Almost out of sight, and certainly outside sceptical minds, the private sector has risen to economic dominance. In 2013, there were 12 million private firms and 42 million proprietorships. By looking at the national and provincial data, Nicholas Lardy at the Peterson Institute for International Economics in Washington has spent literally decades ploughing through Chinese data, and concludes that the private sector has not been in retreat since 2008. Whatever their deficiencies, data are consistent over time and across the economy. This corroborates extensive field work by Research-Works.

With meticulous attention to definitions as well as detail, Lardy's ground-breaking *Markets over Mao: the Rise of Private Business in China* gives objective observers the reality. In all three major sectors — primary, secondary and tertiary — private companies now lead. Private farmers dominate agriculture. The state employs a mere 1% of agricultural workers producing only 3% of output, compared with almost 100% in the 1960s and 1970s communes. In manufacturing, the state's share of industrial output has fallen from three-quarters in 1978 to one-quarter in 2011. In services, the trends are equally telling. Private sector retailing in 1978 made just 0.1% of sales; by 2008, it was half. When foreign private firms like Walmart, Carrefour, Lotus and RT-Mart are included, it was 60%: the state's share has fallen to about one-fifth. In wholesaling, on the same basis, the private share is over half. In restaurants and catering, it comprises two-thirds of sales and 80% of employment, while in construction it accounts for three-quarters of jobs and two-thirds of output value. In jobs, the private sector provides over half, and almost all job growth since 1978. In exports, the state's share has fallen to only 11% while the domestic private sector has overtaken the once dominant foreign firms. In 2015, Chinese private firms made 65% of overseas direct investment, some $145 billion.

Various measurements show the private sector's much greater efficiency. Private industrial value added was almost double that of the state from 2009–2012: 18.2% compared with 9.2%. Total factor productivity rose 4.3% annually in private firms against 1.7% at state companies from 1978–2004. Return on equity at private firms was 20% in 2009, almost double that of SOEs. Return on assets in 2012 was 13.2% compared with only 4.9% in the state sector: a very consistent pattern. Only cognitive dissonance can deny the data: see Chapter 9.

Access to Capital

Apart from a private sector retreat, the other major myth is that private firms cannot get bank credit or, if they do, it is very much harder to get than for state companies. The data shows otherwise. Central bank data put new bank loans to state entities at just 36% in 2012. Most of the rest goes to private firms. The China Banking Society said the private sector received 52% of new bank lending in 2010–2012. The private share of non-bank funding, almost 40% of total funding, is even higher, with most bankers' acceptances made to private companies and many trust loans to private developers. That is the current reality, yet people still trot out the myth.

I asked a colleague visiting Zhejiang businesses in 2012 to find out if private firms still could not get credit, as some sceptics then maintained. She emailed back that she had stopped asking the question after the first few meetings because everyone laughed, some scornful of her ignorance. Where else, they asked, were banks going to find business growth, apart from private companies? Anyway, individuals and firms had what Asian bankers love, collateral, be it homes, factories or raw land: assets pledged as collateral well below market value. No messy cash flows to calculate — just hard property assets to value. There was no problem lending against bricks and mortar which in China have appreciated as incomes rise.

Does the government, national or local, discriminate against the private sector, as sceptics widely assume? When I asked this, a leading Zhejiang entrepreneur thought he misunderstood the question and looked blank. He could not believe that someone would think that. When he was sure he understood the question correctly, he stated the blindingly obvious. In this "small" town, in a county of just over one million people, local officials rely on him and other private firms to create jobs and pay taxes. These are two key measurements of local growth, on which officials' annual assessments are based. Why would officials discriminate against the golden goose? On the contrary: they try to help wherever they can, aware this furthers their own careers and interests too. What about where state enterprises are more numerous, deeply entrenched and therefore more powerful? Yet, particularly there, think for a moment. Where can local officials find enterprises to create jobs and taxes rather than give problems and be a drain on resources as SOEs can be, especially in one-company towns built around raw materials like iron ore and coal, or their users like steel and other processors? There are exceptions, especially where corruption is involved, but overall, officials know which side their bread is buttered. Very few, if any, oppose private sector lending on ideological grounds.

This on-the-ground research agrees with investment data trends. SOEs' share of investment has slumped from 82% in 1980 to 34% in 2012. The private sector's has risen to almost half: its share of equity market fundraising was over treble that of SOEs from 2010 to 2013. Most importantly, most private sector investment has been driven more by retained earnings than by credit simply because this is a more stable and less risky way to expand. Banks can withdraw credit as policies change or cycles turn, just as they did in 2011 and 2012, causing borrowers great stress. China's economic stability has gained tremendously from the private sector's use of retained earnings to fund investment.

Overall, the private sector is estimated to produce two-thirds of China's GDP. This is consistent with the data, though far from the consensus belief that the private sector is China's very poor relation. That was the case two to three decades ago but no longer.

Roots

The first post-revolution private firms emerged in the 1980s, a few years after the Cultural Revolution and central planning ended. Then, it was very unclear what could reform China's increasingly ailing economy. It certainly was not the private sector. Ideological hostility then did exist: for decades, private entrepreneurs had been demonized as exploiters, pariahs and the class enemy.

Slowly a few individuals began small companies, often under the protection of local officials. These were the firms that could claim a Red Hat (an official or state entity) to hide their private form. Complicating matters further, the Cultural Revolution had caused the loss or end of these entrepreneurs' formal education. They had no training for business management. However, living on their wits and devising strategies on the fly came much more naturally to them than to bookish graduates. What these entrepreneurs learned outside school were political survival skills and how to weave webs of connections, *guanxi,* for protection and profit. There were few scruples about labour exploitation, the environment, regulations or intellectual property. This was Dickensian China, a century after the West did the same.

Private sector pioneers were joined later in the 1980s by a new entity. Town and village enterprises (TVEs) attempted to create a new form of local ownership which removed often apparently failing companies from the government's balance sheet and responsibility. After a brief burst of growth, many became moribund or collapsed. Some, though, especially those with technical skills, managed to survive and grow into sustainable firms with a changed culture similar to the private sector.

A third variant appeared in the 1990s, sometimes directly a result of what even the state media sometimes calls the tragedy of 1989, without usually referring to Tiananmen directly. Unlike the first two groups, these entrepreneurs were often highly educated. It was also greatly disillusioned by the third major blow to China's post-1949 development: the famine-related deaths of 30–40 million people after the Great Leap Forward and the often violent lawlessness of the Cultural Revolution being the first two.

Some sought escape from this turmoil through business, choosing to find a new China not through politics but as far away from politics as possible. More followed in their footsteps in the late 1990s and early 2000s, often in the new field of IT. Not all were so motivated, there were plenty of *guanxi*-exploiting carpetbaggers, but this third group was not simply the crony capitalists seen in much of Asia.

IT's big attraction was that it represented a completely new industry whose significance Beijing did not immediately see, giving it freedom denied elsewhere. There were no major state firms in IT, hence no state monopoly to protect. By the time it became attractive, few state firms were interested as their manufacturing or utilities businesses, often linked to China's surging property or infrastructure booms, were making good money elsewhere. This left IT largely to private firms to develop, mainly outside government control, while gaining the tacit support of economic reformers.

Their leaders were the complete opposite of the Russian oligarchs who capitalized through political connections on state asset privatizations. China's 21st-century private sector was built from the bottom up, *de novo*, responding to consumers' rising incomes with new goods and services or better quality. This *raison d'etre* focused SMEs on customers' needs and rapidly changing tastes, which made them competitive, adaptive and highly innovative. It also instilled good discipline, especially after many failed or came close to failing. Indeed, failure was tolerated, as creative economies require, teaching valuable lessons.

DNA

Apart from motivation, this third group reflects its business experience. Many who succeeded in IT have much in common with early Silicon Valley entrepreneurs who survived the 1990s' dot.com boom and bust before coming to dominate their fields. Shona Brown, formerly of Google, and Kathleen Eisenhardt of Stanford wrote *Competing on the Edge* about Silicon Valley's fast-changing markets and dynamics, much of which applies to their Chinese counterparts.

What is so distinctive? This group differs from its predecessors and even succeeding generations in several ways. Apart from motivation, experience has taught that it is impossible to build bullet-proof businesses. Any advantage is only temporary. As Haier's founder Zhang Ruimin declared, companies can never say they are successful, merely that they hope to move with the times to be in place to catch the next big wave. This is just as applicable to making white goods, which Haier does, as to cutting-edge technology and social media. All now compete on the edge in this disrupted world, constantly innovating, from products to business models. Strategy has to be diverse and complex, defying simple generalization. It must be driven from the bottom up, not top down. Firms need to be nimble and quick. Flexibility is essential in goals and plans: plenty of options should be created. Many of these approaches mesh with traditional Chinese thinking and strategy.

Companies need to reinvent themselves constantly. This is pure *weixin,* with its insistence on permanent renewal: not permanent revolution anymore. Experimentation enables firms to extend knowledge and products into new areas. They have to understand rhythms, as Mao quoted from the classics, to seek truth from facts. If companies are too slow they will be overtaken, if too fast they will be too early and fail. Timing and sequencing are critical.

The most successful firms stay ahead by expanding into new areas, building scale and competing. They continually adapt and modify, at home and abroad. The three IT giants, the BATs (Baidu, Alibaba and Tencent) in particular, have done this for the last few years, rapidly extending their reach to secure new beachheads in the ever-changing new economy. As management consultant Edward Tse of Gao Feng says, Chinese companies do not necessarily have solutions immediately, but they skillfully adapt strategy and execution, pushing forward, taking risks, reacting quickly to opportunities, constantly searching either for small gains for a temporary advantage or for larger ones to build scale to create lower costs and new markets.

This inevitably gives them influence in China disproportionate to their numbers. Millionaires became billionaires and some make the lists of the world's wealthiest people. They mix, talk and co-invest with their peers in the US, are photographed with Bill Gates, Warren Buffet and Mark Zuckerberg, while also appearing at Davos, on Bloomberg television and sitting on global advisory boards. Golden geese, they are very aware of their position: privileged and vulnerable. As China's richest man, Wang Jianlin, said, "Be close to government, but far from politics." They have their own thoughts and opinions but recognize the unwritten rules. Few understand this group better than Edward Tse who has known most of the leading entrepreneurs since their early days whilst working at leading consulting firms Boston Consulting Group, Booz and McKinsey. What major point does his *China's Disruptors* make?

This group is very aware of how much change the private sector has brought since the 1980s and how much this has benefited China: its worth. Leading entrepreneurs, though, do not question China's system publicly, they merely move rapidly beyond it. They are content to work within the existing system. They do not want to confront it. They know their place and space, value and limits. The government and private sector alike, true to their Daoist roots, assume disorder is natural and chaos to be avoided. They instinctively believe that complex systems, which the Chinese economy and polity certainly are, need constant monitoring and oversight to get the best results. Otherwise, China will render itself, in Tse's words, "impotent through cacophony and inefficiency, like the US and others".

These entrepreneurs are not ideological about markets. Instead, they see markets as a means to an end. In modern China this also serves the nation's goal for greater prosperity: again, wealth, power and national dignity. Rather than sharing a political ideology, three core elements unite them — national pride, ambition and cultural heritage. Like the elite in olden times, they feel a responsibility to society, including for the environment, which is the patrimony this generation hands on to the future.

Like business leaders in the rest of Asia, they now appear at official events, at home and abroad, be they about the internet, trade promotion or investment. Jack Ma makes himself useful in personal diplomacy with Donald Trump. Cementing acquaintance with government thinking and officials is undeniable but it is not the only reason. As in Singapore, there is a strong concept of "national service". There is also an obligation and duty to speak out: see Chapter 3 "Elite". Tse quotes Victor Wang of MTone Wireless who feels he has an "inescapable historical responsibility", and, as someone sincere about the need for reform, has the right to influence the state so that China moves peacefully to become a modern nation with the rule of law and individual autonomy. Wang feels that entrepreneurs and others should be accommodated within the current system rather than change the system. He helped launch the China Entrepreneurs Forum in 2000 to further this end, part of the informal infrastructure providing the glue that binds things together in changing times.

A common view among this group is that the government and private sector have distinct roles. Government should drive economic development by investing in infrastructure, education, R&D and large SOEs. The private sector drives standards, creates variety and boosts efficiency through competition while meeting the needs of SMEs and consumers. There are trade-offs between growth, efficiency and control. Government and entrepreneurs recognize this but disagreements are unlikely to come out into the open. The broad elite, like the ruling party, discusses this internally but not in public.

The Example of Zhejiang

Zhejiang is an example to the rest of China of what the private sector can do. An average-sized province of 55 million people on 1% of China's land, Zhejiang is China's third-largest exporter, producing 12% of all exports. This can largely be put down to being the most private sector-dominated province, with an inherently entrepreneurial culture that goes back at least 1,000 years. The home of Chinese silk, with significant trade, markets and communications, Zhejiang was at the heart of Jiangnan, the lower Yangzi delta: see Chapter 10.

Although Alibaba was founded in Zhejiang's capital of Hangzhou, the bulk of the province's manufacturing is not IT-related but light industry. This too has its own dynamic, based on traditional concepts as well as elements and influences from the "competing on the edge" strategy that Alibaba has embraced. After China joined the World Trade Organization (WTO) in 2001, Zhejiang has had both opportunities and challenges.

After 2008, Zhejiang's private sector faced many existential threats. First, it had to reset its thinking, cast in the furnace of China's white-hot export boom that grew annually at almost 28% *a year* after 2001. This may have seemed like a blessing at the time but, when it ended, the boom was clearly a very mixed blessing. Imagine having to expand at 30% to 50% each year, for seven years running, just to keep customers to stay in business. No wonder there was a relentless obsession with short-term growth, capacity expansion, speed, market share and quantity rather than with the long-term, quality or R&D.

To survive, manufacturers had to expand capacity enormously just to secure future orders. They could not be blamed. The pressures were enormous. Prices were often driven down each year, such was the buying power of global firms. Chinese companies could not resist. They could only absorb the pressure and hope to survive by increasing scale to lower unit production costs. There was very little time for detailed corporate strategy or research. Expand or die. That was the only thing that mattered.

All this bred bad habits. In management, there was great focus on the short-term: often an obsession. Who could know if they would even exist in a couple of year's time if they did not immediately secure, meet and deliver the next order. In investment, there was a herd mentality. When one manufacturer found a profitable new line, everyone jumped in to copy. Often, before long, little or no profit was left. In short, conditions were against firms developing skills needed for sustainably profitable, stable businesses.

Lessons

All these challenges, though, taught valuable lessons. One of the hardest to accept, especially for the first two groups of entrepreneurs, was a need for more professional management instead of relying largely on the founder's family. Small and medium enterprises, despite their name, increasingly reached a scale requiring professional management. As their founders near or even pass 60 years of age, succession also becomes an increasingly common problem for many private firms founded in the 1980s.

Either they cannot let go or want their children to take over, a familiar desire from Korea (North and South) to Southeast Asia. Rarely are the results as good as under the founder. Times have changed but families have not. Few second-generation children, too often spoiled by doting parents and grandparents, especially mothers and grandmothers, have none of the steel, resilience or street smarts the Cultural Revolution and its aftermath beat into their parents.

That core Confucian value of flexibility and adaptability had to be learned anew. The first thing manufacturers discovered after 2008 was the need for flexibility in thinking, approaches, business models and marketing. The recent, old ways did not work anymore. New trends emerged. Those companies that focused on business basics stole a march on competitors. Many did not and went to the wall or just withered away.

Markets were changing. So were relations with customers and suppliers. China's home market, which many exporters had avoided due to intense price competition and payment problems, started to look attractive as richer local customers could afford the more sophisticated, export-quality products. Import substitution became a real opportunity for those that could narrow the technology gap with global companies. Branding could expand margins for unknown original equipment makers who previously produced at often razor-thin margins. R&D was no longer an option: it was a necessity, the only way for sector leaders to keep ahead of the copycats. Continuously they had to introduce new models to maintain the quality gap with their competitors and therefore their premium pricing.

Was relocation an answer to growing manufacturing problems, especially costs? There were pluses and minuses. Generally, low value production moved inland or overseas where land and labour were cheaper. Zhejiang kept three things: higher value-added work, corporate headquarters and R&D. Running away rather than facing problems directly was no long-term solution, as my colleague Anna Kieryk observed. Furthermore, Zhejiang has already created substantial critical mass and skills not available elsewhere, building hard-to-copy industrial clusters by moving up the value-added chain.

All successful Zhejiang manufacturers focus on global competitors, at home and abroad. The US, EU and Japan have become more than just end-markets: Chinese companies increasingly search them to acquire technology and distribution. Smaller companies, not just giants like Alibaba and Geely, have already bought overseas firms or brands.

Most successful Zhejiang companies do business with foreign firms, some with global industry leaders. This helps in three ways: firms gain access to often world-leading technology and design; they benefit from knowing the latest global trends; and finally, probably most valuable of all, they learn production skills from foreign partners who insist on much higher manufacturing and governance standards. All this introduces Chinese firms to global best practices, which often launches them into a much higher quality league. After acquiring new skills, they can attract even larger customers, who in turn expose them to still more demanding requirements, which provide even further learning. This virtuous circle enables them to put more distance between themselves and the piranhas, the host of smaller competitors in China and worldwide.

The most successful Chinese manufacturers move beyond pure production. They become more customer-focused, using their local knowledge to solve global customers' problems. For example the West increasingly seeks market intelligence on latest Asian trends and fashion, especially in Japan or South Korea. Chinese companies, with culture and geography on their side, exploit this advantage. Before too long, China itself will become a fashion trendsetter. In terms of fashion awareness, surveys already rank it second in Asia to South Korea, ahead of Japan. Some in China think it is number one already.

Expansion now seems less risky than in the past. That may seem strange, given all the negative sentiment about Chinese manufacturing and competition, but things have settled down after all the frantic demands and challenges of the post-WTO-entry years. After 2008, it has usually been easier to identify and implement expansion than before when markets, customers, management and global trends were much less understood, and when demand grew too fast, making accurate capacity production planning impossible.

Now expansion in Zhejiang is usually much smaller, easier to forecast. Often it is very logical, involving far fewer leaps of faith compared with the start. Making 10% of the world's seemingly ubiquitous dark green and maroon umbrellas, outdoor furniture maker Yotrio can work with world leaders like Ikea and Home Depot, now its relationships are well established. It is much easier to gain trust and orders than in the first place. Price alone is not a sustainable advantage: it quickly reaches its limits. Similarly for Zhejiang Wanfeng Auto Wheel, it is much easier now to work with Honda and others abroad. Nanfang Pump, with its local technological edge, is now positioned at the head of a very large and highly fragmented series of water-related businesses. All this is so much easier to manage than getting started.

After the 2008 slowdown, manufacturers finally had the time and reason to change. This is a blessing even if initially the slowdown appeared a curse. From this grew the second generation of leading private sector companies who moved up the value-added curve, increasingly able to think and operate internationally. In terms of development, these companies are where many of today's corporate leaders were 10–15 years ago. Whether they become the next Alibabas, Huaweis, ZTEs, Sanys, Geelys or Vankes remains to be seen, but there are plenty more aspirants backed by a strong private equity industry which barely existed when the current leaders began their long journey to the top.

Education

Rich, developed economies are generally well and broadly educated; poor ones are insufficiently and narrowly educated. A key factor for any economy is the percentage of workers that has completed 12 years of education. Backed by more learning, they can do far more value-added work than primary school-leavers, earning higher incomes which in turn generate greater consumption.

China is reaping the fruits of its earlier investment in education. It takes a long time, but now brains, not brawn, power economic growth. In 1990, some 37% of workers only had primary school education while 16% were completely illiterate. Therefore, 25 years ago, over half of all workers had only the most basic education or none at all: typical of an underdeveloped economy. People moving from low productivity farming to higher productivity manufacturing have driven three decades of economic growth. Now the number of years spent in the classroom is what counts, not the number of bodies available: quality not quantity.

A transformation in education is critical to economic development, reflected by the increasing use of terms like knowledge economy and innovation. Education is emphasized by Ted Schultz, one of the economists Liu He, Xi Jinping's chief economic adviser, highlights in the foreword to a book on development economists: see Chapter 10. Indeed, Schultz called it educational capital, an idea that created the term human capital, something China grasped millennia ago. The difference today is that education is no longer restricted to the elite, it is pretty well universal. Illiteracy, which holds back development, fell from 33.6% in 1964 to only 4.1% in 2010. Higher education has made equally impressive strides. By 2010, nearly 9% of China's workers had university or junior college education, while another 14% had finished senior secondary school or technical college. Combined, this higher-educated 23% of the working population compares with just 1.7% in 1964. University intake has trebled since 2000.

The power of this change will continue to drive China for at least the next couple of decades, especially as the poorly educated Cultural Revolution generation retires. The post-2000 surge in university enrolment continues to increase the number. Even more importantly, graduates' length of work experience has risen significantly. A graduate at 35 has much more to offer than at 25, one at 45 is more productive still.

So, although China's labour force may decline marginally, its education levels continue to climb significantly; and will for many years to come. Education spending as a share of GDP almost doubled from its 20-year low in 1995 of just 2.3% to 4.3% in 2013.

The focus now is on quality, especially in areas like problem-solving, question-finding and critical thinking, fundamental to knowledge-based economies. As China moves to the next economic level, beyond grunt manufacturing into the secondary and tertiary sectors' higher areas, a broad base of people with 12 years or more education is needed. Not just as knowledge workers in everything from IT to the professions but very importantly as consumers who will provide a growing market for services and high-end goods. A better-educated majority, earning higher incomes, generates domestic demand to support GDP growth.

China now has the world's largest number of university graduates, some 5.7 million each year compared with 3.3 million in the US. In 2000, China had under half the US number. By 2010, it produced 10 times as many engineering graduates as the US. Even allowing for any differences in quality, this is quite a gap and it is growing. Furthermore, significant numbers of US engineering graduates were born in China, and more return as China is increasingly where the opportunities lie: in 2016 an estimated 82% of Chinese students abroad returned home compared with 72% in 2012, which is far higher than that in previous decades.

Informal on-the-job learning for workers and managers alike has been just as important as formal education: practical real-life commercial and production knowledge, not theory. Autarkic, command economy development after 1949 meant China lacked many skills for a market economy. These have had to be acquired on the job during reform in what have usually been very challenging but highly educational times. None have been more challenging than after the 2008 global financial crisis, especially for private SMEs which have become the backbone of China's economy. The crisis hit SMEs the worst, especially exporters. First, western markets collapsed in late 2008 then almost immediately trade credit froze globally, sending Chinese layoffs soaring.

Financial famine then turned into over-abundance as government-primed stimulus flooded China with credit and cash. Welcomed initially, it disrupted product and informal capital markets as boom led to over-rapid expansion and bust. Many marginal SMEs went to the wall: see Chapter 7. Others were already under great stress as sharply rising commodity prices, labour shortages and tighter monetary policy piled on the pain, squeezing cash flows and profit margins. For manufacturers, 2011 and 2012 were the worst of times.

Most that survived emerged fitter, leaner and far more competitive — after a very practical education. Markets taught the efficient management of everything from cash flow, investment, brand and raw materials to labour, land, property and customers. Many lessons, of the sort not taught at business school or in finance classes, were learned. All this difficulty and uncertainty provided entrepreneurs, managers, officials and workers alike with an intense but very valuable education.

R&D

China is ruled by a technocracy that believes in the power of science and new technologies, as James Wilson, the director of Britain's Royal Society Science Policy Centre, and James Keeley observed in 2007. Engineers comprised eight of President Hu Jintao's nine-man Politburo Standing Committee. The ninth was a geologist.

The education of today's political leadership has changed slightly but the essential point remains. China sees technology and science in very positive terms, to be harnessed and developed. Current leaders, some with backgrounds in other disciplines such as economics and law, have a broader understanding of what this means while keeping the same firm faith in the transformative power of science and technology. They do not fear or distrust experts, only the lack of them.

Quadrupling R&D spending to 2.5% of GDP by 2020 from 0.6% in 1995 was anticipated by the 2006 Science and Technology Plan. Leaders hope that innovation will contribute 60% of economic growth. Enterprises, not government, do the lion's share, motivated by profit rather than by the quest for pure research. The R&D levels of leading Chinese companies are respectable by global standards. Huawei and ZTE are where they are today globally because of their R&D, spending some 10% of sales, just like Intel and other US leaders. No longer can it be said that China only does R&C — reproduction and copying — the common jibe only a few years ago. Some numbers may be exaggerated or the benefit dubious, but the fact is that China's R&D has come a long way in the last decade, as shown by the quality of products and processes that have come from it. In 2016 China's ZTE and Huawei topped the world patents filing league in North America, Europe and Japan: China, with a 44% surge, ranked third as a country, just behind Japan.

The increasingly strong R&D culture, as well as plentiful trained workers, has made China a prime research location for multinational firms. As part of global R&D strategies in 2013, there were some 1,800 foreign-invested R&D centres in China compared with just 24 in 1997. China's R&D attraction is no longer all about low cost but more often about scale. Being able to spread R&D costs across a market of potentially 1.4 billion people is a great advantage. China also provides technical scale. Being able to hire thousands to work on research because of the availability of large numbers of qualified graduates is rare elsewhere.

Sometimes research is all about the numbers, and China has the numbers. These begin with almost 2.4 million graduates a year in engineering and science combined, with another 445,000 in healthcare. ZTE's new Xi'an facility will produce 25,000 R&D workers over five years in just one location, where annually it is hiring 5,000. When I asked a Californian biotech company's research head if this would be money well spent, he answered that even if 90% were useless, which was unlikely, 2,500 could achieve a great deal. China also has trial scale. This is particularly important in pharmaceuticals where large numbers of people can be mobilized for trials on a scale unknown in the OECD.

The scientific technocratic culture means China does not fear backing major projects in new areas. These have ranged from high-speed rail to alternative energy and engines, from 4G telecoms and beyond to crop seeds, providing the impetus to new growth areas. Government support comes through tax incentives and grants, including a 15% tax rate for "high-tech" enterprises compared with the standard 25%.

Arguably more valuable even than specific project support is long-term outline planning. This helps investors know where an industry is heading, reducing uncertainty and hence risk. No other major government automatically looks out several decades, providing a higher degree of confidence about long-term demand. Wind turbine makers in 2010 had little doubt what the minimum demand in China would be for their product in 2020: targets and the means to reach them are contained in numerous documents well in advance, attracting foreign as well as domestic investors. Government and market forces alike encourage industry consolidation towards a few major groups in each sector or subsector. This gives winners sufficient scale to exploit.

Government policy offers incentives to speed technological catch-up. China has helped domestic firms share in and thereby acquire the knowledge of leading global technology by offering partnerships with pre-eminent firms through technology-for-market access deals. Foreign firms have not always liked it; some declined. However before too many years, Chinese companies have often developed their own technology, with or without foreign joint ventures. Railway equipment is one example where this strategy first opened up a substantial domestic market, then exports. The government generally sets high standards for its own procurement, especially in high technology: second-best is generally not good enough, especially if safety is involved. Switzerland's ABB has dominated electricity transmission equipment because of its quality.

Companies do not have to be large to be leaders, nor do they lack models to emulate. To embolden the next generation of entrepreneurs to invest heavily in R&D, there are enough examples of pioneering Chinese entrepreneurs such as Jack Ma of Alibaba and Liang Wengen of Sany, as well as companies like Huawei and ZTE, which have successfully used R&D to acquire sector leadership. The bookstores of any Chinese airport or railway station are full of their words, wisdom and videos, either by themselves or by academics and consultants. They feature widely on the covers of magazines, the internet and television. *Fortune, Time* and *Forbes* have their Chinese imitators, and plenty of material to fill them.

New Sources of Growth

Outdated mental pictures cloud many views of China's economy. Images are stuck largely in ideas of where Western economies were in the late 19th and early 20th centuries: heavy industry with steel plants, coal-fired power stations, metal-bashing shipyards and car assembly lines. There is little room in this image for 21st-century new-economy industries where China is often among the leaders. Then there is geography, which, like history, is generally unknown.

Geographically, China can be described in many ways. It can be viewed as a continent, just 5% smaller in area than the US with a population several times larger, or it can be thought of as a score of megacity clusters, which is where much of its growth occurs. What is most misleading is to think of China as simply one single, uniform country. That mars any clear understanding of its new main growth areas and industries. Much of China's initial post-1978 economic takeoff happened along its 1,200-mile coastal strip from Beijing through Shanghai to Guangzhou. The rest of China was hardly in the picture.

This ignores the 840 million people in central, western and northeastern China, some 61% of the population: the main basis of future growth. The three regional laggards are very similar in terms of disposable annual income, around Rmb 22,700 ($3,440), some 28% below eastern China's Rmb 31,500 ($4,773). Collectively the 61% now accounts for over half China's GDP. In 2015 only 13% of China's middle class lived in inland China. By 2022, McKinsey projects this will treble to almost 40%. The path of inland China's catch-up has been lit by the early coastal developers: it knows what to do. There are of course structural differences, which is why Chongqing, for instance, with its 33 million people, has been designated to find how to combine urban and rural growth with reform. Some two-thirds of Chongqing population was rural but government aims to provide urban facilities to all, from good-quality healthcare and education to infrastructure like water and waste treatment.

Demographic trends reinforce this reversal. With more jobs now available inland, fewer people flock to work on the coast. Between 1995 and 2013, eastern China's resident population grew 26.5% while the other three regions rose by only 5%–6%. That is the past. A striking reversal is underway as inland rural China now migrates first to its provincial capitals and prefecture cities. Here people are closer to home, nearer their families, can speak their own language or dialect and eat their own cuisine. Income differentials are no longer so great. The annual population growth of 20 main inland provincial capitals is forecast at 2.7% in 2011–2020, compared with 1.8% in the previous decade: 50% faster. In contrast, the growth of coastal China's major cities should fall from 3.0% in 2001–2010 to 2.3%: one-quarter slower.

The newest regional growth opportunity is not within China at all but along and beyond its 14 land borders. China hopes to spark more regional growth with a series of initiatives to bind Asia closer together through trade, infrastructure, funding and common interests. Reviving the historic Silk Routes by land and sea in the Belt and Road Initiative, China aims to rebuild links with West Asia, the Middle East, East Africa and, finally, Europe, redrawing the world's geopolitical and economic map along the way: see Chapter 14. Apart from new geographic areas of growth, there is considerable scope in new industries like IT, e-commerce, logistics and transportation. These are the stuff of daily media reports and whole books, so no need to describe them here in detail. Merely note they substantially offset declining growth in more mature old industries like textiles, shoes, steel and cement.

These four major long-term growth drivers — private enterprise, education, R&D and new areas — explain China's continued high growth, but the negative narrative on China takes a more pessimistic view. The next chapter considers the negative narrative's four greatest economic charges, from ghost cities, shadow banking and rising debt, to fear of the middle-income trap. Long-term reality shows these come largely from the land of misconception, if not myth.

Chapter 13

Ghosts, Nightmares, Middle-Income Trap and Reality

Pudong is a statist monument to a dead Pharaoh on the level of the Pyramids.

Milton Friedman, 2001

Decades of rapid growth are a testament to China's success in implementing reforms ... success was built on waves of major reforms, and frequent adjustment of policies in line with evolving conditions.

IMF, *China Staff Report*, 2014

Frightening ideas and even more terrifying labels have dominated the sceptical view of China. The spectre of ghost cities, shadow banks, runaway debt and a middle-income trap are enough to give anyone nightmares. Adding to the air of menace are frequent references to zombie companies, financial fragility and imminent collapse. Anyway, surely after such long and frenetic growth, China must be running out of new opportunities?

On closer examination, all fail to live up to their billing. Over time it is possible to see and understand reality. Ghost cities do not exist: temporary areas, yes; whole cities, no. Alarms about shadow banking, debt and traps are the result of fervid imaginations: not illuminating. Those caring about their reputations or short investments should remember Milton Friedman's remark above about Pudong. It is easy to get China wrong from afar, underestimating the dynamic, sheer scale and inherent demand for change in China.

Property and Ghosts

The biggest recent change in Chinese lives has been the quantity and quality of living space. In the past two decades, nothing has come close. Property has been central to China's economy since 2000. Satisfying this most basic need has been the largest driver ever since, responsible both for many achievements and some problems, including perceptions of ghost cities.

The crucial importance of the late-1990's housing reform, which transferred most home ownership from the state to occupants, should not be underestimated. Yet it is generally ignored as just one of many things happening. That is a major misconception. As housing was at the heart of the "shortage economy", it was the single greatest change. Average personal living space would have to quadruple or even quintuple after 1990 if life were to change enough to meet people's constantly rising expectations. China may be barely halfway through the process, despite so much visual evidence to the contrary, which some assume must be overbuilt already.

I was ushered in to meet one of Shanghai's vice mayors in the early 1990s, after the municipal government's economist said his boss's boss wished to see me. Foreign visitors in those days were not so common and the vice mayor wanted me to hear his pitch as to why foreigners should invest in Shanghai. I then headed Merrill Lynch's research for Asia ex-Japan, so presumed he wanted to showcase Shanghai's long-term plans for the glitzy new commercial area of Pudong with its proposed forest of skyscrapers. Instead, the reason was much more mundane: residential bricks and mortar. The vice mayor spoke not about building the new but of tearing down the old, what elsewhere are called slums or urban renewal. This was new.

Residential property development is the most overlooked driver of East Asia's earlier economic miracle. It was about to be repeated on a continental scale. Without the usual lengthy preamble or notes, the vice mayor immediately cut to the chase. "Mr. Peyman: 40% of Shanghai's people each live in four square metres or less of space," he began. I was somewhat thrown. Glancing around the grand meeting room, I noted it could easily house a couple of families. Not a typical local politician's admission in the West, I thought, nor exactly a winning campaign slogan. Somewhat perplexed, I wondered where the presentation was going. Only time would tell.

Shanghai was about to embark on the greatest building boom in world history. It would demolish much of the old city to build more spacious and modern apartments with indoor sanitation, in the process creating new urban and suburban areas as people relocated, many to Shanghai's more sparsely-populated outskirts. After Shanghai, other major cities would follow, and after them the rest of the country. This would take the best part of half a century, much as happened in Europe and America during the 19th and early 20th centuries. None of this was stated directly, but talk of bricks and mortar was no different from the Delphic utterances of former US Federal Reserve Chairman Alan Greenspan: oblique to most but perfectly clear to those who understood, which did not include me immediately.

This construction boom would not only boost the economy but provide plenty of investment opportunities and jobs. China's government knew what was most needed: an end to the acute housing shortage, a world of overcrowding, constantly quarrelling neighbours and outdoor sanitation. That was the new administration's top priority, unspoken but underway. It was what most people wanted too. Shanghai was the pioneer in what would be a vast pilot scheme.

I frequently think back to that meeting a quarter of a century ago as it subsequently shone great light on what happened. No one was talking in such terms then, when China was still languishing in the shadow of June 1989 and living in generally very miserable physical conditions. This was not about Potemkin villages, ghost cities or roads to nowhere but very real need.

Central Role

Residential property has played the central role in China's record-breaking GDP growth over the last 25 years, especially since 2000: arguably twice as important as exports. Combined with all related construction and manufacturing, residential housing comprises about 25% of China's GDP.

Shanghai's vice mayor doubtless saw home-building generating two great growth waves, cycle after cycle. First the physical building, when people would buy as much space as they could afford, followed by the second wave, when people with rising income and subsequently accumulated savings would fill the space with white goods, upgrade furniture and improve finishing. These waves would repeat themselves until China's per capita living space reaches the northeast Asian average of 32–35 square metres, probably around 2030. Of course there have been booms and busts, three main ones in fact, but the enormous pent-up demand for decent housing has ensured each bust has been followed by recovery. The latest upturn began in 2015, broadening out in 2016 and 2017.

Households often spend 25%–35%, sometimes up to half, of their income on housing, first saving for the down payment then to service the mortgage. The positive economic linkages have fuelled economic growth, ranging from rising real estate demand to new types of financing, and from growing government revenues to much larger markets for white goods. However this building boom is often characterized only negatively as creating ghost cities, financial fragility, overcapacity and corruption. What is being missed? Think of the linkages.

Booms need construction materials from cement and glass to steel and copper; then machinery like excavators, pile drivers, cranes and cement mixers, and, most important for job creation, construction workers. All require investment and funding. Homebuyers need finance, so bank mortgages developed. New institutions emerged like credit trusts and the stock market, rather than banks, to meet the bulk of developers' funding needs. Land sales to developers became a principal revenue source for many local governments, though painful when demand shrinks, straining balance sheets. All these elements are connected in an increasingly well-developed funding loop, even if at times things become temporarily very stretched.

Demand has been driven by high household income growth (wages mainly), supported by rising productivity, education and R&D. This flows into bank deposits and increasingly into "shadow banking" assets. Do not be alarmed, all will be explained later: Chinese shadow banking is not generally shadowy. Boosting demand were mortgages, only made possible by revising China's constitution in 2002 to allow private ownership of property: a ticklish concept in a communist country.

With booms and busts, property cycles will drive the economy until there is enough living space for all who can afford it. Understanding this process requires detailed knowledge of real estate's evolution in China. Property has indeed contributed to overcapacity, capital misallocation and rising debt, but this is either largely temporary or normal as economies develop, as the section on debt will explain. Generally, capital has been allocated by the markets, even if not always wisely at times, but that is the prerogative and way of markets. Pent-up demand and homebuyers' ability to finance it soundly through rapid income growth have ensured the economy did not collapse, even during property cycle downturns. Prices have merely adjusted and, in fact, become increasingly affordable in most cities during the last decade.

Ghost Cities

Urban myths do not come much larger than the claim that China is littered with ghost cities. These are something that, remarkably, mainly only some foreigners can see. The fact is there is no rash of ghost cities spread out across the whole of China, about to collapse the economy and financial system.

What do exist are temporary ghostly areas where rapid urbanization has driven housing construction on a truly China Scale, with row upon row of empty apartment blocks waiting to fill up, which they invariably do — as anyone who visited Pudong around the turn of the millennium knows but Milton Friedman could not see. It is not a new phenomenon, except to first-time visitors or those who have never been to China. Nor is it an error of development or misallocation of resources but an unusual, even a surprisingly *laissez-faire*, part of China's answer to its still-serious housing shortage. Markets, initially at least, are left to do what they generally do best, allocate resources.

The first major wave of accelerated urbanization in China, including much empty space, occurred in the late 1990s. This was when Beijing, Shanghai and Guangzhou, the capitals of China's three coastal regions and gateways to its hinterland, developed the Chinese model for rapid urbanization. Redevelopment on steroids, initially complete with bamboo scaffolding, would be a good description. The overcrowded unsanitary city centres were largely flattened. These made way for much more valuable commercial and upmarket residential real estate, just as once happened in London, New York, Hong Kong and Singapore. Compensation to the original dwellers funded their purchase of much higher-quality living space, typically on the outskirts of the existing town or in new adjacent rural areas like Pudong in Shanghai or Zhengdong in Zhengzhou, where land was much cheaper.

These new areas were subject to the same criticism levelled at ghost cities today — gross misallocation of capital by misguided state planning. Admittedly, Pudong commercial real estate had 80% vacancy in the late 1990s but oversupply soon disappeared as Pudong's GDP grew at 22% per annum. Within three to five years, most new areas fill up no matter how ghostly they appear at the start. Ghost areas are not a financial disaster waiting to happen. The phenomenon is best explained by China's property shortage, rapid urbanization, upgrading and scale. With such a backlog of demand, even with annual completed housing almost doubling since 2000, per capita urban space is still 30%–40% below the average of northeast Asia. Providing space in this way is logical and works, even if there are excesses, periods of indigestion and, for some observers, an eerie sense of the supernatural.

The construction boom is far from over. China still needs about 60% more housing. With per capita space demand likely to expand by almost another 50% while China's population could grow 10%, residential space may not peak before 2030. On top of that will be replacement of poorer-quality homes. China's average living space is still hardly half of Europe's, little over a third of the US and barely 60% of Japan, Taiwan or Korea. At 24 square metres, it is even over 20% smaller than public housing in Singapore. There seems no reason why China's average per capita should not approach the living area of its

Asian neighbours, even if it still lags 10%–15% behind the likes of Germany, UK and Australia.

Will all this bring risk to developers and, consequently, the banks, as sceptics fear? The financial implications are not so threatening. Most phases of a typical developer's project break even financially after 50% of units are sold. Therefore they are not a major burden on the financial system, neither does that much property sit on developers' balance sheets. Most is placed firmly on household balance sheets, the strongest part of China's finances: either as property assets or as part of wealth management products funding developers. The vast majority of homebuyers, borrowing from banks, can service their mortgages perfectly well.

Where will all the demand come from? Take one of the two most famous ghost cities, Zhengdong in Zhengzhou, the capital of Henan. A Research-Works survey found the largest source of Zhengzhou's housing demand is first-time buyers, comprising 38%, usually with help from parents and relatives, while property upgraders account for another 32%, many from overcrowded city centres or similarly rundown areas. Investors comprise 16% of buyers, mostly local people who have left the province but intend to return or buy for their parents, while the remaining 14% are people who have moved into the province to work: a solid foundation for demand, almost all from local people.

Vacancy is another worry. Government data shows that unsold (not empty) space is only 1.8% of China's total urban residential space — not the enormous overcapacity many imagine. If this were even three or four times greater it would still not be excessive for an economy undergoing such rapid change, especially considering high single-digit or even double-digit annual household income growth. Emptiness does not mean unsold, just empty: this is where ghosts exist in the misconceived financial equation.

As for emptiness, 70% of residential property is occupied on average within two years of a development phase being completed, and nearly 90% within five years. This is not uncommon in other parts of Asia. It does mean that an estimated 10% of housing stock is unoccupied, but this is the result of custom, shaped by convenience as well as the sheer scale and pace at which China urbanizes. Just-in-time delivery would not work in a country the size of China that is growing at such speed. Surplus stock avoids continuous (and inflationary) shortages like in London. Think of empty space as short-term inventory or a market signal about overpricing in a fast-moving, complex and very large market. Developer and bank funding is attuned to these realities, as their continued profitability confirms.

Scale is the next concern: very hard to grasp. The numbers are China Scale writ large. One way to understand the fastest-growing part of today's property picture is that China's main focus this decade, without announcing it explicitly, is to transform some 20 provincial capitals into true capitals with all the amenities and infrastructure of any capital city in the world. This includes everything from high-quality offices and housing to convention centres, museums and parks, along with the same job opportunities in administration, healthcare, education, sports, recreation and entertainment. Transforming all the capitals of Europe within two decades would be the equivalent.

Building these provincial capitals requires more qualified personnel for construction and services: everything from engineers to logistics, lawyers to teachers. Often, the capitals lack these skills, especially professional skills, which they lure with higher pay from other cities within the province and outside. These highly-qualified personnel earn above-average salaries, further boosting demand for property.

Here comes the scale. The provinces of these 20 inland capitals have a combined population of 827 million people, an average of over 40 million: each larger than most European countries or US states. The 20 provinces combined have more than double the population of North America and 60% more than the EU. This is the logical next phase in China's development that began with the three gateways to China — Shanghai, Beijing and Guangzhou — driven by the same forces of rising incomes, inward migration and shrinking household size. All this hardly suggests massive oversupply for long, unless the laws of market economics have been suspended, which they have not. Ghost areas are temporary. They have existed around China for over two decades without bringing down the financial system or the main developers, let alone most households. There is no sub-prime crisis about to explode.

At China Speed, change at the ground level happens surprisingly quickly. Zhengzhou's new area of Zhengdong was the hot subject of a misconceived CBS *60 Minutes* documentary in 2014. Andy Rothman videoed the same scene for the Matthews Asia website two years later: it looked very different and very occupied. Clearly, Zhengdong no longer deserves the moniker of ghost city after just half a decade of rapid growth. Zhengzhou has a population of 7.4 million while its province Henan has 94 million people, more than any country in Europe or any US state. Neighbouring Shandong, Hebei, Anhui, Shaanxi, Shanxi and Hubei provinces add a further 358 million people, for whom Henan historically has served as an important crossroads at the heart of central China. Together, Zhengzhou and its hinterland totals over 450 million people, 44% more than the entire US and more than post-Brexit EU. Yet Henan is just one province, and not even the largest in China; Guangdong and Shandong are bigger.

The sheer scale of these emerging capital cities is hard to appreciate. The scale explains why ghostly appearances disappear very rapidly — there are so many people to house. In fact, if developers had priced their Zhengdong properties more affordably in the first place, the homes would have sold much faster, avoiding their temporary ghostly appearance altogether. Instead, developers waited several years for incomes to catch up with prices while road and rail infrastructure linked the new district to existing urban centres to make them more valuable: normal profit maximization.

I first visited Zhengdong in 2005 when it was just starting to create a new town outside the heavily congested old town. For a province of 94 million people, this seemed sensible. Few foreigners had heard of Zhengzhou, let alone Zhengdong, before it became a byword for ghost cities and supposed gross misallocation of capital. How many can recall it now, let alone place it on the map? Yet Zhengzhou was first a capital during the Shang Dynasty in 1600 BC due to its supremely strategic location. To give the new district of Zhengdong a central focus, up went the convention centre and museum, facilities that capitals anywhere in the world usually have, be they national or state — yet deemed by some to be a hubristic or socialist waste of resources. The implied disapproving message being that China is a poor country that should not indulge in such baubles, and an unspoken suggestion of corruption.

New areas take longer to fill than city centres for four very logical reasons. Initially, they lack transportation links, facilities, jobs and development coordination. Infrastructure invariably lags behind residential construction but catches up very fast. New districts usually start as rural areas with no industrial facilities. Then, as more and more companies relocate or expand their factories and offices, more employees live there. Since its opening, over 5,000 enterprises had moved into Zhengdong by 2014. Some homebuyers, though, may still wait a few years before moving from the old city. There are good reasons, as anyone who has visited a new residential development in China knows.

Although the homes themselves have been completed, the project is often still a building site. This is because, in China, homeowners usually prefer to do their own finishing, which involves a great deal of interior remodelling, generating much noise, dust and noxious fumes. After a couple of years, renovation becomes more bearable so occupancy rises in a phase that, on paper, was finished (because it was sold) several years previously. Even then, some facilities, from sufficient shops and recreation to transportation, may still be lacking. Therefore, if people can, some leave property empty for as long as possible. These include retirees, keen to get away from the old city's noise and pollution but wanting to avoid the initial disruption of a semi-permanent building site; young couples who purchase property ahead of their need; and parents who buy long-term for their children, fearing that prices will become unaffordable.

The fact that most project phases are sold within one year of completion while occupancy reaches 90% within five years obviously refutes the assertion that Zhengdong is a permanent ghost city. Prices reflected this, up over 25% in 2013 alone, more than in any other major Chinese city that year. The overhang of unsold property was clearing quickly. The new district's residential population grew from 300,000 in 2009 to more than one million in 2013, up by 35% annually. The number of primary schools more than doubled since 2006 yet the demand for places exceeded capacity. In Zhengdong's early days, people talked about how few lights were on at night; by 2015 people complained of insufficient parking space. Such is the life cycle of a typical new Chinese urban development.

Property bubbles have certainly existed, but there is much muddled thinking about them. Those who write cavalierly about both property bubbles and ghost cities do not seem to understand that it is hard to square the two together with the laws of supply and demand: one or the other may hold, but not both for long. Of course there have been property bubbles and will be again. They have been a constant feature of Asia's recent development, so China has not departed from the norm. To comfort the worriers, what can also be said is that Chinese property prices have risen in cycles but have always returned to what is affordable. Bubbles have deflated without collapsing the financial system.

Shadow Banking

With no banking system in the Western sense of the term to develop, China reformed its financial system in its own way, causing nightmares for those unfamiliar with change or history. Eschewing any Big Bang, China followed the path outlined by traditional thinking: gradualism, pragmatism and taking a 360-degree view. Now its banking system provides the basic services an increasingly sophisticated economy needs. Rather than being financially fragile, what has evolved is steady financial deepening and, with it, increasing stability, a perfectly normal transitional phase in economic and financial development.

"Shadow banking" is a sinister, negative and very misleading term. In fact it can be very good news hidden under a very bad name. There is nothing especially shadowy about it except for the assumption it is the same as shadow banking in the US, in the shadows, not subject to banking regulation. However, in China, it is a misnomer: all these activities are now regulated. China has no sub-prime mortgage or related banking time bomb ticking away.

Far from being threatening, these non-bank financial intermediaries (NBFIs) such as credit trusts, credit guarantee companies, leasing companies, pawnbrokers and micro lenders which comprise shadow banking play a crucial role in the final major stage of transforming China's financial system. NBFIs force banks to compete, teaching them to price risk better. "Shadow banking" in China is essentially regulated non-bank funding. For decades, everywhere called this non-bank financial intermediation, never "shadow banking" with its sinister, misleading connotations. Outside this there is still an informal capital market that includes Wenzhou-like lenders (see Chapter 7) but is relatively small and will probably be absorbed by formal finance as in Taiwan and South Korea.

NBFIs show how China's traditional evolutionary and exploratory approach has achieved change without derailing reform or the economy. First, identify the long-term objective: to prevent systemic failure. Then improve risk management of credit, liquidity and funding; increase transparency of products and borrowers; provide continuous monitoring and better regulation; reduce exposure to a single borrower; and avoid mismatch of loan tenures. A long list, but all connected.

China's NBFIs can do all this, harnessing the skills they have honed since credit trusts were allowed in 1978 to set market interest rates. Not only were these skills superior to those of state banks, but so were levels of service. Largely from hard experience, the regulators learned how to regulate better. They were up against a particularly innovative industry, nimble in keeping one step ahead of regulators. It all takes time and patience. NBFIs' great virtue is they enabled interest rate liberalization by stealth, even before this began in 2012 at the banks. In the process, the allocation of capital and access to it improved. Just one decade ago, banks directly provided the bulk of all funding in the financial system, over 80%. Constrained by the central bank's interest rate caps, they felt no need to compete aggressively, if at all, let alone make interest rates reflect the real risk of a loan. Now there is more competition and less risk.

Overlooked have been significant improvements in financial products, notably in information available to investors. Professional advisers like Jason Bedford, previously an auditor with KPMG China before becoming China financial institutions analyst with UBS Securities, believes the standard of disclosure in trust product prospectuses has improved markedly since 2010. This has been driven by a combination of growing investor risk awareness and trust company caution to avoid the legal consequences of product mis-selling. All parties know they could be held to account for any failing. Competition, as theory would expect, has driven innovation. Among other things, trusts or their investors can now take equity stakes in projects, get board representation and insist on strict loan covenants. All improve investors' positions.

The China Banking and Regulatory Commission (CBRC) has shown itself to be a proactive and pretty effective regulator, capable of enforcing its will in what could very easily be the Wild East. Both in designing regulation and monitoring market behaviour, it has shown ability. The fact market participants say the CBRC stifles innovation suggests it is probably following a prudent path: the middle way and gradualism rule. The CBRC has real enforcement powers. These include withholding licenses for new business and branches. For more serious infringements it can require assets be brought back onto the balance sheet, hitting profit directly by forcing banks to pull capital away from income-generating assets to restore capital adequacy. A more personal punishment is that it could affect senior bank staffs' annual appraisals, compensation or even careers which are monitored by the party's central organization department. In particularly serious cases, the CBRC can bring about a change in management.

There is, though, one negative. Reform first highlights systemic weaknesses, giving an impression to some of great but unquantifiable fragility, beyond sight, control or even hope. Vocal doubters fixate on them. Many editors, journalists and headline writers cannot resist the opportunity to make alarming suggestions such as linking China's shadow banking with US sub-prime lending, despite the fact that there are very important definitional differences. The sinister connotation has stuck even though it is not reality.

Debt

Alarm bells rang when markets realized China had the world's largest non-financial corporate debt, just when credit growth exploded in 2009 by 99%. Both were true. Images of zombie, rusting manufacturers on state life-support fed fears that banks would soon be in crisis and GDP growth would collapse. That was nine years ago. Neither has happened.

Instead, the rapidly rising level of Chinese debt growth moderated significantly after 2010 before picking up again in 2016, though still within what is considered the upper limit of acceptability. Even this definition is debatable as the true test is simply a borrower's ability to repay. Generally, a strongly growing developing economy like China is more capable of repaying its debt than a mature, stagnating one in the West. Furthermore, China is the world's largest creditor nation whereas the US is the world's largest debtor in terms of internationally held debt. China's short-term foreign debt is just 8% of GDP while long-term is only 5%; those of the US is at 32% and 66% respectively. This is not the same as the amount of domestic debt, but it speaks to a very different background picture to any assumed by the negative China narrative. Moreover, China is growing about three times faster. Even if the US reached 3% GDP growth, it would still be under half of China's. So why all the fuss? Something seems to be wrong, some perspective and context required. The answer lies largely in debt's components and trajectories being misunderstood.

In one very important way, China was fortunate when the 2008 global financial crisis struck. It had relatively little debt. Consequently, doubling credit in 2009 was less risky than many imagined. This was especially so at the national, public sector, financial sector and household levels: see Appendix: Debt Comparisons. Banks had very little exposure to finance because China's capital markets are very underdeveloped compared with those in the UK, EU, US, Hong Kong or Singapore where complex derivatives and other forms of financial engineering caused the systemic global collapse. This underdevelopment also means that Chinese companies use banks as their main source of funds, just as firms in much of the West did until about half a century ago. This high dependence on bank lending was the problem for sceptics, but they missed the overall picture.

China could afford the stimulus and high corporate debt. These could be managed over time, providing China a path out of the global financial crisis in a way that no other major economy has done. With a low amount of overall debt, high corporate bank debt was nowhere near as threatening as numbers suggested. Indeed, the rapid rise in debt illustrated its economic and financial transformation, as will be explained in a moment. It also meant China could use the banks to stimulate the economy without creating a crisis of its own. Debt overall could balloon under the stimulus to 262% of GDP by 2013, as measured by Simon Ogus of independent economics research firm DSG, but still be lower than that of any of the other major world economies. Ogus calculated that debt-to-GDP at the end of 2016 for China was 308%, US 310%, EU 532%, Japan 549% and UK 765%.

A more accurate way to view China's debt, therefore, is that up until 2016 it still had the *lowest* overall debt-to-GDP ratio of any major economy, not the highest. It may in future slightly exceed that of the US but still be well under that of the EU, Japan and UK, all of which are likely to grow much more slowly. China's 2016 household debt was only 47% of GDP compared with 79% in the US and 87% in the UK. For many in China, especially the older generation, debt is still a four-letter word. Credit card debt is rarely rolled over. Some 75% of cars are bought with cash. Home mortgages are smaller, with a 20%–30% cash deposit normal. Borrowers repay as fast as possible in this still generally debt-averse culture, though credit card issuers put their hopes in more free-spending Millennials. Financial sector debt is just 36% of GDP compared with 255% in major OECD economies due to China's bond and equity markets being relatively undeveloped, partly because it has been very cautious about derivatives. CBRC head Liu Mingkang, even before 2008, said, "The simpler the better". Despite China's SOEs, public sector debt in 2016 was only 70% compared with the 137% average of leading global economies.

So, the debt numbers are not alarming in themselves, but what of the fact that it takes more credit to generate China's GDP growth. This must be bad? Not unless increasing modern home ownership is bad and living in often substandard and overcrowded housing is good. Remember the acute housing shortage and the 2002 constitutional change that legalized mortgages. Even then, initially only the more financially sophisticated used them. Only since the 2009 housing cycle began have most homebuyers borrowed from banks. Of course, that means more debt but usually very manageable debt in an economy at full employment. Yukon Huang, former head of the World Bank in China, explains.

> Much of the recent surge in the credit to GDP ratio is actually evidence of financial deepening rather than financial instability as China moves towards more market-based asset values. If so, higher credit ratios are fully consistent with the less alarming impressions that come from scrutiny of sector specific financial indicators,

Huang wrote in the *Financial Times* in 2014. That is the key point that many miss.

A rapid rise in the credit-to-GDP ratio is normal for any economy at China's stage of development. It is a sign of progress, described as finanacial deepening. Mortgages enable people to buy better housing much sooner than they could without credit: their welfare improves. Mortgages and related activity, most very sound, account for much of the debt increase. The alternatives are highly undeveloped or barter economies, which are almost debt-free but not lauded as desirable models to emulate: otherwise North Korea, anyone? There is of course an acceptable limit, of which China has been very aware since 2011 when priorities changed to tighten monetary policy after the stimulus had achieved its purpose.

Local government debt has attracted far more attention than it merits. Legally, there is no distinction in China between local and national government debt. All such debt is on the national government's balance sheet. It is true that local debt numbers were unknown in 2008, but the National Audit Office established that 56% was funded by banks, 12% by NBFIs and 10% by bondholders, a fair spread. However, it does not constitute misallocation as almost all is needed to maintain China's long-term growth, overwhelmingly for much-needed infrastructure as well as affordable housing.

The national balance sheet can support all this. China is not only still growing relatively rapidly, promising higher revenues and taxes, but the state also owns all the land and many other assets. Plenty of other countries are in a far more worrying position when it comes to contemplating their debt ratios, with minimal growth: Japan at 549% or UK at 765%, anyone? Are there other ghosts to bust or nightmares to end?

Middle-Income Trap

Sounds nasty, the middle-income trap. Conjuring up images of being stuck in thick, gooey mud, possibly even in quicksand, unable to get out: enough to focus any mind. There is a hint of even further danger: a trapdoor lurking, waiting to spring open and plunge the unwary to their doom. No one would take such a prospect lightly.

The term middle-income trap was conceived in 2007 by economists Indermit Gill and Homi Kharas. It may appear somewhat academic until some long-term trends are known. From 1870 to 1913, Argentina was the world's fastest-growing economy, the late 19th century's equivalent of today's China. Angus Maddison, pre-eminent in his field, calculated in 2007 in *Contours of the World Economy 1–2030 AD* that Argentina's real GDP grew twice as fast as the world average for over four decades, ranking 10th out of 65 economies. Convergence with the US economy was in sight but never happened. By 2008 it had fallen back to 28th by Woo Wing Thye's estimate. Might China be the next Argentina? Especially as only eight out of 101 middle-income non-Confucian economies reached high-income status after 1960: a very disturbing thought.

However, five of the eight Confucian economies *have* reached high-income status. That should settle the nerves, as long as China follows its neighbours. China ranked 64th out of 65 in 1913, long before communism, and 65th from 1960–1975, long after the 1949 revolution. Reform raised China to 40th by 2008. Vietnam has made similar strides. Only North Korea remains the stubborn Confucian laggard. China's climb should continue as the long-term thinking has been done out to 2030 and much growth is already in place.

Growth Exhaustion

China must be running out of growth opportunities? Not at all. New higher growth industries and regions can largely offset slowdowns as parts of China's economy mature. First among new growth engines are three major IT-related investment hubs and clusters that have blossomed in the north, east and south: Beijing, Hangzhou and Shenzhen. Smaller ones are scattered elsewhere. All benefit from and compete with each other nationally, possessing their own local investment ecosystems, just as Silicon Valley had in the 1980s. E-commerce and services also drive growth from medicine to tourism.

Is China creating new Haiers and other arch-exponents of change? Some 16,000 new firms are registered every day. This is 1970s Hong Kong or 1980s Taiwan with China Scale. One afternoon in 2015, I met three companies in Hangzhou, all part of the new wave. Some use the science of tomorrow, others harness IT knowledge and data mining to provide new services and convenience to meet old needs.

Guahao.com is a health portal connecting patients with doctors online to solve a very Chinese problem. Getting to see a doctor in China is very time-consuming. Normally, people take half or even a whole day off work to visit a doctor, not just for themselves, but to accompany relatives. Entire families of three generations swarm around Chinese hospitals, hoping for an appointment with a top specialist. China has medicine on an industrial scale. Treatment is still in the shortage economy as the supply and retention of doctors has lagged behind rising incomes that have driven demand. Visiting a major hospital in the morning is like entering a railway station at rush hour: very stressful. Therefore people are happy to pay for the convenience of Guahao to avoid the stress and the waste of their increasingly valuable time — previously a wholly unappreciated concept.

The frontiers of new technology are being pushed by other Hangzhou companies like Shining 3D and Digital China Union. Developing software systems, Shining is China's leading 3D printing company. Using metal powders, plastic, paper and silk, it makes body parts, especially replacements for teeth, bones and human organs, including silk hearts. Yes, as incredible as it may sound. Zhejiang is the millennia-old home of silk whose advanced knowledge enables it to use the natural fibre to replace vital organs, including hearts. Shining 3D's R&D spending in 2015 was a very high 25% of sales. Even when sales increase substantially it still aims to spend 10%–15% on R&D, as any aspiring world leader would.

Digital China Union may seem much more prosaic but is potentially equally transformative. It designs content for online sales platforms, furniture manufacturers and retailers which enables people to visualize how a piece of furniture would fit in their home: seeing is believing. Customized online to meet a buyer's precise tastes and specifications, this saves the retailer expensive display and storage space, freeing up working capital, meaning lower costs, while customers get greater convenience by saving time: win-win. Manufacturing is subcontracted to others, who are abundant in Zhejiang. These are just three of the firms in China's real economy, moving up the value-added curve by harnessing innovation.

Long-Term Thinking 2016–2030

To continue to grow, China just has to continue using its change management playbook. Of course different strategies will be needed as China has lost some of its strongest original advantages. The China Price is no more. All that surplus labour, which flowed into factories largely from rural areas to make China the world's cheapest manufacturer, has gone. That is the fact, so new paths are sought, largely using traditional concepts as Japan, South Korea, Taiwan, Hong Kong and Singapore did.

Asia's recent past has lit the future. Extensive research and field work, *yanjiu*, is still integral to policy formulation, as the *China 2030* study into the challenges China faces showed. Jointly conducted by the Development and Research Centre of the State Council, the Ministry of Finance and the World Bank, it aims to build "a modern, harmonious and creative high-income society". Learning lessons, including from the experience of other countries, is still very much the way.

China 2030 laid out in 2011 its medium-term economic thinking to be detailed in three upcoming five-year programmes. Now the basic foundation has been set, apart from spreading to the interior knowledge gained from developing coastal provinces, new policies will upgrade the whole economy. *China 2030* outlines ideas in services as well as initiatives to shape global financial architecture through institutions like the Asian Infrastructure Investment Bank. For manufacturing, specifically, there is *Made in China 2025,* plus the Belt and Road Initiative to grow its economy overseas: see Chapter 14. Apart from agriculture, which finally may get a major upgrade in the next decade, the economy's main challenges have now been thought through and necessary changes outlined.

Made in China 2025

To a surprising extent, China is just Singapore writ very, very, very large. China, though, has not yet paid such close attention to industrial upgrading as Singapore. The focus previously was to reform China's industrial structure, while constrained by historical baggage and concern for jobs. With its urban work force barely growing since 2012, unemployment is no longer the central issue. China can now more actively upgrade its technology, workers' skills and incomes, as Singapore did when it reached full employment in the late 1970s. The scale China has chosen is of course so much greater but the principles remain the same. Widely respected as having the world's best mechanical engineers, Germany is an obvious example from which to learn as it has already planned its next steps in industrial upgrading through Industry 4.0. *Made in China 2025* is China's version of the same process, only starting from a lower level.

Industry 4.0 is global manufacturing's Next Big Thing, linking networks of real time information between cyber–physical systems, the Internet of Things and the Internet of Services. Great productivity claims are made for providing real time information to automate processes. These range from restocking inventory to forecasting and diagnosing mechanical failures. Big data and sensors communicate real time information to people, machines and other data users, decentralizing decision-making, increasing speed and boosting efficiency. 4.0 is not confined to manufacturing. Cities can use similar systems and some services too.

Germany approached conceptualizing 4.0 very carefully, organizing many working groups to consider not just technology but related long-term factors like climate change, healthcare and communications. The German Ministry for Education and Research started about 100 joint projects in 2011 involving universities and 67 research institutes across a wide range of topics, especially in the Internet of Things, networks and artificial intelligence. Beyond technology, Germany carefully considered legal, social, economic and employment issues. The private sector and trade unions were involved, as in Singapore. This inclusive, holistic, 360-degree approach to future challenges impressed China, resonating with its thinking.

Like the scale of China's urbanization, the ambition of this fourth industrial revolution is unprecedented. China has set three goals. First, to close the gap as far as possible between Chinese manufacturing and world leader Germany by 2025; then, by 2035, to reach a middle-ranking position among those who have attained 4.0; and finally, to be the leading global manufacturer by 2045. Again, the basic unit of time in Chinese governance is the decade.

4.0 anticipates changes as great as any the world experienced during the first industrial revolution when machinery harnessed steam and coal power; the second, when electricity drove mass production; and the third, when IT and automation began to revolutionize manufacturing. The fourth revolves around digitalizing the whole economy and society to "optimize life", as Dr Luo Jiafu, Vice Chairman of the Sino-German China Association for Industry 4.0 in Düsseldorf puts it. Already, for 10–15 years, some German companies have used software and enterprise resource planning in accounting, production, logistics and sales to re-engineer their operations: Siemens claims it has reached 3.8, while automakers are over 3.0. The German average is estimated at 3.0, while in China the average is said to be about 2.0, with many manufacturers below that.

Ironically, Germany designed its 4.0 programme in 2011 to protect it from US and Chinese competition. However China's top leaders were so intent on acquiring the knowledge they persuaded Germany in 2014 to cooperate with China. Germany's reason for accepting is equally compelling. The reason is simple, reflecting one of China's overlooked but growing strengths. If German factories in China do not upgrade, their firms may well fail globally. They need China to succeed. All others are in the same position. For their China operations to succeed, German firms' Chinese suppliers and customers also have to be 4.0-compatible. This will help make 4.0 the new global standard in manufacturing by ensuring it is used to the maximum. Put simply, without Chinese firms using and developing similar systems, 4.0's usefulness will be limited. As with more and more things in the world, from avoiding climate change to disease control, China is critical to global success. Everything is interconnected.

Can China live up to Germany's hopes? Critical to the success of 4.0 is the private sector's curiosity, which in China is very evident and not in doubt, especially among industry leaders and younger entrepreneurs. More challenging may be the need to constantly test, test and test again. That is not so ingrained in the culture. Time will tell. The important thing is that China has a sense of where it is going. Through *yanjiu* and experimentation it has adapted foreign systems before, without necessarily copying the entire blueprint. This will be an evolutionary process to upgrade its industrial base that, if successful, will be revolutionary.

In 2015 China issued its *Made in China 2025* white paper after some 100 engineers from the Chinese Academy of Social Sciences spent over a year looking at 4.0 to figure out how to implement it in China. Taking a 360-degree view, targets were set for everything from R&D, production and costs to CO_2 emissions and green energy. The Ministry of Industry and Information drives the process, reporting to a working group headed by the vice premier responsible for China's economy who reports directly to the premier.

Ultimately though, its success will depend on independent entities, most in the private sector. That is good as it forces a major overhaul of all China's existing systems from IT to cloud computing, bandwidth to reliable connectivity. Can China make this great technological leap?

"No doubt," is the confident answer of a German company's technician responsible for implementing 4.0. When asked why, he replied because China has always achieved what it sets its mind to doing, echoing Professor Michael Enright's point to doubters about Chinese policy: see Chapter 5. How long will it take? The technician calculates his company's Chinese operations will get to 4.0 by 2025.

Why is he so sure? Simply because China already has major private sector providers of the infrastructure, firms like Alibaba, Baidu and Tencent. After them, many firms provide the specialist knowledge. With local knowledge and cultural affinity, they can design the applications needed in what is likely to become the world's largest user of 4.0.

China 2030

China 2030 aims to do for the overall economy, including finance and services, what *Made in China 2025* hopes to do for manufacturing: transform them by using markets and commercial considerations rather than outdated ideology and vestiges of central planning. Li Keqiang oversaw the *2030* report before becoming premier, providing substantial input for the 13th five-year plan from 2016–2020 as well as laying out all the challenges that China is likely to face and proposals to address them. Nothing was rushed into action. The party and government were given four years to consider it further: classic Chinese gradualism. Some parts may only be emphasized in the 14th or even 15th plans in the 2020s.

The *Financial Times*' chief economic commentator Martin Wolf called it a "remarkable document". Statist planning language is no more: see Appendix: *China 2030* for excerpts. *2030* recognizes that economic development gets harder as a country reaches technological frontiers. It makes explicit that innovation cannot be achieved through government planning, saying government intervention may even retard growth: no mean statement, given China's history since 1949.

Individuals and the private sector are critical. *2030* acknowledges that with the rise of the middle class China needs to empower people to contribute to development. This requires "granting rights to encourage broad participation". What might that mean? Furthermore, it states the government must reduce its role in production, distribution and resource allocation. Instead it should focus more on designing and implementing policy along with the regulatory framework. China's new private sector leaders could have written much of it: see Chapter 12 DNA.

Intellectual Property

One of the most frequent China questions is about intellectual property (IP). The presumption is that IP protection in China does not exist or, if it does, only on paper, leading MNCs to contemplate leaving. Closing in China seems highly unlikely as most MNCs see it as their major market before too long: many have reached this point already. That, though, is not the only reason. According to leading IP lawyer Luke Minford of Rouse and Co. in Beijing, "remarkable progress has been made over the last five to 10 years" to protect intellectual property in China. The courts are developing fast with three special IP courts, four trial tribunals and almost 400 other courts authorized to hear a range of IP cases. Some 75% of IP owners succeed in winning their cases. For foreign firms it is even higher.

In 2004, I asked a Taiwanese law professor what the prospects were for IP in China. Somewhat to my surprise, and going well against the negative narrative, he answered they were very promising. The law is good, so are the judges, he asserted. He should know, he trained many of them while they studied in the US or Taiwan. Minford's verdict in 2016 is that the judges are now experienced, while judgements are consistent and show little bias. His 30,000-case database from all over China bears this out.

The main reason I have always been optimistic about IP protection over the long run is that most cases involve Chinese suing Chinese: almost 99% of IP cases in 2015. Attitudes towards IP theft change when the owners are local. To use the private equity jargon, China now has skin in the game. There are still, though, many people acting in bad faith, especially in smaller cities, but behaviour in Tier 1 and 2 cities has improved greatly, Minford observes.

MNCs can take comfort from Chinese courts listening to foreign judgements, especially from Germany and, in some areas of law such as copyright and patents, from the US. Going to court is also a lot faster and cheaper in China than in the US or EU. However in sophisticated cases, most probably involving two MNCs, they would be very unlikely to choose Chinese jurisdiction, simply because China's courts have yet to handle cases involving disputes among global leaders at the cutting edge of technology. That will doubtless change.

Private Equity Funding

China's volatile stock market gets a great deal of attention but China's early-stage financing does not. The reverse should be true. Unlike many equity cultures which evolved in their own formalized, well-regulated and transparent markets, China has done the opposite by embracing its existing informal markets before wholeheartedly adopting alien systems like Western stock markets.

China has plenty of successful entrepreneurs, who started with nothing, looking to invest surplus funds. They happily accept more risk in anticipation of commensurately higher rewards. Investors in the West have known from the 19th century to the dot.com era that the best opportunities in fast-growing, transitional economies often lie outside the stock market. In many ways, early stage investment (venture capital, private equity, buyout firms and hedge funds) is much more important for China's long-term growth, which has to come largely from private sector creativity and ambition. China now has a very robust early stage investment ecosystem. Only the US invested more than China in private equity in 2015, some $60 billion against China's $32 billion, three times greater than in the EU. Apart from the US, China is the world's only early-stage market with a self-sustaining system where companies can get sufficient funds throughout a project's life. This is helped by the market's size, depth and liquidity. Considering the US industry has been institutionalized for 60 years whereas China's is barely 15 years old, that is quite an achievement and overlooked strength.

Chinese investors are familiar with the risks of early-stage investment. Many entrepreneurs started out being funded informally by families and friends, knowing risks are high, so concepts must be equally ambitious. Failure is frequent but Chinese investors have little problem with that as the flip side, historically, has been so attractive. This positions China well to move up to high-income status: yet another reason China can avoid the middle-income trap and the other nightmares some imagine.

People

Millennials China's Millennials are now the largest, most sought after group of 15–29 year-old consumers in the world. They outnumber the entire population of the US. For most, the top priority purchase is a home: 70% of Chinese Millennials own their home compared with 35% and 31% of US and UK Millennials.

Graduates University enrolment trebled after 2000 to become the world's largest. Chinese ability and ingenuity should not be underestimated: already seven Chinese firms are in MIT's 2017 Smartest 50 Companies list.

Consumers

Let the market decide. That was the 3rd Plenum's major reform in 2013, a year that also showed how capricious markets can be in China. Having grabbed some 40% of China's fast food market with almost 4,000 outlets, KFC was hit by concerns over bird flu and other adverse events. Now it is Starbucks that is making the running with a reputation for understanding Chinese consumers' rapidly changing tastes, not just in beverages and décor but also in using innovative technology.

Disneyland The Magic Kingdom in Shanghai welcomed 11 million visitors during its opening year, 10% above Disney's target.

Tourism Chinese are now the world's most numerous tourists, over 120 million in 2016. No longer just in large tour groups, Xiao Yu from Guangxi is seen outside Milan Cathedral on his 2014 round-the-world solo cycle tour.

Technology

Mobile Payments Chinese are rapid adopters of new technology. Above, even vegetables are bought by mobile payment. In 2016, mobile transactions exceeded $5 trillion, 50 times more than in the US.

London Taxi The iconic London Taxi maker is now owned by Zhejiang Geely. The Chinese firm also bought Volvo Car Group, which in 2019 will be the first major manufacturer to sell only hybrid or electric vehicles, heralding the end of the petrol engine era.

Drones Privately-owned and Shenzhen-based, DJI is the world's leading maker of civilian drones. This unmanned aerial vehicle sprays wheat in Jiangsu.

High Speed Train High-speed rail has become China's global calling card but ever-higher technological frontiers are being opened in artificial intelligence, quantum communications and space.

Chapter 14

Finding the Morning Sun to Avoid a Chaotic Era

My favourite song is Tomorrow Will Be Better.

13-year-old, Heshan, Guangdong, 2017

Creativity really is the fuel of growth and transformation.

Shaun Hargreaves Heap, King's College, London, 2015

When I asked a friend's 13-year-old nephew his favourite song, he named *Tomorrow Will Be Better*. This was not in cosmopolitan Shanghai or innovative Shenzhen but in a fourth-tier town, unknown to most Chinese, called Heshan. Only a decade before, when I first visited Heshan, it had one dusty main street, inevitably called *Renmin Dadao*, People's Avenue, and a down-at-heel city centre with a single unprepossessing hotel. On the western shore of the Pearl River Delta, which lagged far behind the boom cities of Shenzhen and Dongguan on the eastern shore, Heshan is becoming one of China's newest boom towns thanks to its location in the Guangdong–Hong Kong–Macau Greater Bay Area, the world's largest economic unit, having overtaken Tokyo Bay's industrial belt. One of the world's longest sea bridges, which incorporates a 6.7 km-long underwater tunnel, connects the previously underdeveloped western Pearl River Delta with Hong Kong, once the world's only gateway to China.

The catchy 1980s Taiwanese song *Tomorrow Will Be Better*, (itself inspired by Quincy Jones' arrangement of *Do They Know It's Christmas?*

which is better known for its chorus *We Are The World)* may sound cheesy, even propagandistic, but no more so than the Rogers and Hammerstein lyrics of *Oklahoma!* that captured the optimism of 1940s America with its chorus of "Oh, what a beautiful mornin', Oh, what a beautiful day, I've got a beautiful feelin', Everythin's going my way!" with no mention of the absence of black civil rights or bad air pollution, which in Los Angeles stung the eyes. Broadway looked beyond these scars to the fulfillment of the American Dream. Now it is the turn of Chinese to enjoy their version of the better life. After experiencing the last four decades, this is now the expectation of most Chinese: a better tomorrow.

China's change since 1978 has been like night and day. The difference is enormous, its breadth telling, but what of the future? At the midpoint of a seven-decade economic transformation, China is progressing from a largely very poor pre-industrial economy to a high-income post-industrial one. Already it is a higher middle-income economy by World Bank definition. Achieving high-income status requires the main driver of economic growth to shift from investment to consumption. This is well on track.

New Era

The first two sentences of the preface to *China's Change* were written in late summer 2017. They are that "Asia and the West face similar challenges. Both need to renew themselves as mounting disruption forges a new era." Without knowing that "new era" would be the two defining words of the party's 19th Congress in October, they come as no great surprise to people living in it every day in China. This new era, though, is not just for China but the whole world, which is why a prologue about accelerating global disruption is necessary before launching into the thesis of *China's Change*.

Understanding the context puts China's ability to conceptualize, implement and manage change in perspective, while shining light for everyone on how to handle an era of great change driven by technology, demography, connectivity, along with migrations of wealth and work.

This is the new global reality. "Change is everywhere and the pace seems to quicken," Lyric Hughes wrote in her 2016 *EconVue* year-end review. Geopolitical and economic ramifications are many. "If 2016 has taught us one lesson, it must be humility in the face of history," Hughes continued. History and its offshoot, philosophy, are relevant again.

By the time Xi Jinping had completed his near three-and-a-half-hour report to the 19th Congress, few could have been unaware of the change in tone. Confidence oozed from every statement. Deng Xiaoping's 1981 economic goal of reaching a moderately prosperous society had been reached and 700 million people (the World Bank head says 800 million) have been lifted out of poverty.

Now, Xi declared, is the time to set new goals. Eliminating all poverty is the first, by 2020. Looking to the medium-term from 2020 to 2035, Xi talked of building on this increasing prosperity to focus on global innovation leadership, people's rights and social civility. By 2050, the goal is for China to be an advanced nation in all respects: material, ethical, social and ecological, as well as happier. How did this seemingly sudden three-decade vision and new goals materialize? Apart from the economy having developed to where this is possible, Xi has played his political cards astutely. "Collective" political leadership proved increasingly ineffective in the last decade, enabling Xi to consolidate power more quickly than most imagined.

With two-thirds of the ruling Politburo now firmly identified with him, Xi is free in his second term to push through his plans. Immediately, he addressed the two most obvious potential threats to China's stability, the financial system and corruption, by establishing institutions to oversee financial stability, economic development and clean governance. Three priorities are set, deepening reform and opening up, with special emphasis on the latter; the rule of law; and the environment, which occupied an estimated one-tenth of his speech. The pursuit of a better life and happiness rather than pure growth is now the explicit goal, admitting that over-rapid growth had been unbalanced and created major issues.

A goal for China to become an active member of the community of nations received the longest applause during Xi's speech. Within three weeks, Xi was in Vietnam at the Asia-Pacific Economic Cooperation annual meeting. Following on from US President Donald Trump, who gave his vision of America First and the offer of bilateral trade negotiations to the region's heads of government and top executives, all of whom had benefited greatly from freer multilateral trade, a.k.a. globalization, Xi made the same pitch to keep global trade open as he had at Davos in January. Holding the lectern firmly, Xi promised more regional cooperation and urged the region to take global initiatives. With geography and funding on his side, China moved one step closer to the centre of the world's stage. What gives Xi and China confidence to do all this now?

Economy

China's economy has four strong overlooked pillars to support its transformation, even as parts mature and structural problems remain to be fixed. A dynamic private sector now dominates; very demanding but fast-adopting consumers, especially Millennials, keep firms on their toes while lapping up innovation; R&D, which James Wilson and James Keeley in 2007 called the most ambitious research programme since John F. Kennedy embarked on the moon race; and education, where two decades of investment is paying off with higher-qualified and therefore higher-paid workers who can consume more. In addition, high-growth new industries drive China up the value added curve while previously lagging regions, with 60% of its population, have begun to catch up with earlier growth leaders in coastal China. This is all amplified by China Scale and China Speed. Supertankers don't stop suddenly; there is still much momentum and time to alter course if need be.

What does this mean in practical terms? McKinsey estimates that China's new car market in 2022 will exceed that of the US and EU *combined*— in 2016 it already led the US with 23.9 million sold against 17.5 million; China's middle class will reach 550 million by 2022, the Washington-based Center for Strategic and International Studies calculates; China was the first country to file one million patents in one year; it accounts for half the world's e-commerce transactions and 40% of delivered packages; Chinese tourists spend over $250 billion on foreign travel; and in the former home of foot-binding, some 60% of the world's new female billionaires live in China.

Nonetheless, alarm about financial fragility and potential economic crisis persists in the negative narrative. Since of all foreign institutions, the International Monetary Fund (IMF) has more access to China's economic technocrats, done more in-depth macroeconomic research on China's economy and advised China much more than any Wall Street firm or financial commentator, it is instructive to look at the IMF's annual review of China's economy in August 2017, a year when sceptics still abounded.

The IMF concluded that household debt growth slowed in 2017 (and may slow further in 2018 as property cools more); economic rebalancing continues with consumption contributing nearly two-thirds of growth, the highest amount since 2000, before supercharged economic growth went on a tear; the current account surplus is estimated to be down to 1.4%, well off its 10% peak; and the IMF raised its GDP forecast a notch to 6.8%. Reducing fears about zombies and overcapacity, it subsequently detailed that zombie loans to loss making state companies comprised only between 5% and 9% of corporate debt, while the major overcapacity industries of steel, coal, aluminium, cement and plate glass made up just 19%. This was less than the fearful consensus had imagined and, if properly managed, not enough to bring down the financial system.

Overall, the IMF believes China's transition to a more sustainable growth path continues as reform "advances across a wide domain"; coordination between politicians and regulators continues to improve with important actions taken on financial risk; corporate debt is growing more slowly, reflecting restructuring initiatives; and overcapacity reduction targets have been met in the major areas of steel and coal. The IMF considers that the renminbi remains broadly in line with fundamentals, while over $3 trillion of foreign exchange reserves is more than adequate: $2 trillion would suffice. The IMF has already stated China's existing importance in saying that "China's continuing strong growth has provided critical support to global demand".

Geopolitics

As China's economy continues to strengthen and open up, inevitably its global geopolitical position will change even more. By 2025, China will very likely overtake the US to become the world's leading economy: it is already the largest trader. Apart from China's actions, much will depend upon the response of the West and Japan to China's re-emergence after nearly 200 years of relative steep decline. If they fail to acknowledge China's economic strength, they will anyway face the fate of King Canute, who could not stop the rising tide.

China's force is sheer numbers, not water. Furthermore, what is not in doubt is that some, if not all, of India, Indonesia, Pakistan, Nigeria, Brazil and Bangladesh will continue in China's wake of growing relative economic size and, therefore, influence. China is just the first wave of large emerging economies taking their place in global councils during the 21st century. The trend from a unipolar world to a multipolar one will be relentless. China's accelerating global importance will increasingly help achieve global goals and resolve problems from global trade, jobs, standards, security and epidemics to determining success, from Germany's Industry 4.0 initiative to corporate global industry leadership, as Japanese automaker Toyota has found to its cost.

Think of China's ruling party as the Development Party pursuing a better life by attaining the goal of Wealth and Power. This is a 21st-century development state just as Germany is, providing direction by considering hard the long term and speaking in a soft but firm voice. It is comfortable with cooperation, competition and inclusion beyond its narrow borders. Another way is to think of it as the Business Party or China Inc, just a much larger version of Singapore Inc, run like a modern corporation with a business development department. Considering that the latter created the likes of Singapore Airlines, Development Bank of Singapore and the Central Provident Fund, this is not an alarming prospect. China can win soft power in areas where the West is significantly absent, such as through its infrastructure expertise in the Belt and Road Initiative and elimination of its own poverty, the single largest in the world when it began almost 40 years ago.

History and Philosophy

Humility in the face of history resonates with Chinese thinking. History is the raw material for philosophy. 19th- and 20th-century Europe was no stranger to this idea. Indeed for almost 200 years, it was full of the sound of thunder emanating from the forces of history clashing before succumbing to a belief in the End of History. For China, historical forces and lessons are very much alive, and not just in the ruling party. Matthew Hu of Beijing's Courtyard Institute observes that interest in history and China's heritage is rising among the young. Whereas in a recent visit by Buddhist abbots from Japan the youngest was over 70 years old, their Chinese counterparts were in their 30s and 40s. He quotes a Native American who, when asked why he was sitting by the side of the road, answered that he was waiting for his soul to catch up with so much change. The same could be said increasingly in China.

Change is a grey word in English. In Chinese it is dynamic, profound and nuanced with many meanings. The philosophy behind it deals with long-term, holistic thinking, rather than short-termism; complexity, not over-simplification; cooperation beneficial to all sides, not zero-sum games. Major concepts like harmony and stability may sound mushy to Western minds, but they do speak to the values of peace, prosperity and inclusion which address contemporary issues like spent treasure on unending wars, insecurity, left-behind communities and austerity.

Many ideas like pragmatism, flexibility, education and improvement were held strongly by the Victorians who took Britain to world power, and by other European societies that followed in their path to full employment and a better life. Zhao Ya'nan, back from Edinburgh Napier University with her masters in international business management, notes that the West's long-time stability makes people resist change. Stability has closed people's eyes to what can be reality, and therefore does not think about its value. China does not have such a problem because recent history has taught valuable lessons about taking stability for granted, learning the perils of instability and the inevitability of cycles. This has bred a determination that is built into so many Chinese entrepreneurs and ordinary people, migrant workers especially. Ya'nan says, "I think everything is possible. If you want to do something, you can make anything happen." She continues, "That is why I am fearless in my travel. I know what I can do and what I cannot do." Fearlessness: the hallmark of entrepreneurs everywhere. In Southeast Asia it is the Can Do mentality.

Darwin devised his Theory of Evolution not because he answered the problem he set out to solve, but by discovering he was asking the wrong question. Framing the right question led him to conceptualize evolution. Needham discovered that difference can be just different but not wrong. Long-term thinking knows that a decade is the basic unit of time in complex societies. Instant solutions are rarely long lasting: impatience is punished. Fundamental change, especially structural change, takes time. Everything is a work in progress: constant review, *weixin*, adjusts thought to the times and circumstances.

UK Science Minister David Willetts in 2015 commented that "we need to raise our game" when reflecting on the fact that Britain pioneered the use of graphene but China was now the leader in developing it. Australian China specialist Stephen Fitzgerald noted that, "We are living in a Chinese world but don't have the relationship to match it." Much thought has to go into understanding how China thinks and how handling its re-emergence works best. It is not so hard: many of the ideas were familiar to the West when it rose to global dominance. Maybe China's long-term thinking and approaches to problems could inform Emmanuel Macron's proposed European conventions in 2019.

What might a changed future look like? Here are some future snapshots ranging from business, global governance, geopolitics and economics, to philosophy, China's change, and whether others can find paths out of their twilight.

Healthcare: The Biggest Surprise?

Healthcare is the top concern for many Chinese, making it potentially the biggest business surprise. China always had the need, now it has the means. Worth $116 billion in 2016, George Baeder estimates China's market may reach US spending by 2030. Yet global pharmaceutical companies admit they did not see this coming, an echo of the US auto industry in the 1970s grossly underestimating Japan.

Today's generation sees nation building through engineering, maths, science and knowledge rather than politics, as their parents and grandparents did. The wheel has turned full circle, back to the days of 1919's May Fourth Movement that lauded Mr. Science, along with Mr. Democracy and enlightenment. This is the generation not just of reform but, more importantly, of opening up mentally.

All this is happening as Big Pharma faces four major headwinds in what is a metaphor for the West's challenges and future. Ahead are fewer new blockbuster drugs in the pipeline, costlier government approvals, bestsellers going off-patent and intensifying competition as smaller companies can compete more easily. On top of that, its reputation has sunk badly. The golden era is over. China's market growth is good news; however the bad news is that buyers, not sellers will set prices as China cannot afford to spend US amounts on healthcare. Using its buying power, China has strategies to cut costs and profit margins: good news, bad news, typical of the disruptive future; and as George Baeder and Michael Zielenziger concluded in their 2010 report *China, the Life Sciences Leader of 2020* for consultants Monitor, "By 2030 … the best companies won't just sell to China. They will learn from China."

China has taken a new approach to healthcare by using breakthroughs in genomics, medical record data mining and computer modelling of diseases. All are Western techniques China has mastered, to which it adds traditional strengths of long-term thinking, managing scale and speed. This will be in Western and traditional Chinese medicine (TCM) as well as in collaborations between the two, which could spring the biggest surprises. Tu Youyou won the 2015 Nobel Prize for Medicine for helping cure malaria, a "breakthrough" for TCM recognition: a first. Tu and her team combined traditional Chinese knowledge about herbs with Western techniques and technologies, all within China's medical system.

Chinese medicine has combined such other foreign means as biotechnology, gene tests, molecular biology and diagnostic equipment with traditional treatment like acupuncture or knowledge of tumours. Studying the latest Western techniques, from random grouping to double-blinding and meta-analysis, brings TCM researchers closer to their Western counterparts, driving collaboration. TCM doctors are trained in basic Western medicine, so understanding this is not difficult. Much has already been done to establish herbs' elements and chemical compounds, understanding everything from their efficacy to molecular structure. As acceptance of TCM grows from Australia to the US, there is a slow but steady turning of the wheel, no more apparent than in global business.

Multinational Corporations (MNCs): Reform and Opening up Needed

Nothing threatens the West more than China's challenge to MNCs. With their innovation, quality, flair, convenience or entertainment, from Silicon Valley, Germany, Italy, Middle America or Hollywood, Western firms have led the world since 1945. Now they stand at a major crossroads.

Some of the giants like ABB, GE and VW are truly global firms, having integrated China into the rest of their world operations and *vice versa*. They have evolved with China, completely at home there, able to harness China's energy and opportunity. There are also smaller, younger firms, especially in the new economy and biotechnology, without the baggage of old thinking, which are at the cutting edge of China, technology and global business. However, there are many more foreign companies that need to learn from them. MNC morale and self-belief is eroding as home markets stagnate and global competition intensifies. Few respond well to this disrupted world. Many complain about unlevel Chinese playing fields, blaming referees and tools alike, nostalgic for easier days when they felt warmly wanted, and the new China markets, particularly high-end segments, effortlessly drove global profits. That has all changed. Now the worst wallow in self-pity, complaint and victimhood. These are costly distractions from the fundamental reality — leading Chinese companies are increasingly competitive and will only get more so.

Yet some MNCs do very well in China, largely because of long-term thinking and commitment. Germany's VW arrived to explore the potential even before China started to open up in 1978. Now, helped by China, VW is the world's bestselling carmaker. Swiss ABB also stands out, regarded by peers as having among the best foreign understanding of China, its culture and what drives it. Manufacturing and energy conglomerate GE may have some businesses maturing but finds new ones to replace them as China's economy upgrades and its Belt and Road Initiative opens up new markets outside China. In 2016, these earned sales of $2.3 billion. By the end of 2018, it expects to have bid for natural gas turbine and other power equipment contracts worth $7 billion along the Belt and Road path. Winners view the world much as leading Chinese firms do, ruthless in self-criticism. They embrace China's re-emergence as an opportunity while keeping their eyes and ears wide open.

Intellectual property theft is the most common concern. British engineering group IMI decided there is only one answer: innovate faster so copiers cannot keep up, buying more time for new models to earn premium pricing. That means spending real money on R&D, often 10% of sales. This is what makes world leaders, not sitting on faded laurels. IMI has more reason than most to be concerned: it has nuclear technology to protect. Among other precautions, separate stages are manufactured in different locations: sensible, practical and not exactly rocket science. Where there is a will, there is a way: too often the will or focus seems lacking back home in the corner suite. China's markets are no longer the fast tracks to success they were before 2008, when careers and reputations were easily made. Often, competition has intensified, sales growth slowed and expatriate careers gone sideways, at best. This need not be so. IMI also took a radical approach to China by hiring many more Chinese in senior positions. An Australian change management and cultural systems expert came in as CEO, speaking both Mandarin and Shanghainese; out went foreigners from 28 of the top 30 positions and up went China profits.

Such wrenching corporate cultural change is bound to meet resistance. Strong will, leadership and great understanding from the very top at corporate headquarters is required to make it work. The problem is that many CEOs cannot handle ideas of which they have no real experience, particularly trends that directly threaten them personally: baffling and disturbing. Instead of bringing to China what worked in the West, MNCs would do better to see what works in China, then transfer the knowledge globally, which is how Chinese competitors will next make inroads, this time not just in peripheral Africa or Latin America but in MNC home markets of Europe and the US: an inside-out strategy, as consultant John Hoffman calls it.

One consultant is particularly scathing about some MNCs, proclaiming, "Ignorance can no longer be excused." Constant rotation of executives in and out of China has to stop. Firms have to build long-term dedicated China teams. The right mindset and corporate culture has to develop, along with appropriate systems and decision-making processes, all attuned to China's importance and reality. These have to replace outdated notions of what China can learn from foreign firms: that catch-up has mostly happened.

Despite having the great advantage that Chinese consumers generally have a better impression of foreign products than their own, poorer MNC results are starting to show. The foreign share of China's smartphone market has fallen from 55% in 2011 to under 15% in 2016, and Apple's China sales fell for the first time, ranking it a mere fourth behind Oppo, Vivo and Huawei — none household names in the West yet. In 26 fast-moving consumer goods (FMCG) categories, from groceries to toiletries, snacks to shampoos, foreign firms' market shares have fallen continuously since 2011, according to consultants Bain/Kantar. In 2016, MNC sales rose by 1.5% but their Chinese competitors' sales grew 8%, despite the fact that most growth was in premium products, supposedly MNCs' strong suit. Chinese firms gained share in 18 categories, MNCs in only four. Consultants China Skinny commented that, "Foreign firms do not understand the Chinese market as well as they could, their marketing strategy isn't tailored enough and they don't move as nimbly as domestic brands."

This is three decades after many first entered China. Proctor and Gamble had to bring in a new China head to address problems. A turnaround is not impossible but does require deep China knowledge, including about changing tastes, sophistication, regional differences and use of digital media.

Reform and opening up seems just as appropriate for many MNCs today as it did for China in 1978. Most important of all, do not underestimate China. Humility does not always come easily to once-unchallenged Western firms. Three decades ago, Chinese companies had a lot to learn, "now they have much to share", as Edward Tse puts it diplomatically. Some MNCs are more amenable than others to learning from China. The same goes for global institutions.

Global Governance: Change Needed After 70 Years

Resistance from established powers to rising economies is normal. Similarly, stronger developing economies naturally want seats at the top tables of global finance and trade. Not surprisingly, after 70 years of change, the post-1945 Bretton Woods world order needs new architecture to accommodate the increasing heft of developing economies and financial systems. China's change is the main driver of this reformation.

China now has the single largest banking system, with double the assets of the US. At the frontiers of finance, China is a world leader in fintech, judged to be ahead of the US or EU. Chinese third-party mobile payments more than trebled to $5.5 trillion in 2016 while US mobile payments rose 39% to just $112 billion: one-fiftieth. Over half Chinese mutual funds are sold online. China, "the most wired nation on earth", has "much to share" and teach. As Nicholas Veron of Bruegel (Brussels) noted in his 2016 report *China's New Economic Frontier* for the Peterson Institute for International Economics, "This system [of global governance] has not sufficiently adapted to the new reality of China's prominence, and has instead remained unsustainably centred on incumbent North Atlantic financial systems. This … is not in the interests of the incumbents, China or the world as a whole."

Progress, though, has come sporadically. Considerable behind-the-scenes cooperation between China, the US, IMF, World Bank and UN went unremarked before the 2016 G20 Hangzhou Summit. Much background work was done to address the world's deep-seated economic woes. Instead of focusing on current crises, there was real long-term thinking. Development became an important growth strategy, commitments were made to the UN's 2030 sustainable development goals, while the presidents of the world's two largest polluters, China and the US, signed the Paris Climate Change agreement. This was very different from the normal crisis-reactive summits, all about the short-term but changing little or nothing in the long run.

China brought to the G20 its process for change: using extensive consultations and focused expert working groups to set goals, then to identify means of implementation. Consensual agreement led to more commitments than ever. In finance, the IMF agreed to devise a reformed voting structure; on trade, members pledged greater openness, even if their sincerity was questionable; ideas on innovation and improving efficiency came from China, on tax from the US, and on over-capacity from manufacturing nations. New global approaches were finally heard to address old problems, even though international forums are notoriously slow in making decisions.

Managing complexity comes naturally to China because of its size and historic turbulence. Large organizations and crisis management are very familiar. Beijing's ideas to reform global finance will spread into global rule-making for one simple reason: as the world's largest trader, China has a great interest in world economic health. It needs to keep the financial and trading systems open and stable by influencing multilateral agencies like the IMF, World Bank and WTO. The financial crisis of 2008 proved the global financial system is not working. Once China has put its own financial institutions in order, it will look to help shape global financial architecture even more actively. China already has had technocrats in senior positions in these institutions, like the well-regarded Zhu Min who was a deputy director of the IMF from 2011 to 2016.

Friction will inevitably grow with China's growing economic might but, with enough goodwill or at least appreciation of common interests, nothing that cannot be managed. There are, though, potential flashpoints. Chinese thinking is at odds with conventional Western belief over some fundamentals, starting with a traditional Chinese view that finance should serve the real economy, not be an end in itself. In fact, finance works best as an enabler for the real economy otherwise it distorts and destroys, as it did in 2008. China recognizes that competition in financial markets is fundamentally different from that in manufacturing and has to be regulated accordingly: see Chapter 10. Traditional China had its reasons for ranking businessmen last in the social scale after scholar–officials, soldiers and farmers.

Securing China's Borders and Foreign Relations

Avoiding being boxed in is China's primary security goal: containment in strategic jargon, the US and Japan in reality. Time and size are on China's side, as long as it is patient, which is why Deng advocated China should keep its light hidden, promoting good relations with all. Recent events, however, have jolted this low-profile approach, with Japan aiming to revise its pacifist constitution, disputes in the East and South China Seas and the US defending a new concept of the Indo-Pacific. While maintaining peace and development, adapting to these challenges is likely to remain China's priority as building a high-income economy greatly strengthens its long-term strategic position.

Securing the borders, a millennia-old concept in China, brings great glory to those who achieve it. Making China's borders safe by reducing threats and tensions begins internally with Tibet, Xinjiang and Hong Kong. Beijing issued white papers in 2015 on both Tibet and Xinjiang, focusing on continued economic development but indicating that alone is insufficient. With the Dalai Lama ageing and some Xinjiang Uighurs linked by China and the US with al-Qaeda and ISIL, China's focus on both provinces is likely to become more apparent.

Maintaining stability with Hong Kong and Taiwan through greater economic integration into the mainland will continue to be the goal, but the 2016 government change in Taipei and Hong Kong protests make it more challenging. To deepen integration, the Guangdong–Hong Kong–Macau Greater Bay Area initiative is one response, mimicking other successful bay areas around the world from New York and San Francisco to Tokyo. A new Hong Kong chief executive provides another opportunity to address domestic concerns, especially housing that for most young people is unaffordable. Further afield, the world is changing even more fundamentally.

The end of the Vasco da Gama Era is nigh, Australian international relations specialist Coral Bell observed in 2007. Unchallenged Western dominance over the non-Western world is coming to an end. Anticipating this, Prime Minister Gough Whitlam, when opening Australia's diplomatic relations with China in 1973, was clear about two things. The relationship placed China on par with other world powers while Australia had to look after its own interests and be able to say "No". The first Australian Ambassador to China, Stephen FitzGerald, relating this in 2017, spoke of achieving it by building trust and confidence so that Australia could be a "friend at court", able to speak truth to power in both regional and global affairs. In turn, Australia will need much greater education about China, along with a self-reliant foreign policy. Others can do the same.

There need not be conflict, even with the US, despite much bellicose talk before the start of the Trump presidency. Rapid acceptance of the One China principle to guide US–China relations signified the re-emergence of *realpolitik*. Despite differences, Xi and Obama had worked well together on climate change and reversing Iran's nuclear programme. China now seeks other areas to engage Trump, including Chinese-created jobs in the US and opportunities in China by changing some trade and investment rules.

Most pressing problems today, though, are global, not bilateral, be they nuclear proliferation in North Korea, refugees in Europe or potential pandemics like Ebola. China's win-win approach may be a cliché but creating a new culture of cooperation will be far more effective than reducing everything to a zero-sum game of endless confrontation.

Permanent differences have to be managed. As a retired US diplomat reflected, 98% of diplomatic problems are managed rather than resolved.

Geopolitical Economics

Economics and finance will play a major role in securing China's borders. Beijing's focus on driving Asian economic integration faster is helped by establishing new funding institutions like the Asian Infrastructure Investment Bank, the New Development Bank and the Silk Road Fund. In addition, China is pushing the decade-old APEC idea of a Free Trade Area for Asia Pacific (FTAAP) and supporting the Asia-wide Regional Comprehensive Economic Partnership (RCEP), particularly after Donald Trump scuppered the Trans-Pacific Partnership (TPP).

Nothing, though, is likely to be as significant as the Belt and Road Initiative that could potentially transform the countries to the west of China, all the way to Europe. Affecting over half the world's people and 60 countries, the idea was unveiled in 2013 to help develop a 4,000-mile reinvention of the land and sea routes that connected Europe with the Pacific in the days of Marco Polo and before. Funding and building roads, railways, ports and pipelines are meat and drink to China.

Former World Bank economist Justin Lin Yifu, in a 2016 *Project Syndicate* piece, explained the initiative's economic logic: countries with surplus labour can generate growth for two or three decades through labour-intensive manufacturing, just as China did for 30 years. China has 85 million low-skilled manufacturing jobs which, over time, it could transfer abroad as it upgrades its workforce domestically. When Japan did the same in the 1960s it had only 10 million such jobs, while South Korea, Taiwan, Hong Kong and Singapore combined had just 20 million when they followed suit — not China's 85 million.

Industrialization and modernization can go together, Lin believes. Markets can be created for more-developed economies, including China. Passing through such troubled countries as Pakistan and

Afghanistan, the initiative has the potential to transform their societies or pull China into a mire of its own making. In 2030, the world will have a better sense, and by 2050 it could be considerably different or the initiative could become China's Vietnam. Such speculation is outside the scope of *China's Change*; suffice to say the initiative has all the hallmarks of traditional Chinese thinking — vision, scale, managing large resources, long-term planning, strategic and holistic thinking.

Such a possibility was probably not in the minds of US military planners when they conceived the Pivot to Asia, even though it has the potential to repeat the 19th-century Great Game for influence in Eurasia, though through cooperation, commerce and development rather than arms. China's initiative has been swiftly executed: a classic *taiji* strategy to catch an opponent off balance. Embodying "peace and cooperation, openness and inclusiveness, mutual learning and mutual benefit," as Xi Jinping put it, Edward Tse concluded in the *South China Morning Post* in 2017 that this provides a vision of a new global order based on soft power rather than brute force.

Philosophy: New Thinking for the West?

Much is made of Xi Jinping's China Dream. More startling to the world could be the vision of two of the foremost Western translators of Chinese philosophy and literature of the last 80 years, Arthur Waley of Cambridge (see Chapter 1) and David Hinton of Cornell.

Hinton hopes that China's traditional philosophy of pragmatism and morality can guide contemporary America. In 2013, he wrote,

> [The US has] certainly witnessed the same kind of catastrophic cultural collapse in this last century as China did in Confucius's time and the insights that emerged so long ago from China's similar experience could well play a significant role in whatever renewal may take place here over the next millennium.

The third-most popular course at Harvard in 2017, after introductions to economics and computers, is Chinese philosophy, taught by

Chinese history professor Michael Puett. In *The Path: A New Way to Think About Everything*, he and Christine Gross-Loh reveal "how the timeless wisdom of ancient Chinese philosophers can transform the way we think about ourselves". One *Guardian* reviewer commented that "ancient Chinese philosophers … were trying to answer the same big questions we still ask". Disillusioned with the Western idea of finding self or that History Ended with the collapse of the Soviet Union, this may appeal to younger people searching for a different understanding of human behaviour and events. Confucian practical wisdom could yet know a wider audience and application if Harvard students are any guide.

The Age of Improvement: The Supertanker is Turning

So much has changed over the 40 years since I first looked across to China from Coloane. Back in the summer of 1977, the distant shore was inhabited by just a few fishing families. In 2016, some 20,000 people lived there in Hengqin, transformed through a pilot scheme. By 2020, some 200,000 should work in this special economic zone for trade, tourism, entertainment and finance, hosting Hong Kong and Chinese banks' back offices, the world's largest marine attraction, Ocean Kingdom, and courts that stage the women's professional tennis tour: grunts, thuds and all. This is China today, still changing at surprising pace.

The supertanker continues to turn. With so much change in the last 40 years, it is hard to imagine China's economic recovery and re-emergence stopping now. There is simply too much momentum in spite of the problems and setbacks — or maybe because of them. All have provided lessons that have been studied, discussed and disseminated within the system that supports China's change. As some of its original engines burn out, most notably surplus labour, cheap land and rapidly expanding export markets, change comes from upgrading and new areas to keep China growing. Not at the previously breakneck pace but at rates that most other countries would envy.

In many ways, China from 1978 to 2015 passed through its Age of Improvement, as Asa Briggs called Britain's industrial, political and economic change between 1783 and 1867. It was far from complete in 1867, very much a work in progress, but improvement was well underway. Over half the population lived in towns, the environment was heavily polluted, there was great wealth, much poverty and high income inequality, and it was far from having universal suffrage: women would not vote for another half century. Yet there was palpable improvement. The same can be said of China today.

China's Great Change: 1978–2015

China's Great Change from 1978–2015, its extraordinary scale, speed and length, gives it a significance of unique magnitude. It is literally different from anything else in history. With India doing much the same, the world has moved into an increasingly unpredictable but transformative era.

No economy can change at such speed for so long without facing major problems. That has been China's story in the 1980s, 1990s and 2000s, so there is no reason it will not have problems again: problems *but also* progress. 700 million people escaping poverty is not a minor footnote to history, nor is the emergence of a 250 million middle class and the world's most sought-after Millennials. These are historic, world-defining and world-changing events.

China already has been the Greatest Show on Earth for many Chinese, like Xiuyun and her family. Yet China's economic transformation has barely reached its mid-point. However, two forces that drove the first half, industrialization and investment, are almost exhausted. The surplus of rural workers moving to much more productive urban jobs has dried up. Heavy investment in infrastructure and housing, with all the associated investment in steel, cement and related plants, has slowed.

China's growth, though, is not over, merely changed, moving at a more measured pace. Consumption overtook investment to comprise over 50% of GDP in 2015, a defining moment as the crossover will continue for another 35 years or so before China becomes a mature economy with slow average GDP growth of 2%–3% around 2050. For now, an annual real average of 5% looks possible over the next 15 years: slightly more in the next five years. In the second half of this 70-year fundamental change, China will become much more apparent to the rest of the world, increasingly leading global news bulletins and moving markets.

China has to be the Greatest Show on Earth for those concerned with business, economic, social, political and world affairs, especially for those interested in development and transformation, history and real life drama: there is no need for reality TV. China is tuned into raw reality in real time. No longer merely a rapidly growing emerging economy, it is already a global force in new products, processes and thinking. For global impact, growth in percentage terms is no longer the criteria. On a much larger economic base absolute quantity is what counts: China's growth exceeds US, EU and Japanese growth combined. Chinese entrepreneurs will help change the world, not because that is their goal, but simply because everything is now so interconnected, amplifying their significance.

The second half of China's change will likely be another great show for the Chinese. Even more significantly, for the first time it will be the Greatest Show on Earth for Non-Chinese: not that many realize it yet. Soon they will. Just as the US left its economic and cultural footprint all over the world after 1945, as Britain did in the 19th and early 20th centuries, so will China, in its own way, over the rest of this century. Parts of Asia, Africa and Australasia see it already. By around 2025 China could well be the world's largest economy and a major source of capital. Economic determinism does not come any clearer than this.

Greatest Change Ahead: To 2030

China's period of Greatest Change may last from 2016–2030. Underway in a world increasingly disrupted by accelerated shifts in wealth, technology, demographics and connectivity, China is central to all four. No surprise then that China's presence is felt in ways it was not even five years ago. Apart from economic development, there is technological advance.

China has a growing sense it is on the brink of making major technological breakthroughs. The tech and scientific communities are decidedly upbeat. Global low economic growth does not cast a shadow in this part of China. Already, Huawei's phones send better quality photos than brand leader iPhone, US tech investors say. Indeed Apple leased 769 patents from Huawei in 2015 while Huawei only leased 98 from Apple. WeChat is better than Skype: try it. Google works with and learns from Tencent on the Whisper messaging app. China leads the world in civilian drones and automated personal flight, Wall Street analysts aver about two major industries of the future, both led by private Chinese firms. It is also competing with the leaders in electric and automated road vehicles. China in 2016 built the world's largest and most powerful radio telescope as well as the world's fastest supercomputer, which for the first time was made completely with Chinese processor chips, five times faster than anything in the US.

Nothing shows China's scientific research progress like the world's first quantum satellite, Micius, launched in 2016. Named after 5th-century BC Chinese philosopher and scientist Mozi, who is credited with conducting the first optical experiments, Micius uses quantum physics and its theory of entanglement to send "uncrackable" communications. In 2017, the scientific journal *Nature* reported that transmissions had travelled as far as 1,400 km between base stations in China and the Micius satellite. Tim Byrne, a quantum physicist at New York University's Shanghai campus called the achievement "truly remarkable", noting that the previous longest distance a quantum communication had travelled was 143 km. This is a major step in preventing "hacking". Could online cyber identity theft one day be a thing of the past? No longer is China's technological edge just in trains.

Apart from the Micius achievement itself, China's changing relative position in science is most telling. China's quantum communications is based on work done by Vienna University Professor Anton Zeilinger who since 2001 tried unsuccessfully to interest the European Space Agency in launching a similar satellite. One of his students, Pan Jianwei, helped get funding, and now Zeilinger advises China. In 2016, China spent $10 billion on basic research, including quantum physics, up from $1.9 billion in 2005. US annual federal funding for quantum physics is only $200 million even though a 2016 Congressional report said it would enhance national security and that funding fluctuations are setting it back. Long-term thinking, vision and perseverance are shaping China's future while their lack is hurting others.

More mundanely, back on earth, the wheel keeps turning. China now has over half of India's smartphone market, yet another OECD citadel falling to Chinese pricing and innovation. After becoming the Workshop of the World, Chinese firms now Go Out (abroad) with their capital and production systems. So do their ideas. China, once a great copier, is being copied. Just as Alibaba, Baidu and Xiaomi were dubbed the eBay, Google and Apples of China, now there are imitators of Chinese firms from Indonesia's Tokopedia to India's Snapdeal and Nigeria's Konga. Globally, Gao Feng says, China leads "in the emerging industries of internet finance, new social media, artificial intelligence, virtual reality, augmented reality and intelligent transport". The BBC even reports China-inspired copycat attempts to establish bike sharing in Oxford.

Connectivity has linked almost all main Chinese cities, often by time- and distance-shrinking high-speed rail as well as air and highways. Hence, Shanghai Disney's catchment area: 300 million people within three hours' land travel, almost as many as the entire US population. Another billion can fly within three hours to Pudong airport, some 15 minutes from the Magic Kingdom. Abroad, the Belt and Road Initiative aims to link China with Europe through Eurasia, influencing West Asia, Southeast Asia, the Middle East and East Africa, redrawing the world's economic and geopolitical map. Like the East Asian Economic Miracle, it could be world-changing.

There are many sceptics about China: some ideological, others in denial, and many just plain confused by its size and unfamiliarity. Sceptics feel that having travelled so far, China's arrival at a modern (Western presumably) model must be imminent, otherwise something is seriously wrong: like tired, anxious children asking "Are we there yet?". What they do not grasp is that after so much change, the final 10% can take 50% of the time and effort: reform's equivalent of the last mile in delivering cable services, something the Warring States official history knew over 2,400 years ago. Patience, endurance and perseverance are virtues: a decade is the basic unit of time for real change to occur. China has the thinking tools to adapt to its New Normal of slower growth, among them the idea that change never stops, new cycles just begin: Asia's eternal cycle of birth, death and rebirth.

In China's Greatest Change, three main Chinese forces — consumers, companies and understanding change — will shape the globe just as dramatically as cheap labour and the lowest-priced goods did during China's Great Change, probably more so. McKinsey forecasts that China's urban households earning over $25,200 will jump from just 4% in 2010 to 54% in 2030. In terms of global urban consumption growth from 2015–2030, the consultant calculates that China's 15- to 59-year-olds will account for 18% while the US will contribute only 10%. With some of the most adaptable, flexible and long-term-thinking firms, which are also very nimble and effective in the short-term, private sector sharks will take down many of the state- and even foreign-owned whales, becoming the largest life in the corporate oceans. They will need to be swift as even smaller and more ferocious Chinese piranhas are in hot pursuit. Further pressure comes from China's famously-demanding customers, who trust so little. As Bill Clinton could have said "It's The Consumer Stupid": all very competitive and, again, economic determinism at its most basic.

Creativity: What China and Western Peaks Have in Common

Creativity is often central to how Chinese manage change. Creative ways are found to escape from systems or circumstances that are not working. This applies as much to government as to individuals, to regulators as to firms. Naturally, ideas can only take root in Chinese soil if they are compatible: not all can be transplanted successfully from foreign lands. Therefore China must be understood in its own terms and context, with a philosophy based on its history.

That said, leading Western societies at their peaks, from Athens to Florence, Vienna to Silicon Valley, have had much in common with traditional Chinese culture and history, notably in terms of origins, approaches, thought, arts and business. Indeed Hangzhou, with a population of two million during the 13th century, dazzled Marco Polo whose own city of Venice comprised a mere 50,000. During the Tang Dynasty (618–907), nothing in the West compared with Chang'an (Xi'an) that boasted half a million people while no European city had more than a few thousand. This curious and cultivated Tang China on the original Silk Road was very open to the world, even employing foreigners as high officials.

Creativity requires continuity with the past, not a break with it: though often it benefits from a new setting. Transitions are disruptive, with an increasing free-for-all in ideas, as China is finding as social media and Internet evolve; some friction and tension may even aid creativity, while collaboration, another common feature in creative peaks, also helps. Outsiders with new eyes often see what the mainstream does not, as migrants did in Vienna and Silicon Valley.

Vision, a love of paradox, comfort with ambiguity and ease with complexity are common to creative societies. So is tolerance of failure. Nervous optimism is in the air. New possibilities are envisaged simply because other new ideas have succeeded. Some come from overseas, others from the past. The peaks of Western creativity therefore had much in common with today's China, down to the fact, as Eric Weiner pointed out in *The Geography of Genius,* that Greece was a great copier: copying the alphabet from the Phoenicians, maths from Babylon, literature from Sumeria and medicine and sculpture from Egypt. Today's China has merely followed in an age-old tradition, just as the US did by ignoring international copyright laws into the 20th century.

All valued history: Freud collected archaeological artifacts during Vienna's peak. In a thought that could have come from the *Yi Jing*, Steve Jobs said of Silicon Valley, "You can't really understand what is going on unless you understand what came before." He could have added that knowledge of cycles is also useful, as his own life personified.

Creative societies ask the right questions. Socrates and Confucius lived thousands of miles apart but both understood the importance of discovering truths through the right form of questioning. Problem-finders such as Charles Darwin are more important than problem-solvers, in Weiner's words. They are the real innovators, not the mere nerd. Breadth of knowledge is more conducive to discovery and creativity than mere specialization: think Leonardo da Vinci, Renaissance Man.

The mainspring of these societies is also similar. Many reacted to a near-death experience: Greece from war, Florence and the Italian Renaissance from the Black Death, and Silicon Valley from the Vietnam War and corporate America's ossification. For China, it has been the Great Leap Forward and the Cultural Revolution. Hitting rock bottom motivated both China's individuals and official class to find a new path. The latter suffered the most from the violence and disruption caused by the lack of due process and arbitrary rule. All creative societies thrive on challenge, obstacles and even chaos. The Brexit decision, potentially triggering an eventual breakup of the EU, should be a near-death experience that prompts much soul-searching and rethinking in Europe.

Many of China's newly-minted billionaires sought security far away from politics in business, even though that was hard to do in the 1980s and 1990s. Only in the 2000s was private business officially tolerated. With the quest for personal safety and development came a desire to restore the nation's position. China's new billionaires share three powerful forces — pride, ambition and cultural heritage, as Edward Tse observed. Just as Florence sought to replace Rome, so Hangzhou, Shenzhen and Beijing seek to join, if not replace, America as the leading creative centres and powers. How plausible is this? The Medicis, Bill Gates and Steve Jobs would have had much in common with the Mas, Jack and Pony, of Alibaba and Tencent respectively, and the now literally millions of Chinese entrepreneurs starting to hit their stride. All of history's most creative cities have been empowered by a demanding, increasingly discerning and appreciative audience: a rapidly growing market of wealthier consumers. This is very much true in China today.

Previously deprived consumers, seeking innovative goods and services of the highest order, are rapid adopters.

When Travis Kalanick, co-founder of Uber, pronounced in 2016 that in five years time Beijing would have more creativity, innovation and entrepreneurs than Silicon Valley, it must have come as a great shock to many in the West. Creativity is critical to change. As Professor of Political Economy at King's College, London Shaun Hargreaves Heap noted, creativity really is the fuel of growth and transformation.

Kalanick's prediction is unthinkable to those who see China collapsing or, at the very least, stagnating. The prediction must have shocked US Vice President Joe Biden who in 2015 challenged people to name one Chinese innovation. Kalanick's words also defied the assumption that China's education system is based on sterile, rote learning instilled by Confucianism and communism, as a 2014 Harvard study asserted. Furthermore, China lacks the supposedly self-correcting mechanisms of free markets and democracy. Yet in 2017 the *MIT Technology Review* ranked seven Chinese firms among the world's 50 Smartest Companies. How can this be if China lacks critical thinking and problem-solving that are central to creativity? Again, Western assumptions about China are flawed. Much though has changed. When asked to name one leading world-class Chinese company in 2002 when I first moved to China all I could offer was Tsingtao Brewery. I had never heard of Alibaba, Tencent or barely two-year-old Baidu. That is China's change.

Paths to New Paths

This book's purpose is to show that understanding China's change can help other countries, firms and individuals find new paths, while answering the question whether China can continue to contribute significantly to world growth: it can. *China's Change* also indicates how China will fare in an increasingly disrupted world: generally well, as traditional philosophy helps navigate the Greatest Change of the next decade and more.

For almost 4,000 years, *weixin* has taught individuals and rulers to review and renew constantly. The ruling party's almost 100-year history teaches many strategic lessons, some from traditional thinking, others new to modern times. Along with accustoming people to change, the party's greatest impact has been the ability to regroup after setbacks, before analyzing the main problems and devising corrections. Pragmatism has replaced ideology, while moderation and harmony have removed political extremism and struggle. Successful Chinese policy reflects such traditional thinking, learned from its long history and harsh lessons from the violent disruption of the heavily ideological 1950s and 1960s.

Long-term perspective fits the near-term into an overall continuum, enabling people to sequence change more effectively. Stability, harmony, moderation or other priorities can serve as goals while pragmatism, flexibility, gradualism, restraint, self-criticism and a 360-degree holistic approach help achieve them. Understanding cycles, research and field study, *yanjiu*, followed by pilot schemes and continual renewal, *weixin*, are plain common sense. Endurance, patience and perseverance should shape behaviour. Cultivating good people was always the Confucian basis of good government through education, morality, integrity and responsibility to society. All these 20 essential traditional ideas can be applied anywhere.

China's advance need not mean that other societies will fall back, let alone fail. The US and Europe have their strengths, but also their challenges. The US's traditional ability to renew its institutions has never been more important. Europe's longer history and professed moderation, as well as the pragmatism of countries like the UK, needs to come to the fore in policy and political debates instead of being bogged down fighting old battles from the extremes. Asia has the East Asian Miracle and its own philosophies, including Confucianism, to help find new paths. This is not about Chinese exceptionalism but about the realities of an emerging multipolar world where demography, not military might or recent history, increasingly shapes influence through a new form of democracy: market-driven economic democracy with one middle income, one vote.

Living in China, surrounded by all the change, experiencing it every day, makes it hard to avoid concluding that China will again be a world-leading economy. Still a work in progress, China's change will be the Greatest Show on Earth as it becomes a significant part of the new equilibrium that emerges from the growing disruption of the next 15 years or so. No other country possesses the twin strengths of China's scale and momentum, except possibly India. All need to understand China's change better if they are to remain economic or world leaders, while others can find new ways out of poverty, the middle-income trap or stagnation.

As *No Ordinary Disruption* concludes, "Those who understand the magnitude and the permanence of the changes that we are now witnessing, reset their intuitions accordingly, and see the opportunities will shape the new world — and they will thrive." After 40 years of observing China, there seems no reason why China should not thrive, given the ability of its individuals, firms and government to cope with disruption through flexibility, adaptability and managing challenges by understanding change. It is not a zero-sum game.

If other countries find new paths, they too should thrive in a new stable equilibrium. So, why not look to China for clues? China has been the world's largest economy (and may well be again soon) three times in the last 1,400 years, reinventing itself each time it has stumbled. Having captured the "Promethean energy" that created the West's post-1800 dominance, China is now recovering from its sharp relative decline. If the West copies China's change manual, there could be another dramatic, unexpected turning of the tables in world history. This seems much more achievable than when China sought to regain its "Wealth and Power" in 1978.

If the West and parts of Asia, however, fail to manage change, they may enter an increasingly chaotic and relatively poorer period as China did two centuries ago. For as Liu Cixin, the first Chinese winner of the Hugo award for best science fiction novel, wrote in *The Three-Body Problem*, "Other than Stable Eras, all times are Chaotic Eras.... It is morning but the sun does not always rise in the morning. That is what a Chaotic Era is like." Finding the morning sun to avoid painful chaos is China's quest. Others too can catch the sun again if they understand how to manage change.

Appendices

Understanding China

Accessibility is No Longer a Problem or Excuse

No longer is there any excuse to believe that China is unfathomable, mysterious or inaccessible, nor is it true that little is known or written about China in English, nor that much of what is written is in turgid academic prose or is badly translated. There are now numerous sources to help understand China. Neither is travelling around China so difficult these days. For a continent, it is surprisingly well connected. Scale can be a barrier not just physically but mentally too. True, China is a lot of work, often hard work, but it is not inaccessible and is well worth the effort.

Contemporary novelists provide a very comprehensive picture of China. Nobel literature laureate Mo Yan is very well-translated into English; however, he is often dismissed as a functionary of the Writers' Association with the presumed leaden, compromised prose that is assumed to emanate from such a position. Nothing could be more wrong. Mo's vigour, sense of colour, taste, smell, sound and sensation, as well as his sarcasm, humanity and discussion of what haunts contemporary China give many insights into its recent past. The Cultural Revolution hangs over his generation like a dark and permanent cloud. Highlighting wrongdoing by officials fits with post-2012 thinking. This is political discourse by code, often in the raw. Bad individuals and flaws in the system can be drawn in fine detail as long as this does not advocate the party's overthrow. This is the recognized limit.

Mo does for China what Gabriel Garcia Marquez did for Latin America and Ben Okri for Africa. Mo's Magical Realism bursts with life, vitality and sheer power, illuminating a world that is otherwise closed to foreigners. Most readers start with *Red Sorghum* because Zhang Yimou's famous film of the same name was based on part of it, though arguably the least interesting part. The *Republic of Wine* and *Life and Death are Wearing Me Out,* as well as Mo's short stories in *Shifu, You'll Do Anything for a Laugh*, have a much more modern setting and even more vivid prose. Liu Cixin won the world's leading Science Fiction prize, the *Hugo Award*, in 2015 for *The Three-Body Problem.* Based on the Cultural Revolution and intergalactic warfare between civilizations, it is an allegory for the US and China. Yu Hua's *Brothers, Chronicle of a Blood Merchant* and *China in Ten Words* have deservedly won praise for depicting what lies behind China's recent history, economics and social change.

Plenty of other Chinese novelists have been translated into English, chronicling the last four decades in a large variety of settings. These include Ma Jian, whose internal journey around China and himself in *Red Dust* in the early 1980s was very evocative of post-Cultural Revolution China. The *New Yorker* described *Waiting,* by another prize-winning novelist, Ha Jin, as a "suspenseful and bracing tough-minded love story". Qiu Xiaolong's Inspector Chen detective novels paint the picture of turn-of-the-millennium China through the lives of ordinary people caught up in a system which is increasingly tested and strained by all the rapid change that economic reforms unleash.

Translation has become much better, or at least it sits more comfortably with modern readers trying to fathom China. Howard Goldblatt has captured the vitality and essence of among others Mo Yan and Jiang Rong. There are other outstanding translators not just of literature but of philosophy as well. Fortunately, modern translations are much easier to understand than the dry, often stilted prose of a century or more ago when the Chinese classics were first translated into English. David Hinton's *The Four Chinese Classics* and John Minford's *I Ching* and *The Art of War*, together with their insightful commentaries, bring an unexpected clarity to a philosophy that many foreigners previously considered arcane, opaque and difficult to comprehend.

There are plenty of foreign writers too, who are well worth reading. Indeed Jonathan Woetzel, who opened McKinsey's China office in 1995, says that the reason foreigners get China wrong is because they have not read enough (or any) Jonathan Spence. Professor of Chinese studies at Yale, Spence brings alive whatever he is explaining, especially in his historical novels. *Treason by the Book* and *Return to Dragon Mountain: Memories of a Late Ming Man* are a good start. He has illuminated China's past and thinking in a way that for foreigners is very easy to grasp.

Those writers with much less familiarity with China but great knowledge of other societies can also be illuminating. In his novel *The Ten Thousand Things* John Spurling recreates late Yuan China, as John Keay does for over three millennia of history in *China: A History.* In *Mao: A Life,* Philip Short pulls together all the key strands without it being either a hagiography or a demolition job.

Beneath these overarching accounts of China has come more in-depth consideration of the major individual themes that bear on the economy: the rise of the private sector, modernization and transformation. Some are academic, many others are by journalists writing the first drafts of history. They all help fill some of the many voids that previously existed. Five books from academe stand out. On long-term thinking and managing change, David Shambaugh's *China's Communist Party: Atrophy and Adaptation* takes the real case of how China set about analysing the collapse of the Soviet Union and Eastern Europe so as to learn lessons from the experience. If anything proves that China has its own way of approaching policy and its implementation, this does.

Nicholas Lardy's *Markets over Mao* analyses in meticulous detail the rise of the private sector to overtake the state sector in size. This completely refutes the popular argument since 2008 that the state is advancing and the private sector is in retreat. In diplomacy, strategy and *realpolitik,* Henry Kissinger's *On China* should not be spurned by his critics. On Sino–US relations and thinking, Kissinger concludes that "different histories and cultures produce occasionally divergent conclusions". On modernization, Orville Schell and John Delury's *Wealth and*

Power follows "China's Long March to the Twenty-First Century": Wealth and Power is a central theme for today's China. On transformation, there is Ezra Vogel's *Deng Xiaoping and the Transformation of China*, full of detail on the political and economic transition Deng charted after 1978.

Pulitzer Prize-winner Ian Johnson's *Wild Grass: Three Stories of Change in Modern China* does the same for society. Without this background, much of today's China lacks the crucial context. Journalists have dug down into narrower but still often seemingly too-large-to-grasp issues that bear on the political economy. On the party, Richard McGregor in *The Party* has made its organization and practices comprehensible to audiences beyond academe. On the environment, Jonathan Watts' *When a Billion Chinese Jump* takes a broad sweep through the problems and attempted solutions, while Jiang Rong's *Wolf Totem* addresses the environmental balance through the battle between animal and man, herders and farmers, in a novel set in Cultural Revolution Inner Mongolia. Tom Miller's *Urban Billion* considers all that urbanization's epic transformation entails. In even more detail are the stories of some of the individual actors in this drama as recounted in *The China Price* by Alexandra Harney and by Leslie Chang in *Factory Girls*. On health, there is nothing to compare with *Fat China* by Paul French and Matthew Crabbe that has some truly eye-popping forecasts on disease rates and, hence, likely future costs.

The last well-written, easy-to-read book on China's economy was *When China Shakes the World* by James Kynge, published in 2006, though it is mainly about events in the 1990s and the start of the 2000s. China has changed a great deal since then. That is the problem. By the time something is written it is already out of date, one decade later it is almost ancient history at the speed China changes, as Mark O'Neill once observed, which is why presumably he sticks to history. However a new strain is emerging that captures China in all its change. These include the already mentioned *No Ordinary Disruption* with the China section written by McKinsey's Jonathan Woetzel, *China's Disruptors* by Edward Tse and James Stent's *Transformation of Chinese Banking*.

Keeping abreast of China and all its change may seem daunting as there is now plenty online, from official to unofficial. The problem is quality, not quantity. For quick succinct summaries, *China Economic Review's* daily top five stories catches most of them. Executives at Alibaba look to *China Skinny* to monitor the fast-changing Chinese consumer. In five minutes a week one can learn much more from the *Skinny* than anywhere else on modern social, e-commerce and media trends.

Travelling around China is so much easier than it was even 10 years ago. Clean, safe and affordable accommodation is available at Motel 168, Home Inn, Star of Jinjiang and their lookalikes. All major cities have a full raft of five-star luxury business hotels, while Banyan Tree brings its unique calm charm to luxury resorts in out-of-the-way parts of China. Wild China creates bespoke holidays for those curious to know much more about China and to travel off the beaten track. Ctrip provides easy online travel services while good bus networks connect almost everywhere in China with frequent transport to the nearest town and the rest of the country beyond. High-speed rail is just the icing on the cake for the world's largest travelling population. A decade before, almost none of this even existed.

For background on current affairs, history and culture, there is enough to keep people in touch with contemporary China through Chinese television. The English and documentary channels of China Global Television Network with English commentary or subtitles are available overseas through cable: Jiang Zemin baffled Rupert Murdoch by insisting that part of a proposed media deal in China required that he helped with China Central Television's distribution abroad. Murdoch must have imagined that this would not appeal to anyone. In fact, it is a mine of information in English about China, even if many overseas would disagree sometimes with its interpretation. *Dialogue* with Yang Rui and *World Insight* with Tian Wei give a view of how China sees things and why it is doing what it does. China is no longer unfathomable but remains a lot of work. Hopefully *China's Change* fills a gap to help understand China.

Main Characters, Terms and Abbreviations

Philosophers
Confucius (Kongzi*) (551–479 BC): First of the wandering scholars who made morality and rituals (ties that bind) central to individual actions and governance.

Mencius (Mengzi*) (372–289 BC): Expanded on Confucius, with more emphasis on benevolence.

Laozi* (6th century BC): Founder of Daoism, "the Way that cannot be named".

Zhuangzi* (369–286 BC): Follower of Laozi, critic of Confucius.

Strategists
Sunzi* (544–496 BC): Author of *The Art of War.*

Zhuge Liang (181–234): Premier of Shu, immortalized in the novel *Romance of the Three Kingdoms.*

Leaders
Mao Zedong (1893–1976): Communist Party Chairman and ruler of China (1949–1976).

* "Zi" means "Master".

Zhou Enlai (1898–1976): First Premier of People's Republic of China, head of government (1949–1976).

Deng Xiaoping (1904–1997): Paramount leader and main force for economic reform (1978–1992).

Jiang Zemin (1926–): Party General Secretary (1989–2002) and President of China (1993–2003).

Zhu Rongji (1928–): Premier (1998–2003), architect of post-1992 economic and financial reform.

Hu Jintao (1942–): Party General Secretary (2002–2012) and President of China (2003–2013).

Wen Jiabao (1942–): Premier (2003–2013).

Xi Jinping (1953–): Party General Secretary (2012–) and President of China (2013–).

Li Keqiang (1955–): Premier (2013–).

Finance and Economic Officials

Liu He: chief economic adviser to President Xi Jinping.

Liu Mingkang: founding head of banking regulator the CBRC (2003–2011).

Zhou Xiaochuan: central bank governor (2002–).

Historic Figures

Qin Shihuang (259–210 BC): founded China's first centralized state in 221BC.

Tang Taizong (598–649): the model emperor of what many regard as China's golden era.

Wang Anshi (1021–1086): Song premier overthrown by conservative forces for his state activist policies.

Kangxi (1654–1722): Fourth Qing Emperor credited with taking the Manchu dynasty to its zenith.

Cixi (1835–1908): Empress Dowager whose conservatism led to the end of over two millennia of imperial rule.

Chiang Kai-shek (1887–1975): KMT leader who ruled China from 1928–1949.

Places

Guangdong: Largest province by population, GDP and exports, China's southern gateway.

Hangzhou: Capital of Zhejiang, new economy hub, home to Alibaba, near Shanghai.

Shenzhen: Identified with Deng, a village in 1978 that became one of the first four Special Economic Zones, has overtaken neighbouring Hong Kong for innovation and population.

Zhejiang: China's most private sector-dominated province and third-largest exporter.

Zhengzhou: Central China's northern crossroads, capital of Henan and disappeared ghost city.

Terms

guanxi: connections and information networks.

junzi: virtuous person.

xun: an imperial or high official's inspection tour.

yanjiu: research and field work.

hukou: residence rights.

Abbreviations

CBRC China Banking Regulatory Commission: regulates banking in China.

CSRC China Securities Regulatory Commission: regulates stock and bond markets.

DRC Development Research Centre of the State Council: government policy research arm.

GDP Gross Domestic Product: value of domestic economic output.

GNI Gross National Income: measures nation's income including from overseas.

IMF International Monetary Fund: Washington-based, responsible for global financial stability.

KMT Kuomintang: ruled China until its 1949 defeat in the civil war before retreating to Taiwan.

MNC Multinational Corporations: companies operating worldwide.

NGO Non-Government Organizations: organizations independent of government or state.

NDRC National Development and Reform Commission: China's top macroeconomic organization and coordinator, evolved out of central planning.

OECD Organization for Economic Co-operation and Development: Paris-based organization for mature economies.

Rmb Renminbi: 6.8:$1.00[†] in July 2016.
Renminbi: 6.6:$1.00 in December 2017

SME Small and Medium Enterprises: short-hand for private companies, some are very large.

SOE State-Owned Enterprise: national, provincial or local government-owned.

WTO World Trade Organization: global international trade regulator.

[†] In this book, all dollar amounts refer to US dollars.

Pronunciation

There are numerous online sites explaining the pronunciation of *hanyu pinyin* spelling. Just two sounds do not exist in English: *x* is "sh" and *q* is "ch".

Main Dynasties and Periods of Chinese History

Xia	c.2070–1600 BC
Shang	c.1600–1046 BC
Zhou	c.1046–256 BC
Spring and Autumn Period	771–476 BC
Warring States Period	476–221 BC
Qin	221–206 BC
Han	206 BC–220 AD
Three Kingdoms	220–280
Jin	265–420
Sui	581–618
Tang	618–907
Song	960–1279
Yuan	1271–1368
Ming	1368–1644
Qing	1644–1911

China's turbulent history makes for a complicated time-line. Precise beginnings and ends of dynasties are disputed, so I have used the most common definitions. Less-consequential dynasties have been omitted. This is a simplified version, stripping out details that signify when dynasties ruled different areas or lost territory, usually to the Xiongnu from the western steppes. The Zhou Dynasty is divided into West and East, Han also into West and East but interrupted by the Xin, while the Song's loss of territory breaks it into Northern and Southern eras. Given China's size, there were times when parts were ruled by different dynasties. The Qing took almost 20 years to consolidate its rule, longer than the Qin lasted. Three of China's most famous periods were not even dynasties — the Spring and Autumn Period, Warring States Period and the Three Kingdoms.

Debt Comparisons

%	Total Debt	Household	Corporate[1]	Public Sector	Financial Sector	Foreign Debt[2] Short-term	Long-term
	Debt As a Percentage of GDP: 2016						
China	**308**	47	155	70	36	8	5
Hong Kong	**510**	66	113	44	204	22	52
Japan	**549**	60	78	243	168	52	19
Singapore	**607**	85	97	136	203	2	51
EU	**532**	64	92	90	285	n.a	
UK	**765**	87	80	113	485	n.a	
US	**310**	79	45	102	84	32	66

Notes:

1. Corporate debt for Hong Kong and Singapore is for 2015: excludes non-resident, non-financial credit for use overseas.
2. Foreign debt for Hong Kong and Singapore: excludes financial sector.

Source: Dismal Science Group (DSG).

China 2030: In Its Own Words

The DRC–World Bank report is significant for what it says. The language of statists, let alone central planners, is gone. In its place are words that indicate the fundamental changes that may well lie ahead for China. It highlights six priority reform areas:

- Structural reforms for a market-based economy.
- Accelerating the pace of innovation.
- "Go green".
- Promoting social security for all.
- Strengthening the fiscal system.
- Seeking mutually beneficial global relations.

Extracts:

1. "Redefining the role of government, reforming and restructuring state enterprises and banks, developing the private sector, promoting competition, and deepening reforms in the land, labor, and financial markets."
2. "The role of the government and its relationship to markets and the private sector need to change fundamentally."
3. "A modern society [which] is industrialized and urbanized and enjoys a quality of life that is on par with the Western world."
4. "When a developing country reaches the technology frontier, the correct development strategy ceases to be so straightforward. Direct government intervention may actually retard growth, not help it. Instead, the policy emphasis needs to shift even more toward private

sector development, ensuring that markets are mature enough to allocate resources efficiently."

5. "The role of the private sector is critical … innovation is not something that can be achieved through government planning."
6. "The expanding middle class is increasingly vocal in its demand to participate in the discussion of public policy. This demand points to a broader need to empower people to contribute to the … development efforts, to be creative, and improve standards of living through their own efforts. The government should respond ... to these needs and grant rights to individuals, households, enterprises, communities, academia, and other nongovernmental organisations through clear rules that encourage broad participation. By doing so, the government can gradually transfer some of its previous functions to society at large, allow nongovernmental players to form networks in new and interesting ways, and create space for innovation and creativity."
7. "While the government needs to withdraw from direct involvement in production, distribution and resource allocation, it will need to focus greater attention on designing and implementing the policy and regulatory framework that empowers others to participate in economic decision-making so that the desired outcome of rapid, inclusive, and sustainable growth is achieved. To play this role, the government will need to transform itself into a lean, clean, transparent, and highly efficient modern government that operates under the rule of law."

Not many economic documents would include that "social values and high moral standards will be important. There is widespread concern in China over many recent instances of 'moral failures'". It is not just about economics, it is about the next major attempt to modernize its society. Doubtless there will be opposition along the way but the next generation of leaders, like Deng Xiaoping in 1978, seems to have concluded that there is no alternative to fundamental reform. Using the World Bank to work with the DRC enables them to raise the issues that they will have to address. It feels like Zhu Rongji using WTO entry as an excuse to override entrenched vested interests. Much rides on it.

Read their words:

http://www-wds.worldbank.org/external/default/WDSContentServer/WDSP/IB/2012/02/28/000356161_20120228001303/Rendered/PDF/671790WP0P127500China020300complete.pdf

Source: Research-Works, March 2012.

Bibliography

Bonavia, David (1980). *The Chinese*. New York: Lippincott & Crowell.

Briggs, Asa (1959). *The Age of Improvement*. London: Longmans.

Chang, Gordon (2001). *The Coming Collapse of China*. New York: Random House.

Chang, Leslie (2008). *Factory Girls*. London: Picador.

Dawson, Raymond (1967). *The Chinese Chameleon: An Analysis of European Conceptions of Chinese Civilization*. Oxford: Oxford University Press.

Dobbs, Richard, Manyika, James and Woetzel, Jonathan (2015). *No Ordinary Disruption*. New York: Public Affairs.

de Waal, Edmund (2015). *The White Road: A Journey into Obsession*. London: Vintage.

Fitzgerald, C.P. (1935), revised (1976). *China: A Short Cultural History*. London: Barrie and Jenkins.

French, Paul and Crabbe, Matthew (2010). *Fat China: How Expanding Waistlines are Changing a Nation*. London: Anthem Press.

Fukuyama, Francis (2014). *Political Order and Political Decay*. New York: Farrar, Straus and Giroux.

Geoffroy-Dechaume, Francois (1967). *China Looks at the World*. London: Faber & Faber.

Graham, A.C. (1965). *Poems of the Late Tang*. London: Penguin.

Harney, Alexandra (2008). *The China Price*. New York: Penguin.

Hinton, David (2013). *The Four Chinese Classics*. Berkeley: Counterpoint.

Ho, Kwon Ping (2016). *The Ocean in a Drop: Singapore the Next Fifty Years*. Singapore: World Scientific Publishing.

Jacques, Martin (2009). *When China Rules the World*. London: Allen Lane.

Jiang, Rong (2009). *Wolf Totem*. London: Penguin.

Johnson, Ian (2004). *Wild Grass: Three Stories of Change in Modern China.* London: Penguin.

Keay, John (2008). *China: A History*. London, Harper Press.

Kissinger, Henry (2011). *On China.* London: Allen Lane.

Kong, Xianglin (2010). *Confucius.* Beijing: Foreign Languages Press.

Kroeber, Arthur (2016). *China's Economy*. New York: Oxford University Press.

Kynge, James (2006). *China Shakes the World.* London: Weidenfeld and Nicolson.

Lardy, Nicholas (2012). *Sustaining China's Economic Growth After the Global Financial Crisis*. Washington, DC: Peterson Institute for International Economics Press.

Lardy, Nicholas (2014). *Markets over Mao: The Rise of Private Business in China.* Washington, DC: Peterson Institute for International Economics Press.

Lau, D.C. (1963). *Lao Tzu: Tao Te Ching*. London: Penguin.

Lieberthal, Kenneth (1995), revised (2004). *Governing China: From Revolution Through Reform*. New York: W.W. Norton.

Lin, Paul T.K. and Lin, Eileen Chen (2011). *In the Eye of the China Storm.* Montreal: McGill-Queen's University Press.

Lin, Yutang (1937), reprinted 1998. *The Importance of Living*. New York: Harper.

Liu, Cixin (2006). *The Three-Body Problem*. London: Head of Zeus.

Maddison, Angus (2007). *Contours of the World Economy 1–2030 AD*. Oxford: Oxford University Press.

Maugham, Somerset (1922). *On a Chinese Screen*. London: Jonathan Cape.

Miller, Tom (2012). *China's Urban Billion*. London: Zed Books.

Minford, John (2003). *The Art of War*: New York: Penguin.

Minford, John (2014). *I Ching*. New York: Viking.

Mitter, Rana (2014). *China's War with Japan 1937–1945*. London: Penguin.

Mo, Yan (1992). *The Republic of Wine*. New York: Arcade.

Mo, Yan (2001). *Shifu, You'll Do Anything for a Laugh*. New York: Arcade.

Naughton, Barry (2007). *The Chinese Economy: Transitions and Growth*. Cambridge, MA: MIT Press.

Naughton, Barry (ed.) (2013). *Wu Jinglian: Voice of Reform in China*. Cambridge, MA: MIT Press.

Osnos, Evan (2014). *Age of Ambition*. London: Vintage.

Paulson, Hank (2015). *Dealing with China.* New York: Hachette.

Perkins, Dwight (1986). *China, Asia's Next Economic Giant*. Seattle, WA: University of Washington Press.

Perkins, Dwight (2013). *East Asian Development: Foundations and Strategies*. Cambridge, MA: Harvard University Press.

Pomerantz, Kenneth (2000). *The Great Divergence*. Princeton: Princeton University Press.

Puett, Michael and Gross-Loh, Christine (2016). *The Path*. New York: Simon and Schuster.

Sawyer, Ralph and Sawyer, Mei-chun (2014). *Zhuge Liang: Strategy, Achievements and Writings*. North Charleston: Create Space Independent Publishing Platform.

Schell, Orville and Delury, John (2013). *Wealth and Power: China's Long March to the Twenty-First Century*. London: Little, Brown.

Shambaugh, David (2008). *China's Communist Party: Atrophy and Adaptation*. Washington, DC: Woodrow Wilson Center Press.

Short, Philip (1999), paperback (2004). *Mao: A Life*. London: John Murray.

So, Billy K.L. (ed.) (2013). *The Economy of Lower Yangzi Delta in Late Imperial China*. Abingdon: Routledge.

Spence, Jonathan (1999). *The Search for Modern China*. New York: W.W. Norton.

Spence, Jonathan (2001). *Treason by the Book*. London: Peguin

Spence, Jonathan (2007). *Return to Dragon Mountain*. New York: Viking Penguin.

Spurling, John (2014). *The Ten Thousand Things*. New York: Overlook Duckworth.

Steinfeld, Edward (1998). *Forging Reform in China*. Cambridge: Cambridge University Press.

Steinfeld, Edward (2010). *Playing Our Game*. New York: Oxford University Press.

Stent, James (2017). *China's Banking Transformation: The Untold Story*. New York: Oxford University Press.

Temple, Robert (1998). *The Genius of China: 3,000 Years of Science, Discovery and Invention*. London: Prion.

Tse, Edward (2015). *China's Disruptors*. New York: Portfolio Penguin.

Vogel, Ezra (2011). *Deng Xiaoping and the Transformation of China*. Cambridge, MA: Belknap Harvard.

Waley, Arthur (1938). *The Analects of Confucius*. London: George Allen and Unwin.

Watts, Jonathan (2010). *When a Billion Chinese Jump*. London: Faber & Faber.

Weiner, Eric (2016). *The Geography of Genius*. New York: Simon & Schuster.

Winchester, Simon (2008). *Bomb, Book & Compass*. London: Viking.

Xi, Jinping (2014). *The Governance of China*. Beijing: Foreign Languages Press.

Yu, Dan (2010). *Confucius from the Heart*. London: Pan.

Yu, Hua (2004). *Chronicle of a Blood Merchant*. New York: Anchor Books.

Yu, Hua (2011). *China in Ten Words*. New York: Anchor Books.

Yu, Hua (2009). *Brothers*. London: Picador.

Acknowledgements

China's Change would not have been possible without the help of many people. First and foremost, Maria Yang Tse Oy who provided great support and insight. Particularly helpful during the writing have been Shaun Hargreaves Heap, Tony Hall and Andrew Sheng, as well as Katie Abu, George Baeder, Ed Barlow, Jason Bedford, John Berthelsen, David Brown, Janice Cotton, Tony Doniger and Liza Lunt, William Fu, Gerhard and Robin Greif, Tom Gurney, Ceinwen Jones, Anna Kieryk, Patricia King, William Knight, James Kynge, Ralph and Jasbeena Layman, John Minford, Ng Kok Song, Cristian Ramirez, Gary Rieschel, Andy Rothman, Ulrik Trampe, Wang Tao, Andrew Williams, Yang Fuqiang and Zhao Zhenyi. All read parts or all of the manuscript as it emerged, giving very helpful critiques and suggestions.

Navigating the route to publication was no less complicated. I am very grateful for the help of Rick Borsuk and Nancy Chng, Philip Bowring, Felicity Bryan, Claire Chiang, Toby Eady, Kelly Falconer, Paul French, Alex Harney, C.J. Hwu, Martin Jacques, Jerome Lacroniere, Chris Lewis, Jim Levine, Mark O'Neill and Louise do Rosario, Zaria Rich, Greg Rudd, Samir Shah, Elaine Steel, Tjio Kay Loen, Toh Han Shih, Mike Tsang, Zhang Qian and Zhang Wei.

Other advice and insights into China's change have been given by Francis and Helen Altarejos, Lawrence Ang, Pieter Bottelier, Mark Bowers, David Brown, Mark Chennells, Gerard Choy, Ajit Dayal, Clinton Dines and Jeronia Muntaner, David Dodwell, Michael Enright, Graham Earnshaw, Fan Gang, Andrew Hall, Ho Kwon Ping,

John Hoffman, Kai Hsu, Benny Hu, Yukon Huang, Charles Hutzler, Will Hutton, Ian Johnson, Bill and Audrey Kazer, Koh Boon Hwee, Kim Kihwan, Arthur Kroeber, Raphael Lam, Nicholas Lardy, Kenneth Lieberthal, Benjamin Lim, Michael Lipper, Charles Liu, Lo Bobo, Thomas Luedi, Ma Jun, Jeremy Mark, Brook McConnell, Luke Minford, David Murphy, Rod Oram, Simon Ogus, Tom Orlik, Rick Petree, Nick Platt, Bruce Richardson, John Ross, Vasuki Shastry, Choedchu Sophonpanich, Edward Steinfeld, Jim Stent, Tang Min, Michael Taylor, Teo Kim Yong, Edward Tse, Ezra Vogel, Jonathan Woetzel, Xiao Gang, Xu Yemin, Michael Yang, Leslie Yap, Zhang Longmei, Wesley Zhao, Zhao Ya'nan and Zhou Ping.

Special thanks to Dong Lixi at World Scientific for reaching out just as the manuscript was being completed, saving much anxiety. Then for so professionally stewarding *China's Change* to publication. Thanks also to Sharon Khoo and Judy Yeo for their very helpful and painless copy editing.

About the Author

After graduating in Politics, Philosophy and Economics from Oxford in 1973, **Hugh Peyman** co-authored with Richard Hall *The Great Uhuru Railway: China's Showpiece in Africa* (Gollancz 1976), then moved with Reuters in 1977 to Hong Kong before joining Asia's leading business, politics and economics magazine the *Far Eastern Economic Review* where he worked in Hong Kong and Malaysia.

Peyman began over 35 years of investment research in 1981, heading Asian Research ex-Japan for Merrill Lynch and Dresdner Kleinwort Benson, based in Singapore, before founding Research-Works in 1999 to do independent long-term Asian research for global asset managers. He speaks to investors, companies and students about China. He has lived in Shanghai since 2002.

Index

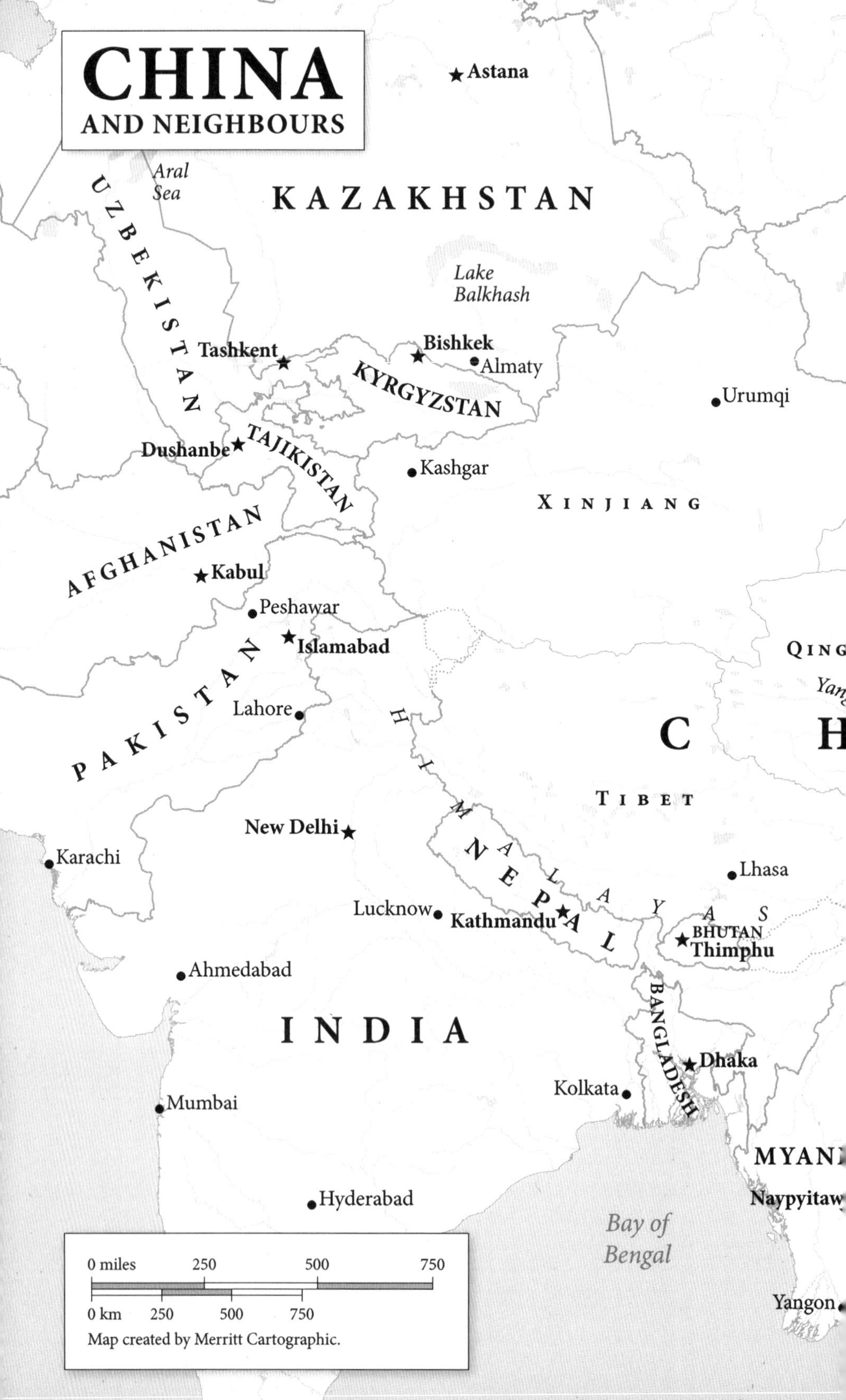
CHINA
AND NEIGHBOURS
Astana
Aral Sea
KAZAKHSTAN
UZBEKISTAN
Lake Balkhash
Tashkent
Bishkek
Almaty
KYRGYZSTAN
Urumqi
Dushanbe
TAJIKISTAN
Kashgar
XINJIANG
AFGHANISTAN
Kabul
Peshawar
Islamabad
QING
Yan
PAKISTAN
Lahore
HIMALAYAS
C
H
TIBET
New Delhi
Karachi
Lhasa
Lucknow
Kathmandu
NEPAL
BHUTAN
Thimphu
Ahmedabad
INDIA
BANGLADESH
Dhaka
Kolkata
Mumbai
MYAN
Naypyitaw
Hyderabad
Bay of Bengal
Yangon
0 miles 250 500 750
0 km 250 500 750
Map created by Merritt Cartographic.

RUSSIA
Lake Baikal
Ulan Bator
MONGOLIA
GOBI DESERT
INNER MONGOLIA
HEILONGJIANG
Harbin
Vladivostok
Changchun
JILIN
Shenyang
LIAONING
Sea of Japan
NORTH KOREA
Pyongyang
Seoul
SOUTH KOREA
BEIJING
Beijing
Tianjin
TIANJIN
Hohhot
Yellow
Ordos
Yinchuan
GANSU
NINGXIA
Taiyuan
SHANXI
HEBEI
Shijiazhuang
Yellow Sea
JAPAN
Jinan
SHANDONG
Qingdao
Xining
Lanzhou
Yellow
Zhengzhou
I N A
Xi'an
SHAANXI
HENAN
JIANGSU
ANHUI
Nanjing
Hefei
Shanghai
SHANGHAI
East China Sea
SICHUAN
HUBEI
Yangzi
Wuhan
Hangzhou
Ningbo
Chengdu
CHONGQING
Chongqing
ZHEJIANG
Nanchang
Wenzhou
Okinawa
Changsha
JIANGXI
HUNAN
GUIZHOU
Guiyang
Fuzhou
FUJIAN
Taiwan Strait
Taipei
Quanzhou
Xiamen
Kunming
TAIWAN
YUNNAN
GUANGXI
GUANGDONG
Guangzhou
Dongguan
Shenzhen
HONG KONG
Hong Kong
Zhuhai
Nanning
PACIFIC OCEAN
VIETNAM
Hanoi
MACAU
Haikou
LAOS
HAINAN
South China Sea
Vientiane
PHILIPPINES
Manila
THAILAND